D0908136

Farm Journal's COOK IT YOUR WAY

Farm Journal's
COOK IT
YOUR WAY

Edited by **NELL B. NICHOLS
AND BETSY McCRACKEN**

Recipes edited by **PATRICIA A. WARD**
FARM JOURNAL ASSISTANT FOOD EDITOR

Drawings by **Maureen Sweeney**
FARM JOURNAL ART STAFF

Doubleday & Company, Inc., Garden City, New York 1979

COOK IT YOUR WAY is syndicated internationally by
UNIVERSAL PRESS SYNDICATE
Copyright © 1977, 1978 and 1979 FARM JOURNAL, INC.
ISBN: 0-385-13099-6
Library of Congress Catalog Card Number 77–73333

Contents

CHAPTER ONE

Cook It Your Way

Just as soon as speedy cooking by microwaves became practical for the average kitchen, someone turned around and invented the slow cooker. And why not? Your days are different, with different demands on your time. So it makes sense to cook with different appliances—fast, slow or in between—depending on your plans for the day.

This book gives you alternate ways to cook or finish such favorite foods as Swedish Meatballs, Down-home Pot Roast, Beef Burgundy, Sweet-sour Pork, Bean Soup, maple-flavored New England-style Sweet Potatoes, spicy Pumpkin Bread, Cherry Cobbler and many other tempting recipes.

The basic recipes, originally perfected for oven or range top cooking, have all been tested and adjusted for cooking in the microwave oven and/or in various portable appliances. As you finger through the recipe pages, you'll see that each recipe gives you a list of ingredients followed by a choice of two, three or even four cooking methods. To save heating the big oven, you can bake some of the breads and desserts in your slow cooker or electric skillet; the toaster-oven is another possibility. You can speed up a stew by using the pressure cooker or the microwave oven, if you have one. You can do Chinese stir-fry dishes in an electric wok, electric frypan or in your old iron skillet on top of the range. Or in the microwave oven.

You can decide which method to follow, depending on the time you have available, or the appliance you prefer to use. (This book points out how you can conserve oven heat, for example, to save energy.) The cooking time for each method is printed in bold face type; you can see at a glance how many minutes or hours it takes to cook the dish. Here's how it works:

When you are going to be away from home several hours or most of the day, you might choose the 8-hour method and put food in the slow cooker before you leave the house. Dinner will cook without supervision while you are gone. Or you may prefer to cook the same dish in minutes in the microwave oven after you get home. The weather may influence your choice: almost everyone votes for cool cooking on hot, humid days. The number of people you'll have gathered around your table at mealtime may dictate which method you'll use.

Saving Energy in the Kitchen
Every day, newspaper headlines and TV newscasts report on the energy situation. And the rising costs of electricity and gas as reflected in your utility bills have also alerted you to the need to conserve energy. In Chapter 2, we describe some of the techniques you can adopt to save gas and electricity; in many cases, it's a matter of being aware of waste.

True, the amount of the energy that can be saved in the kitchen is small compared to the energy used to heat and cool your home, to heat water and to run your automobiles. But every "drop in the bucket" counts. Add the savings made in one kitchen to similar reductions across the country and the magnitude of the accomplishment becomes impressive.

Multiple-Method Recipes
Women have asked, "Will my favorite recipes turn out well if I cook them in different appliances?" The answer is no—not always—not without adjustments. The multiple-method recipes in this book show you how to make the necessary adjustments when you move from the range to one or another of the appliances. All versions of each recipe have been tested.

The basic method is given first: cooking the dish on top of the range or in the oven. Then specific directions follow for cooking the same dish in one or more of the following appliances: microwave oven, slow cooker, toaster-oven, electric frypan, electric wok and pressure cooker.

Even with adjustments, however, the same recipe may not give identical results when cooked in different appliances. So when you try these recipes with a choice of cooking methods, adopt a give-and-take attitude. To save time, be prepared to surrender some subtlety of taste, texture or appearance. With multiple-method recipes, cooking becomes a game in which you trade values. Play it to win. For example:

Baked in the conventional oven or toaster-oven, Grandma's Apple Betty takes 40 to 50 minutes. You can microwave the dessert in 10 to 12 minutes. Or you can cook it in the slow cooker for 2½ hours—and be gone from the kitchen. Only the oven's dry heat will give your pudding a crusty brown top, but the convenience or time saved by microwave or slow cooking may compensate. And your family may not even be aware of the choice you make, especially if you top the warm pudding with scoops of ice cream. Someone lifting his spoon is bound to say, "It tastes great—like apple pie à la mode."

How Cooking Methods Change from One Appliance to Another

The toaster-oven is usually interchangeable with the conventional oven except that it has limited capacity. If you are filling only one 8-inch square pan or equivalent, the toaster-oven will bake it for you at a one-third savings in energy over heating the conventional range oven. However, the home economists who tested our recipes observed that food tends to brown faster in the toaster-oven. That's why, in the recipe for Brownie Pudding Cake, for example, you are directed to lay a piece of aluminum foil over the dessert after 20 minutes' baking time. This will protect it from browning too much as it finishes baking.

When we moved the cooking of a dish from one appliance to another, our home economists considered many variables besides cooking time and the amount of electricity and/or gas consumed in the cooking. We adjusted recipes, if necessary, to make the size of the recipe match the capacity of the different appliances or pans used. Through repeated testing we found the right size to cut vegetables for cooking in the pressure cooker, slow cooker, wok or electric frypan; and the optimum measure of liquid for sauces.

Some of the time differences are startling. Depending on which appliance you use, Family Meat Loaf takes from 18 minutes to 8 hours to cook. Spreading ketchup on the top improves the appearance of loaves cooked in the microwave oven, slow cooker and electric skillet. Adding an extra egg to the meat mix for the slow cooker helps bind the ingredients together so the loaf slices neatly. This loaf, incidentally, must be formed as a round loaf so it will fit into the cooker without touching the sides of the cooking well. For the other appliances, the meat mix is pressed into traditional loaf pans.

You'll notice a change in the cooking temperatures in some of the recipes—often the difference between success and failure. To cook custards in the electric skillet, the temperature setting is only 220° F. With the vent in the lid closed, the custards steam to perfection. But baked custards require an oven temperature of 325° F. Obviously, the skillet is much more economical of energy. What about taste? The custards from conventional oven, electric skillet and microwave oven are equally delicate, smooth and velvety; however, the baked dessert has a drier top than the other two.

The custard recipe is also a good example of how a recipe needs to be changed to fit the capacity of the appliance used. You can easily bake 8 cups of custard in a water bath in the conventional oven. A 12-inch electric skillet will accommodate 6 custard cups. Our directions for the microwave oven tell you to bake only 4 cups at a time— cups are arranged in an 8-inch square glass baking dish filled with an inch of water. In the oven or skillet, the baking time is 40 minutes; in the microwave, 6 to 6½ minutes for each 4 cups.

Taste and Eye Appeal

Taste-testing is an important ritual in adapting recipes for cooking in several convenient appliances. Testers frequently expressed a preference for crusty-brown oven-baked foods over those baked in a skillet or by microwave. However, we found ways to "fool the eyes" and give foods a browned appearance. Cherry Cobbler cooked in a skillet is a good example; the biscuits are baked on one side until brown, then turned—like pancakes—to brown on the other side. For microwave cooking, biscuits are dipped in melted butter and rolled in crushed honey graham cereal. Placed on top of the cherry mixture for microwave baking, they come out looking most appetizing.

The microwave oven cooks a half-dozen Raisin-Oatmeal Muffins in 6 minutes and many a busy woman will surrender the crusty tops to bake muffins so quickly—especially when it's easy to give them eye appeal by dipping the tops in melted butter and sprinkling on a cinnamon-sugar mixture.

One of the most frequent adjustments, when a recipe moves from one appliance to another, is the change in amount of liquid. Even though such change may be small, it makes a big difference in the quality of the dish you make. So before you assemble ingredients, read through the cooking method you plan to use and see what modification you need to make, if any, in the measurements.

Unfortunately, there are no precise rules to follow. Each dish, and each type of appliance, has its own requirements. But our multiple-method recipes will show you what adjustments to make. They'll also serve as models for you when you experiment with modifying your own favorite recipes.

The amount of liquid needed for braising depends largely on the amount of evaporation during cooking. When cooked in a Dutch oven on top of the range and in the pressure cooker, Italian Pot Roast needs ¼ cup water. But there is little or no evaporation in the covered slow cooker, so water is omitted in this version.

Depending on the appliance you use, there are variations in the way you prepare vegetables. To assure tenderness, vegetables are cut in smaller and thinner pieces for the slow cooker than for other appliances. Mixed Bean Casserole illustrates a simple but desirable change. The chopped onion—okay for a dish cooked in the conventional and microwave ovens—gives way to grated onion in the slow cooker.

Mixed Bean Casserole is a recipe that gives you great leeway in scheduling your time. You can microwave the beans for 26½ minutes, or bake them in the oven for 1½ hours. Or, if you must be away from home or will be very busy during the day, you can put the beans in the slow cooker for 7 to 8 hours. By late afternoon, they'll be ready to take to a picnic or covered-dish supper. Tote them in the cooker and reheat them (if an electrical outlet is available). The cooker makes an ideal serving dish—an up-to-date bean pot.

If you've always cooked meat-and-vegetable combinations in a Dutch oven on top of the range or in the oven, you know the procedure: start the meat first; add vegetables later so they won't be overcooked. When you use the pressure cooker or the slow cooker for stews and other combination dishes, the vegetables are added at the start of cooking and you compensate for the difference in cooking time by the way you cut up the ingredients. In the pressure cooker, the challenge is to get the meat tender without overcooking the vegetables so they become mushy. The recipe tells you to cut the vegetables in large pieces.

The slow cooker is exactly opposite. Meat sometimes cooks faster

than vegetables, so the vegetables are cut in small or thin pieces. You'll
see this rule at work in a delicious recipe for Lamb Stew with Mashed
Potatoes.

Tender-crisp Foods:
A Good Way to Save Energy and Vitamins

Give credit to the Chinese for inventing the wok and creating a style
of cooking that is extra good to eat and positively pinchpenny in its use
of cooking fuel. Stir-fry foods are small slivers or cubes of food, cooked
in a tiny bit of oil over high heat for minutes only. They retain more
of their fresh flavors, colors and nutrients than foods cooked by other
methods. Properly served, they're still tender-crisp, with a fresh,
crunchy taste.

We've borrowed the technique of stir-frying for many of the recipes
in this book, although the recipes themselves are American develop-
ments using few of the seasonings employed in Chinese kitchens. And
while it's fun to cook in a wok, you can stir-fry the same dishes in your
electric frypan or iron skillet. The recipes also adapt to cooking in the
microwave oven.

People who like the crisp texture and fresh taste of vegetables
cooked in the Chinese fashion are willing to spend some time at the
cutting board. Speedy, economical cooking and delicious taste are their
rewards.

The chapter that follows give you specific information about using
the various appliances to cook the recipes in this book.

When you plan your day with these recipes in hand, you can choose
a meal and a cooking method that will let you "cook it your way."
Our multiple-method recipes work successfully with your different
cooking appliances, thereby adding a lively new spirit to meal-getting.

CHAPTER TWO

Making the Best Use of Your Appliances

When we began recipe testing for this cookbook, one of our goals was to find ways to cook that would conserve energy. This is also an important goal for the manufacturers of appliances. Energy-saving features are built into many of the new model appliances being offered today. If you are shopping for a new range or microwave oven or one of the small appliances, you will want to compare brands and models for their energy use as well as other features you consider important.

However, there are techniques you can use, whatever the age of your appliances, to get better performance from them. In this chapter, we give tips on using your range to best advantage, along with information on the other appliances for which we have recipes in this book: the toaster-oven, electric frypan, electric wok, microwave oven, pressure cooker and slow cooker.

Likely, before you bought any one of your appliances, you saw a demonstration on its use. Or when you unpacked a gift appliance, you read the instruction manual. We hope you keep all of these "use and care" booklets on file in your kitchen. Look through the booklet again after you've used an appliance for a while; see if there's another idea or recipe you might try. The recipes in this book and the information in this chapter will also show you new ways to expand the use of each one of your kitchen helpers.

You and the Conventional Kitchen Range

While manufacturers are now designing ovens and surface units to be more energy-efficient, the biggest effect on fuel savings continues to be how you use the conventional range. You can learn to use less energy when you cook. And if you are determined to make a dent in your utility bills, it pays to concentrate on the oven.

The range oven or wall oven uses more energy than any other kitchen cooking appliance. But it can be managed! Here are ways to bake and roast in the oven with minimum heat waste:

• Before you turn on the heat, check to be sure the oven racks are positioned where you want them.

• When you preheat the oven, time your preparations so that the food is ready for the oven when it reaches the desired temperature—don't let the oven stand hot and waiting. Check how long it takes for your oven to preheat; the time depends on the temperature you select and also varies somewhat from one range to another. Ovens used in our recipe tests take from 8 to 10 minutes to preheat. Memorize the number of minutes it takes for your oven to reach a moderate and a hot setting, and set a timer each time you turn on the electricity or gas. The bell will remind you to put the food in.

• Bake several foods together whenever you can. It takes about the same amount of electricity or gas to bake two loaves of bread, or two pies, instead of one. Freeze the extras. Keeping the freezer filled, but not overcrowded, helps it function more efficiently, too. For oven meals, choose dishes that cook at about the same temperature.

• Curb your curiosity and keep the oven door closed while food is cooking in it. You lose heat each time you open the oven door. According to research, one opening can lower the temperature 25 to 50 degrees. The more peeps, the more heat loss. When checking foods for doneness, hold the oven door open no longer than necessary.

• Thaw frozen casseroles, meat and other foods in the refrigerator to reduce cooking or reheating time.

• Turn off the oven just before cooking is completed—there's enough heat to finish the dish. Take advantage of residual heat in the turned-off oven to warm rolls, pies or coffee breads.

• Save energy and keep self-cleaning ovens at peak efficiency by starting the self-cleaning cycle at once after use, to utilize heat build-up.

Remember the pot roasts and stews we used to slide into the oven, letting them simmer away with little or no attention required? That was when we didn't think twice about heating the oven. In recipes in this book, we've transferred the cooking of many of these dishes to surface units or burners.

Here are suggestions for making best use of your range top:

• Use pans with flat bottoms, sized to match the diameter of the burners or surface units. The 8-inch unit of the electric range consumes about 2,600 watts set on high, while the 6-inch unit consumes about 1,400 watts at the same setting. Obviously, it is extravagant to waste the larger unit on a small pan.

• Adjust burners on gas ranges so that the flame does not flash beyond the bottom of the pan. A steady blue flame indicates proper adjustment. And cooking utensils placed over such a flame are easier to clean.

• Use the correct size pan for the amount of food to be cooked. Food stuffed into a pan that is too small may boil over. A small quantity of food in a large pan evaporates quickly—food may cook dry and scorch.

• Use snug-fitting lids on pots and pans; keep the steam in the pan to cook food faster. And acquire the habit of using a lid when you heat water in a saucepan.

• Draw water from the hot water tap if you need a large quantity—it will shorten cooking time. When food reaches the boiling point, turn the heat down to the lowest point that will maintain the heat you want—boiling or simmering.

• Heat no more water than you need to make coffee or tea.

• Cook soups and stews that require long simmering in large quantities; freeze them in meal-size portions. Reheating cooked food uses less gas and electricity than cooking "from scratch."

• Turn off the gas surface burner when cooking is completed, but turn off the electric unit three minutes before food is done. The electric coils retain enough heat to complete the cooking.

The Small but Mighty Toaster-Oven

When soaring utility bills make you think twice before turning on the conventional oven to bake two or three apples or potatoes, or a wonderful old-fashioned dessert like the fruit crisps, give thanks for the toaster-oven. Foods cooked in it duplicate those baked in the conventional oven. The cooking time is about the same, but the toaster-oven uses about one-third as much electricity.

You need not alter recipes for the conventional oven to bake them in the toaster-oven, but you do have to check the size of the baking pans and casseroles to make sure the oven has room for them. When testing recipes for this book, we used a toaster-oven that accommodates the following baking containers:

> 8×8×2″ baking pan
> 8½×4½×2½″ loaf pan
> 6-cup muffin pan
> 1-quart casserole
> 1½-quart casserole with straight sides
> 4 (6-oz.) custard cups
> 2 (10-oz.) casseroles

You'll find that foods baked in the toaster-oven brown faster than those baked in the conventional oven. It is advisable to keep watchful eyes on the food to determine if browning needs to be delayed. If it does, lay a piece of aluminum foil over the top of the food—be careful that the foil does not touch the heating element. Avoid baking foods that rise above the top of the baking pan or that expand quite a lot in baking, as some breads do. If food comes too close to the heated coils, it burns before it has a chance to bake.

When friends stop for a visit, you'll find the toaster-oven ideal for heating snacks and appetizers in a jiffy—and to perfection.

Assign More Work to the Electric Frypan

As a Kansas country woman says: "The electric frypan is one piece of equipment that always earns its board and keep." Sales records and testimonials from all over the country testify to the enthusiasm for this appliance. However, electric frypans have talents yet undiscovered by many people who use them every day. For instance, you can use the frypan to braise, French-fry, bake and sauté; also to warm food and keep it warm. Many recipes in this book are for dishes traditionally baked in the oven, but are successful surprises when cooked in the frypan. Try Cherry Cobbler or Salmon Loaf with Dill Sauce and see for yourself.

Electric frypans are economical of electricity but when they substitute for the conventional oven, they make their greatest saving. In a California study which compared the energy costs of several appliances, custards cooked in the electric frypan consumed less electricity than those cooked by any of the other appliances. All the test custards were velvety, smooth and tender, but none superior to those steamed in the electric frypan.

We used a 12-inch electric frypan to test our COOK IT YOUR WAY recipe variations, setting the heat control to the following guide:

Simmer	220 to 250°
Full boil	250 to 300°
Medium	300 to 350°
High	350 to 400°
Hot	400 to 450°

Here are suggestions for using your electric frypan:

• If the frypan has a separate heat control unit, set it at "Off" and plug the unit into the frypan, then plug the cord into the electrical outlet. Turn the heat setting to the temperature specified in the recipe. When the indicator light goes off, the correct temperature has been reached and you can start to cook.

• If you think the foods you cook seem to be browning too soon or simmering too fast, you might want to check the accuracy of the thermostat. This is especially desirable in high altitudes. Here is the way to do it. Pour 2 to 3 cups cold water into the frypan. Bring to a full rolling boil. Then slowly turn the dial back until the light goes out. This point is your frypan's simmering temperature; use it instead of 220° in recipe. Remember it. You will now know the setting you need to maintain simmering and to reach a full boil.

• If you wonder when to have the cover vent closed and when to cook with it open, here's a rule to follow. Close the vent when moist heat is desired, as in simmering, stewing and braising. Open it for dry heat as in baking. Some of the recipes in this book—California Meat Loaf is one—direct you to begin cooking with the vent closed, opening it the last 15 minutes of baking for a finishing touch.

• For some types of cooking, it is difficult to maintain a constant temperature. Two recipes in this book, Homemade Doughnut Balls and French-fried Onions, are cooked in shallow fat. In order to maintain a temperature of 375°, the temperature control is set at 400°. Although only a few onions or pieces of dough are fried at a time, the temperature of the hot oil drops a bit with each addition of food. The higher setting will compensate for this when you want to work fast.

Electric Wok for Stir-frying

If a liking for Chinese cooking has brought a wok into your kitchen, you are probably learning how versatile this appliance is. And if you use the wok as the Chinese intended—to stir-fry foods cut into small pieces—this appliance is miserly in its use of energy. Meats and vegetables cook in minutes.

Anyone who has seen a wok will never forget how it looks. The sloping sides and rounded bottoms of most woks allow you to stir-fry in a small amount of oil. And the shape of the wok—larger at the top than the bottom—make it possible to stir sizable amounts of food without spill-overs.

Even though the wok is a Chinese cooking pan originally designed to fit the Chinese stove, using the wok is not limited to Oriental dishes. The recipes in this book are good American specialties adapted to the stir-fry method of cooking. The Chinese call this method of cooking *frying*, but this terminology is confusing because we have many kinds of fried food in America. That's why we say *stir-frying* or *Chinese-frying*.

For testing our recipes we used an electric wok instead of the traditional Chinese pan. And we used long handled wooden spoons to stir the food—though you may wish to cook Chinese-style, with chopsticks.

• When planning a stir-fry meal, allow plenty of time to prepare the food. To ensure even cooking, all pieces of food should be cut the same size, shape and thickness. Meats and chicken, for example, are usually cut in slender strips and vegetables in thin slices or cubes. All food should be cut and ready before the wok is heated. Arrange cut food within easy reach in the order in which you will add each to the wok for cooking. If you wish to cut and measure the foods a few hours ahead, refrigerate them separately in covered bowls.

• Once the food is ready, heat the wok containing the cooking oil to the desired temperature. Follow the manufacturer's directions.

• Food cooked by the stir-fry method uses a minimum of cooking oil and cooks with a continuous high heat. Calorie counters will appreciate the use of little fat.

• The wok and its cover get very hot during cooking. Avoid touching them unless you use a hot pad or mitt.

• When cooking is completed, turn the heat control to "Off," or to "Warm" if the food is to be served from the wok.

• Cleaning the wok after use is especially easy because of its shape. Let it cool before you wash it; do not pour in cold water to hasten the cooling. Consult the manufacturer's manual to see if your wok may be washed in the dishwasher.

• Bring your wok to the table for entertaining. It is an attractive appliance, fun to use. And its heat-resistant base protects the table. For these special occasions, the "Warm" setting comes in handy.

• In addition to stir-frying, woks may be used for braising, stewing, steaming or deep-fat frying.

• Most of the recipes for stir-frying, or modifications of them, may also be used with an electric frypan and some with microwave ovens.

How Microwave Ovens Work

In microwave cooking, the food is heated by the energy itself—not the air in the oven, nor the dish in which the food is contained. Microwaves pass through glass, plastic and paper and are absorbed by the food. The vibration or friction of molecules excited by the microwaves is what heats and cooks the food.

There are two types of microwave ovens in wide use: the top-of-the-line-oven operates on a power output of 600 to 675 watts. A smaller, less expensive oven operates on 400 to 500 watts. The microwave market is very competitive and an increasing number of settings are appearing on some ovens. Browning units are also provided in a few.

The countertop model is the most widely distributed type of microwave oven. No special installation is required, except that the oven must be plugged into a grounded 115 to 120 volt electrical outlet.

Recipes in this cookbook were tested in 600 to 675 watt microwave ovens. If your oven has an output rating of less than 600 watts, slightly longer cooking times than those specified in this cookbook may be needed. The use and care manual from the manufacturer of your oven will tell you the wattage output of your oven. If not, ask the dealer from whom you purchased your oven.

All our recipes were tested with full power setting, which is available on all microwave ovens, new and old. We specify in our recipes to microwave on high setting. We want as many people as possible to use and enjoy the recipes.

Choose Correct Cooking Containers

Glass, pottery, china without metal decorations, paper, woven straw or wood baskets and microwave-safe plastics are suitable selections as cooking containers. Short-time cooking may be done in paper cups or bowls and on paper plates, towels and napkins—a big help in dish washing. Avoid wax-coated paper containers—heat from food melts the wax.

Always use dishes that withstand high heat when cooking food containing a high proportion of fat or sugar, which heats fast and gets very hot. Wooden and paper containers and baskets are satisfactory for brief cooking and warming of food, but wood may crack and paper and baskets may dry out if left in the microwave oven too long.

Metal utensils and aluminum foil are taboo in most microwave ovens. By reflecting the microwaves away from the food, they prevent cooking. And the microwaves may feed back to the main power tube and cause damage. (Some of the newer ovens are designed to handle small amounts of metal, such as small pieces of foil and TV dinner trays. Check the directions for your oven model.)

If doubtful about using glassware or other dishes you have in the cupboard for microwaving, you can quickly find out if they will withstand heat. Place 1 cup of water in a glass measuring cup. Set cup in dish to be tested. Place in microwave oven. Microwave (high setting) 1 minute. If water becomes hot and dish remains cool enough to be picked up, it may be used. If the dish gets hot, do not use for microwaving.

How to Cook in the Microwave Oven

Timing is the secret to successful microwave cooking. The cooking times given with the recipes in this and other cookbooks may be slightly different than those found in similar recipes in the manufacturer's manual that came with your oven. To prevent overcooking, recipes which are cooked by time direct you to check for doneness after the minimum cooking time. It takes a little practice to get used to the speed of microwave cooking. Many of us have a tendency to let food cook a little longer than a recipe suggests and this usually results in overcooking.

There are several factors which affect cooking time in the microwave oven:

• Amount of food. Small quantities, for 4 or fewer servings, cook faster than more servings. As the amount of food increases, so does the cooking time.

• Temperature of food. Refrigerated foods cook more slowly than warm or hot foods. Timings in our recipes are based on the temperatures at which you normally store the foods.

• Size and shape of food. Small pieces of food microwave more quickly than large pieces. Regularly shaped foods cook more uniformly than irregularly shaped ones.

• Thickness of food. Thin areas cook faster than thick ones. This can be controlled by placing thick pieces to the outside edges with thin pieces to the center.

• Density of food. Fluffy light foods, which are easy for microwaves to penetrate, cook faster than the denser foods.

• Moisture content of food. Moist foods microwave faster than dry foods in small amounts. While stews and soups may be microwaved, they are not as economical in use of time and electricity, because of large amounts.

• Arrangement of food. The position of food in the microwave oven affects the cooking time. Food should be distributed evenly. Round-shaped baking dishes are preferable to oblong or square ones because microwaves penetrate foods to 1 inch from top, bottom and sides. The corners of squares and oblongs receive more microwave energy and may overcook. Microwave-safe ring molds are also good shapes for microwaving.

Follow the recipe you are using for directions about covering the food. Covering helps to prevent spattering and to retain moisture. Our recipes most frequently suggest waxed paper and glass casserole covers. Sometimes paper towels are recommended. Some plastic wrap swells and then shrinks tightly to the dish, causing a mild build-up of steam.

If you wish to use it, turn back the wrap on one side of the dish, leaving about ⅛″ for the escape of steam.

How to Check for Doneness
Check for doneness 30 seconds before the time recommended in the recipe is reached. If the food is not done, cook it 30 seconds longer and check again to avoid overcooking. Some microwave ovens have an automatic temperature probe to help judge doneness in all foods. There are also microwave oven meat thermometers available on the market. They read the internal temperature of foods immediately.

Standing Time Is Important
Frequently recipes specify a definite time for standing after microwaving and before serving. This permits the heat to spread evenly through the food and equalizing the temperature. During this period, the food continues to cook.

What to Do About Browning
Microwave cooking is fast and most foods do not brown during cooking or acquire crisp tops as they do in the conventional oven. Browning dishes are available for use in some microwave ovens. The dish is heated, the food is added and microwaved until brown.

In developing recipes for this cookbook, we added color in many ways as a substitute for browning. Sprinkling with paprika was one of the easiest and most effective additions. It gives such dishes as Chicken Parmesan and Easy Scalloped Potatoes an attractive color. Other times we rolled the food in or sprinkled it with crushed cereal crumbs. Scattering chopped nuts over some dishes contributes pleasant texture or crispness. There are many methods of giving microwaved foods eye appeal. Notice them in this book's recipes.

Adapting Your Recipes to the Microwave
No doubt you have many favorite recipes in your files that you'd like to try in the microwave. There are few cut-and-dried rules to follow in adapting traditional recipes. Variations are so plentiful. The amount

of liquid frequently needs to be reduced. Larger cooking dishes some-times are necessary to avoid spill-overs. Cooking times usually require adjustments. It is a good idea to start testing for doneness when one-fourth of the cooking time given in the original recipe is up. If it is not done, check for doneness often. When you take food out of the oven and find it requires more microwaving, return it for a few minutes and check again. Repeat as often as necessary. As an extra bonus, there is no loss of heat or energy when door is opened as in conventional oven.

The more recipes our home economists adjusted for use in the mi-crowave oven, the more microwaving times of often-repeated cooking processes they memorized. For example, they soon knew how long it takes butter to melt and chopped onion and green pepper added to it to cook until softened.

The final decision is that the best route to follow is to select a simi-lar tested recipe from a cookbook, such as this one, or the oven's man-ual from the manufacturer. Compare it with the recipe you wish to adapt. Notice such things as the proportion of liquid to solid food, the size of the dish in which the food is cooked, the timing, and how much of the food is precooked before it is added to other ingredients, etc.

Be sure to jot down notes on the changes in the recipes you make when cooking with the microwave oven. They will prove helpful the next time you make the dish. And do keep watch over the working mi-crowave oven. It has a timer and, usually, a see-through oven door to help you. And do not hesitate to check for doneness. Better to test too soon than too late.

Pressure Cookers Work Fast

If cooking to save time and money is important to you, the pressure cooker is an appliance you want to consider. Cooking with steam pres-sure is fast; it tenderizes budget cuts of meat. And since the pressure cooker uses the heat of one surface burner or unit—usually for a brief time—it is kind to utility bills.

Recipes in this book were tested using 4- and 6-quart pressure cookers—every recipe indicates the size to use. Following the specific directions for assembling your cooker and the ideas below will help you use pressure cooking most efficiently.

• Foods do not brown in moist heat. If you prefer the improved color and flavor of browned meat, you can brown it before you fasten the cover and build steam pressure. It takes only a few minutes to heat cooking oil in the uncovered cooker for browning.

• While the easiest way to use the pressure cooker is to cook a single food with seasonings, the real saving of energy comes when you cook a combination of meats and vegetables. The trick is to select foods that take the same length of time to cook, so that none will be overcooked. Our recipes do this. Remember it takes longer to cook meats than it does to cook vegetables in the pressure cooker. Both meats and vegetables will be done in the same length of cooking time when you cut the carrots in 3″ lengths, potatoes in lengthwise halves and onions into eighths, as in the Sheepherder's Stew.

• Never fill pressure cooker more than two-thirds full.

• Some foods that foam *should not* be cooked in the pressure cooker. Foam could block the air vent preventing the escape of steam. Play it safe and do not try to cook pearl barley, pea soup, split peas, applesauce, cranberries or rhubarb in this appliance.

• Dried beans require special treatment for cooking in the pressure cooker. The technique suggested in our recipes—Texas Beans with Beef, for example—is to soak the beans overnight in water to cover, adding salt and cooking oil.

Slow Cookers Work While You Are Away

Every woman who works away from home—whether for pay or for community—appreciates coming back to a kitchen filled with the aroma of supper ready to serve. That's the appeal of the slow cooker— the trustworthy appliance that takes over pot-watching when you have to be away all day.

Cooking your dinner in a slow cooker will take roughly half as much energy as baking the same food in a conventional oven—and a little more energy than using a surface unit. Unlike the oven, the slow cooker will not heat up your kitchen—there's a saving on air conditioning in hot weather. The long cooking in moist heat tenderizes the less tender cuts of meat—an aid to food bills. And since all the foods— in many combinations—are added to the cooker at one time, the clean-up is quick. You'll have few, if any, mixing bowls, saucepans or skillets to wash.

Satisfaction from using a slow cooker depends not only on using recipes adapted to it, but also on understanding the appliance, how it will work and what it will do. For testing recipes in this book, we used

3½-quart slow cookers—a good size for a family of four to six. The cookers were cylindrical, the shape of a child's toy drum, with heating element wrapped around the sides of the cooker. On this type of cooker, heat is continuous, not off-and-on, and there are two heat settings, high and low. The cooker has a tight-fitting cover, which is essential to retain the moisture for all-day, no-watch slow cooking.

Slow cookers are available in a variety of shapes, sizes and colors. In addition to those having the heating element wrapped around the sides (there may be a removable liner), there are cookers with a separate heating base. And there are slow cookers that are also all-purpose appliances for regular cooking and deep-fat frying. Some slow cookers have thermostatic heat controls with several heat settings. Because of these differences, it is important to follow instructions in the manufacturer's manual that came with your cooker. Most of the following pointers are applicable to the use of most slow cookers:

• Make sure the cooker with a glass or stone liner is at room temperature before plugging it into the outlet. Turn on the electricity after the food is in the cooker.

• Fill the cooker at least half full of food.

• Since sudden temperature changes can damage the lining of some cookers, *do not* pour cold water or other cold liquid over hot food in the cooker.

• Thaw frozen food before putting it in the cooker—otherwise it delays heating and lengthens cooking time.

• Trim visible fat from meat before placing it in the cooker. Fat floats on top of the food during cooking and seals heat under it. Thus foods lower in the cooker may be overcooked—and when meats are overcooked they become stringy and especially objectionable if you want to slice them for serving.

• Little or no evaporation occurs as food cooks in the moist heat of the slow cooker—and it does not brown. If desired, you can brown meats in a skillet over high heat first, to improve the color and flavor of the dish.

• Meats sometimes cook faster than some vegetables in a slow cooker, which is the opposite of what happens in conventional cooking. Thus our recipes call for dicing carrots, celery or parsnips or cutting them in thin slices and for dividing potatoes into quarters or eighths. Placing vegetables in the bottom of the cooker with meat on top will further assure proper cooking.

• Sometimes the pot liquids in slow cookers are somewhat watery and tasteless; they do not evaporate or cook down as they do in a pot on top of the range. To reduce pot liquids and concentrate the flavor, ladle the liquid into a saucepan and quickly boil it down. To step up flavor, add bouillon granules or cubes; use gravy browners to improve color. Many recipes in this book give directions for thickening juices to make gravy.

• If you are adapting a recipe normally cooked on a surface unit to cooking in the slow cooker, never add more than half as much water as the original recipe calls for—recipes developed for slow cookers always call for less liquid than for conventional cooking.

• Milk, sour and sweet cream, pasta and some soft-flesh fish do not stand up in long slow cooking. Add them near the end of the cooking.

• Use the slow cooker to keep food warm at informal buffet suppers. Some hostesses like to serve baked beans in them. Mixed Bean Casserole is a favorite with some families.

• When in use, slow cookers and their covers may get very hot. Use hot pads or mitts to move them.

• Avoid using abrasive scouring pads and cleaners on the interior of the cooker. They may scratch the lining. Scratches can trap food that cannot be removed in cleaning. It is better to fill the cooker with warm sudsy water and let it soak.

• Some manufacturer's directions permit storing the cooker in the refrigerator, filled with food ready to be cooked, or with leftovers to be reheated. But others advise you not to do this. Follow directions with your cooker. If you do not put the cooker in the refrigerator, the food should be removed and stored in plastic bags or covered bowls in the refrigerator.

• While the slow cooker's greatest help is in cooking main dishes, many of which are practically a meal, we have included a few fun food recipes we hope you'll try. Honey-nut Rolls, an unusual and easy pull-apart bread, attracts favorable attention and wins compliments when served with coffee. Cylindrical loaves of spicy Pumpkin Bread and Banana Bread, sliced and spread with butter or cream cheese, lend a festive air. And Cereal-nut Scramble, an eat-from-hand snack, is too good to miss.

The chapters that follow deliver such recipes to you.

CHAPTER THREE

Soup Sampler

Soups made with recipes in this chapter offer a sampler of the kinds people today most like to sip. Many of them make tempting, satisfying and easy one-pot meals that wait patiently when supper or dinner is delayed.

"When my children tell me they are going to stay at school to practice for the band or play or some other activity," says a Michigan mother, "that is a signal they may be late for the evening meal. On such days I often make a substantial soup. I can reheat it quickly for the latecomers and it isn't much work."

In choosing the right soup for a main dish, check the recipe to make sure it contains some protein food such as meat, chicken, fish, cheese or legumes like dried beans, peas and lentils. Many of the recipes here—Easy Vegetable Soup and Southern Fish Chowder, for example—are satisfying main dishes. If vegetables are scant, add a plate of vegetable relishes, a green or combination salad to the menu.

Representatives of light soups also appear in this chapter. They are good selections for the family or company lunch and make excellent escorts for sandwiches. Creamy Cauliflower and Herbed Tomato Soups are two delicious examples.

Browse through the pages that follow. You will find more recipes for soups that are pleasant to face at mealtime, especially on cold, blustery days.

EASY VEGETABLE SOUP

This flavorful soup can simmer all day in a slow cooker or be cooked in only 12 minutes in a pressure cooker.

BASIC RECIPE — MAKES ABOUT 2¾ QUARTS.

1 lb. ground beef	2 (16 oz.) cans stewed tomatoes
1 c. chopped onion	3½ c. water
1 clove garlic, minced	4 beef bouillon cubes
1 c. sliced carrots	1 tblsp. parsley flakes
1 c. sliced celery	¼ tsp. dried basil leaves
1 c. frozen green beans	1 tsp. salt
¼ c. regular rice	⅛ tsp. pepper

 Range Top: 1 hour cooking time

Cook ground beef, onion and garlic in Dutch oven until beef is browned, about 10 minutes. Drain off fat. Add remaining ingredients. Bring to boiling. Reduce heat and simmer, covered, 50 minutes or until vegetables are tender.

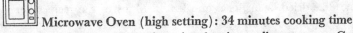 **Microwave Oven (high setting): 34 minutes cooking time**

Use ingredients listed in basic recipe, but in smaller amounts. Crumble ½ lb. ground beef into 3-qt. glass casserole. Cover and microwave 4 minutes, stirring twice to separate meat pieces. Add ½ c. chopped onion, 1 small clove garlic, minced, ½ c. each sliced carrots, celery and frozen green beans, 2 tblsp. regular rice, 1 (16 oz.) can stewed tomatoes, 2 c. water, 2 beef bouillon cubes, 1½ tsp. parsley flakes, ½ tsp. salt, ⅛ tsp. dried basil leaves and ¹⁄₁₆ tsp. pepper. Cover and microwave 30 minutes, stirring every 5 minutes. If soup is too thick, stir in a little water. Makes about 5 cups.

Pressure Cooker: 12 minutes cooking time

Use ingredients listed in basic recipe. Cook onion, ground beef and garlic in 6-qt. pressure pan until beef is browned, about 5 minutes. Mix in carrots, celery, green beans, rice, stewed tomatoes, 2 c. of the water, bouillon cubes, parsley, basil, salt and pepper. Close cover securely. Place over high heat. Bring to 15 lbs. pressure, according to manufacturer's directions for your pressure cooker. When pressure is reached (control will begin to jiggle), reduce heat immediately and cook 5 minutes. Remove from heat. Reduce pressure instantly by placing cooker under cold running water. Add remaining 1½ c. water. Bring mixture to boiling, about 2 minutes. Makes about 2½ quarts.

Slow Cooker: 9 hours 10 minutes to 10 hours 10 minutes cooking time

Use ingredients listed in basic recipe, but substitute long grain parboiled rice for regular rice and thinly slice carrots and celery. Cook ground beef, onion and garlic in skillet until beef is browned, about 10 minutes. Drain off fat. Combine remaining ingredients with meat in cooker. Cover and cook on low 8 to 9 hours. Turn on high and cook until vegetables are tender, about 1 hour. Makes about 2½ quarts.

Note: If more convenient, soup may be cooked on low 10 to 12 hours or until vegetables are tender.

PIONEER VEGETABLE SOUP

There is less liquid evaporation in the slow cooker than range top, so the water has been reduced in this method.

BASIC RECIPE — MAKES 9 CUPS.

2 lbs. cross-cut beef shanks
1½ qts. water
1 tblsp. salt
¼ tsp. pepper
1 c. chopped onion
1 c. sliced carrots

1 c. cubed, pared potato
1 c. cubed, pared turnips
½ c. sliced celery
1 (16 oz.) can tomatoes, cut up

Range Top: 2½ to 3 hours cooking time

Combine beef shanks, water, salt and pepper in Dutch oven. Bring to boiling. Reduce heat and simmer, covered, 2 to 2½ hours or until meat is tender. Add remaining ingredients. Simmer, covered, 30 minutes or until vegetables are tender. Remove meat and bones. Cut meat in bite-size pieces and return to soup; heat.

 Slow Cooker: 6 hours 5 minutes cooking time

Use ingredients listed in basic recipe, but reduce water to 1 quart. Combine all ingredients in cooker with meat on top. Cover and cook on high 6 hours. Before serving, remove meat and bones. Cut meat in bite-size pieces and return to soup. Heat 5 minutes. Makes 11 cups.

MINESTRONE

Corn, green beans or fresh tomatoes can be substituted for other vegetables in the soup—make it different every time.

BASIC RECIPE — MAKES 3½ QUARTS.

1 lb. stewing beef, cut in 1" cubes	¼ tsp. pepper
2 tblsp. butter or regular margarine	1 (16 oz.) can tomatoes, cut up
4 beef bouillon cubes	2 c. shredded cabbage
7 c. hot water	1 small zucchini, thinly sliced (1 c.)
1 medium onion, chopped	1 c. thinly sliced carrots
½ c. chopped celery	1 (15 oz.) can garbanzo beans, drained
2 tblsp. parsley flakes	
1 tsp. salt	1 c. uncooked small elbow macaroni
½ tsp. dried thyme leaves	

 Range Top: 1 hour 50 minutes cooking time

Lightly brown beef in melted butter in 5-qt. Dutch oven, about 10

minutes. Add beef bouillon cubes, water, onion, celery, parsley, salt, thyme, pepper and tomatoes. Mix well. Bring to boiling, reduce heat and simmer, covered, 1 hour 15 minutes or until meat is tender. Stir once or twice during cooking. Add cabbage, zucchini, carrots, beans and macaroni. Return to boiling. Reduce heat and simmer, covered, 25 minutes or until macaroni and vegetables are tender. Stir mixture once or twice during cooking.

Pressure Cooker: 39 to 44 minutes cooking time

Use ingredients listed in basic recipe. Lightly brown beef in melted butter in 6-qt. pressure pan, about 10 minutes. Add beef bouillon cubes, water, onion, celery, parsley, salt, thyme, pepper and tomatoes. Mix well. Close cover securely. Place over high heat. Bring to 15 lbs. pressure, according to manufacturer's directions for your pressure cooker. When pressure is reached (control will begin to jiggle), reduce heat immediately and cook 9 minutes. Remove from heat. Reduce pressure instantly by placing cooker under cold running water. Add cabbage, zucchini, carrots, beans and macaroni. Return to boiling. Reduce heat and simmer, uncovered, 20 to 25 minutes or until vegetables and macaroni are tender.

Slow Cooker: 8 to 10 hours cooking time

Use ingredients listed in basic recipe, but omit butter and reduce hot water to 6 c. Dissolve bouillon cubes in water in cooker. Add beef, onion, celery, parsley, salt, thyme, pepper and tomatoes. Cover and cook on low 7 to 9 hours. Add cabbage, zucchini, carrots, beans and macaroni. Cover and cook on high 1 hour or until vegetables and macaroni are tender. Stir before serving.

FRENCH ONION SOUP

In the pressure cooker, bring soup to 15 lbs. pressure. Then remove from heat. Allow time for pressure to drop.

BASIC RECIPE — MAKES 4 TO 6 SERVINGS.

3 large onions, thinly sliced	½ tsp. salt
¼ c. butter or regular margarine	Dash of pepper 4 to 6 slices French bread,
4 c. hot water	toasted
2 tblsp. beef bouillon granules	¼ c. grated Parmesan cheese

 Range Top: 12 to 13 minutes cooking time

Cook onions in melted butter in large saucepan until tender and lightly browned, about 10 minutes. Stir in hot water, beef bouillon granules, salt and pepper. Heat to boiling; reduce heat and simmer 2 to 3 minutes to blend flavors. Sprinkle toasted bread with cheese. Serve soup in bowls garnished with a slice of French bread.

Microwave Oven (high setting): 26 to 30 minutes cooking time

Use ingredients listed in basic recipe. Combine onion and butter in 2-qt. glass casserole. Cover and microwave (high setting) 16 to 18 minutes or until onions are tender. Stir twice. Add hot water, beef bouillon granules, salt and pepper; mix well. Cover and microwave 10 to 12 minutes or until very hot, stirring once. Serve soup in bowls garnished with a slice of French bread sprinkled with cheese.

 Pressure Cooker: Time to bring to 15 lbs. pressure

Use ingredients listed in basic recipe. Combine onions, butter, hot water, beef bouillon granules, salt and pepper in 4-qt. pressure pan. Close cover securely. Place over high heat. Bring to 15 lbs. pressure, according to manufacturer's directions for your pressure cooker. When pressure is reached (control will begin to jiggle), remove from heat at once. Let pressure drop of its own accord. Serve soup in bowls garnished with a slice of French bread sprinkled with cheese.

Slow Cooker: 6 hours 10 minutes cooking time

Use ingredients listed in basic recipe. Cook onions in large skillet in butter until lightly browned, about 10 minutes. Combine sautéed onions, hot water, beef bouillon granules, salt and pepper in cooker. Cover and cook on low 6 hours. Serve in bowls garnished with a slice of French bread sprinkled with cheese.

BUSY-DAY SPINACH SOUP

Homemade spinach soup that can be cooked in 15 minutes or less— serve this on an extra-busy day.

BASIC RECIPE — MAKES 1 QUART.

1 (10 oz.) pkg. frozen chopped
    spinach
¼ c. boiling water
3 c. milk
2 tblsp. butter or regular
    margarine

1 tblsp. grated onion
1½ tblsp. flour
1 tblsp. chicken bouillon
    granules
¼ tsp. salt

Range Top: 13½ minutes cooking time

Place spinach in 2-qt. saucepan in boiling water. Return to boil, cover and cook 3 minutes. Separate with a fork. Cook 1 more minute. Purée spinach with liquid and 1 c. of the milk in blender. Melt butter in same saucepan, about 1 minute. Add onion and cook 30 seconds. Blend in flour. Add remaining 2 c. milk, bouillon granules and salt. Cook, stirring constantly, 7 minutes or until mixture comes to a boil. Add spinach mixture and cook over medium heat, stirring constantly, 2 minutes or until hot.

Microwave Oven (high setting): 16 minutes cooking time
Use ingredients listed in basic recipe. Microwave (high setting) frozen
spinach in 2-qt. glass casserole, covered, 7 minutes or until tender.
Give dish one quarter turn during cooking. Purée spinach with liquid
and 1 c. of the milk in blender. Microwave butter with onion in same
casserole 1 minute. Stir in flour. Slowly stir in remaining 2 c. milk.
Add spinach mixture, bouillon granules and salt. Microwave 8 minutes or until mixture comes to a boil, stirring every 2 minutes.

CHICKEN-VEGETABLE SOUP

*You'll need to finely chop the vegetables if you choose the slow cooker
method—they cook better.*
BASIC RECIPE — MAKES 2 QUARTS.

½ c. chopped onion
½ c. chopped celery
½ c. chopped carrot
1 tblsp. chopped fresh parsley
Backs, necks, wings from 2
   chickens
1 (8 oz.) can stewed tomatoes

1 qt. water
1 tblsp. salt
¼ tsp. pepper
½ c. narrow noodles, broken up
1 tsp. monosodium glutamate
   (optional)

Range Top: 1 hour 5 minutes cooking time
Place onion, celery, carrot, parsley, chicken, tomatoes, water, salt and
pepper in Dutch oven. Bring to boiling. Reduce heat and simmer, covered, 50 minutes. Remove chicken; add noodles and continue simmering 10 minutes. Remove skin and bones from chicken; return meat to
soup. If desired, add monosodium glutamate. Heat, about 5 minutes.

Slow Cooker: 8½ to 10½ hours cooking time
Use ingredients listed in basic recipe, but finely chop vegetables. Place
onion, celery, carrot, parsley, chicken and tomatoes in cooker. Add

water, salt and pepper. Cover and cook on low 8 to 10 hours. Remove chicken. Skim off fat from broth in cooker. Add noodles and cook on high heat 30 minutes. Remove skin and bones from chicken; return meat to soup. If desired, add monosodium glutamate.

HAM-VEGETABLE SOUP

Leftover baked ham with its bone can be substituted for the smoked pork hocks in this soup.

BASIC RECIPE — MAKES 9 CUPS.

1½ lbs. smoked pork hocks
5 c. water
2 c. tomato juice
1 tsp. salt
¼ tsp. pepper

2 c. shredded cabbage
1½ c. cubed, pared potatoes
1 c. sliced carrots
1 c. chopped onion

Range Top: 3 hours and 10 minutes cooking time

Trim excess fat from hocks. Combine them with water, tomato juice, salt and pepper in Dutch oven. Bring to boiling. Reduce heat and simmer, covered, 2½ hours or until the hocks are tender. Remove hocks from broth. Cut meat from bone, discarding fat and bone. Return meat to broth along with cabbage, potatoes, carrots and onion. Continue simmering, covered, 40 minutes or until vegetables are tender.

Slow Cooker: 10 to 12 hours cooking time

Use ingredients listed in basic recipe, but reduce water from 5 to 3 cups. Prepare ingredients as for Range Top, but finely shred cabbage, cut potatoes in small cubes, thinly slice carrots and finely chop onions. Place trimmed hocks in cooker; add vegetables, tomato juice, 3 cups water, salt and pepper. Cover and cook on low 11 to 12 hours, or 9 hours on low, turn heat to high and cook 1 to 1½ hours. Remove hocks. Cut meat from bone, discarding fat and bone. Return meat to soup.

HEARTY CORN-SAUSAGE SOUP

This robust soup is easy enough to serve on the busiest of days. Delicious cooked all three ways.

BASIC RECIPE   —   MAKES ABOUT 7 CUPS.

1 lb. link pork sausages (12 to 14)

2 medium potatoes, pared and cubed (2 c.)

1 c. chopped onion

½ c. chopped green pepper

1 c. water

1 (16½ or 17 oz.) can cream-style corn

2 c. milk

2 tblsp. flour

1½ tsp. salt

¼ tsp. pepper

1 tblsp. instant minced parsley

 Range Top: 35 to 40 minutes cooking time

Cook sausages in Dutch oven or large kettle until lightly browned on all sides, about 15 minutes. Remove sausages and cut in bite-size pieces. Drain all but 1 tblsp. drippings from Dutch oven. Return sausages to Dutch oven. Add potatoes, onion, green pepper and water. Cover and simmer 10 to 15 minutes or until vegetables are tender. Stir in corn. Slowly stir milk into flour; add to soup and stir well to mix. Stir in salt, pepper and parsley. Cook and stir until mixture thickens and boils, about 10 minutes.

Microwave Oven (high setting): 32 to 38 minutes cooking time

Use ingredients listed in basic recipe. Place sausages in 5-qt. glass casserole. Cover with waxed paper. Microwave (high setting) 6 to 7 minutes or until no longer pink, giving casserole ½ turn after 3 minutes. Remove sausages. Drain all but 1 tblsp. drippings from casserole. Cut sausages in bite-size pieces and return to casserole. Add potatoes, onion, green pepper and water. Cover and microwave 12 to 15 minutes or until vegetables are tender, stirring once. Add corn. Slowly stir milk into flour. Add to soup along with salt, pepper and parsley;

mix well. Microwave, uncovered, 14 to 16 minutes or until mixture comes to a boil, stirring 3 times.

Pressure Cooker: 30 minutes cooking time

Use ingredients listed in basic recipe. Cook sausages in 4-qt. pressure pan until lightly browned on all sides, about 15 minutes. Remove sausages and cut in bite-size pieces. Drain all but 1 tblsp. drippings from pressure pan. Return sausages to pan; add potatoes, onion, green pepper and water. Close cover securely. Place over high heat. Bring to 15 lbs. pressure, according to manufacturer's directions for your pressure cooker. When pressure is reached (control will begin to jiggle), reduce heat immediately and cook 5 minutes. Remove from heat. Reduce pressure instantly by placing cooker under cold running water. Stir in corn. Slowly stir milk into flour. Stir into soup along with salt, pepper and parsley. Cook and stir until mixture thickens and boils, about 10 minutes.

SOUTHERN FISH CHOWDER

An unusual combination of fish, clams and okra. Takes only 13 minutes to simmer on range top.

BASIC RECIPE — MAKES 6 TO 8 SERVINGS.

2 (6½ oz.) cans minced clams
1 (28 oz.) can tomatoes, cut up
2 medium potatoes, pared and cubed (2 c.)
2 medium onions, thinly sliced
1 medium green pepper, chopped
2 cloves garlic, minced
1½ tsp. salt

½ tsp. dried basil leaves
⅛ tsp. pepper
1 bay leaf
2 c. water
1 lb. fillet of sole, cut in 1″ pieces
1 (10 oz.) pkg. frozen okra, cut in ½″ pieces

Range Top: 12 to 13 minutes cooking time

Drain clams, reserving liquid. Place clam liquid, tomatoes, potatoes, onions, green pepper, garlic, salt, basil, pepper, bay leaf and water in large Dutch oven. Bring to boiling. Reduce heat and simmer, covered, 8 minutes or until vegetables are almost tender. Add sole, okra and clams. Return to boiling. Reduce heat and simmer, uncovered, 4 to 5 minutes or until sole is cooked. Remove bay leaf.

Pressure Cooker: 7 to 8 minutes cooking time
Use ingredients listed in basic recipe. Drain clams, reserving liquid. Place clam liquid, tomatoes, potatoes, onion, green pepper, garlic, salt, basil, pepper, bay leaf and water in 4-qt. pressure pan. Close cover securely. Place on high heat. Bring to 15 lbs. pressure, according to manufacturer's directions for your pressure cooker. When pressure is reached (control will begin to jiggle), reduce heat immediately and cook 3 minutes. Remove from heat. Reduce pressure instantly by placing cooker under cold running water. Add sole, okra and clams. Return to boiling. Reduce heat and simmer, uncovered, 4 to 5 minutes or until sole is cooked. Remove bay leaf.

NEW YORK CLAM CHOWDER

Canned minced clams are used in this vegetable chowder. No need to rely on your fish supply market for fresh ones.
BASIC RECIPE — MAKES ABOUT 1 QUART.

2 tblsp. butter or regular margarine	¾ c. water
¼ c. chopped onion	1 (16 oz.) can tomatoes, cut up
¼ c. chopped celery	1 tsp. salt
¼ c. chopped carrot	⅛ tsp. pepper
1 medium potato, pared and finely cubed	⅛ tsp. dried thyme leaves
	1 (6½ oz.) can minced clams

Range Top: 39 minutes cooking time
Melt butter in large saucepan, about 2 minutes. Add onion and celery; cook until soft, about 5 minutes. Add carrot, potato, water, tomatoes,

salt, pepper and thyme. Simmer, covered, 30 minutes. Add clams with liquid; heat thoroughly, about 2 minutes.

Microwave Oven (high setting): 20 minutes cooking time
Use ingredients listed in basic recipe. Place butter, onion, celery, carrot and potato in 2-qt. glass casserole. Cover and microwave (high setting) 7 minutes, stirring once. Add water, tomatoes, salt, pepper and thyme. Cover and microwave 12 minutes, stirring once. Add clams with liquid. Cover and microwave 1 minute.

Pressure Cooker: 10 minutes cooking time
Use ingredients listed in basic recipe. Combine all ingredients except clams in 4-qt. pressure pan. Close lid securely. Place over high heat. Bring to 15 lbs. pressure, according to manufacturer's directions for your pressure cooker. When pressure is reached (control will begin to jiggle), reduce heat immediately and cook 5 minutes. Remove from heat. Let pressure drop of its own accord. Add clams and liquid. Simmer, uncovered, 5 minutes.

NEW ENGLAND FISH CHOWDER

Imagine cooking this chowder in only 18 minutes in the pressure cooker . . . ideal when your time is limited.
BASIC RECIPE — MAKES ABOUT 1½ QUARTS.

3 slices bacon, cut up	1½ c. water
½ c. chopped onion	1 tblsp. parsley flakes
½ c. chopped celery	1½ tsp. salt
1 lb. frozen cod fish fillets, thawed	⅛ tsp. pepper
	2 c. milk
2 c. diced, pared potatoes	2 tblsp. flour

Range Top: 36 minutes cooking time

Cook bacon in Dutch oven until crisp, about 6 minutes. Remove bacon; drain and reserve. Cook onion and celery in bacon drippings until soft, about 5 minutes. Cut fish into bite-size pieces. Add to onion and celery mixture along with potatoes, water, parsley, salt and pepper. Bring to boiling. Reduce heat and simmer, covered, 20 minutes. Blend ½ c. of the milk into flour. Add to fish mixture along with remaining 1½ c. milk. Cook and stir until mixture comes to a boil, about 5 minutes. Serve in bowls sprinkled with bacon.

 Microwave Oven (high setting): 28 to 33 minutes cooking time

Use ingredients listed in basic recipe, but reduce water to ½ c. Lay bacon in 2-qt. glass casserole. Microwave (high setting) 4 minutes or until crisp. Drain bacon and reserve. Pour off all but 1 tblsp. bacon drippings. Place potatoes, onion, celery and ½ c. water in casserole. Cover and microwave 12 to 15 minutes or until vegetables are tender. Cut fish in bite-size pieces. Add fish, parsley, salt, pepper and 1½ c. milk to vegetables. Cover and microwave 6 to 8 minutes or until fish flakes easily. Blend remaining ½ c. milk with flour; stir into chowder. Microwave 6 minutes or until mixture comes to a boil, stirring every 2 minutes. Serve in bowls sprinkled with crumbled bacon.

 Pressure Cooker: 18 minutes cooking time

Use ingredients listed in basic recipe, but reduce water to ½ c. Cook bacon in 4-qt. pressure pan until crisp, about 6 minutes. Remove bacon and reserve. Pour off all but 1 tblsp. bacon drippings. Cut fish in bite-size pieces. Add fish, potatoes, celery, onion, parsley, salt, pepper and ½ c. water to pressure pan. Close cover securely. Place over high heat. Bring to 15 lbs. pressure, according to manufacturer's directions for your pressure cooker. When pressure is reached (control will begin to jiggle), reduce heat immediately and cook 7 minutes. Remove from heat. Reduce pressure instantly by placing cooker under cold running water. Blend milk into flour and stir into chowder. Cook, stirring constantly, until mixture comes to a boil, about 5 minutes. Serve in bowls sprinkled with crumbled bacon.

MIDWESTERN CLAM CHOWDER

Thawed frozen asparagus spears can be substituted for fresh in this recipe—then you can prepare the chowder year 'round.

BASIC RECIPE — MAKES 6 SERVINGS.

1 c. cubed, pared potatoes	1 lb. fresh asparagus, cut in 1"
½ c. chopped onion	lengths
1½ c. water	2 c. milk
1 (6½ oz.) can minced clams	2 tblsp. flour
¾ tsp. salt	2 tblsp. butter or regular
¼ tsp. pepper	margarine

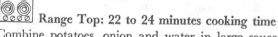 Range Top: 22 to 24 minutes cooking time

Combine potatoes, onion and water in large saucepan. Drain clams, reserving liquid. Add clam liquid, salt and pepper to potato mixture. Bring to a boil. Reduce heat and simmer, covered, 10 minutes. Add asparagus to potato mixture. Cook 7 to 9 minutes or until asparagus is tender. Stir in clams. Slowly blend milk into flour. Add to clam-vegetable mixture along with butter. Cook, stirring constantly, until soup comes to a boil and is slightly thickened, about 5 minutes.

Microwave Oven (high setting): 23 minutes cooking time

Use ingredients listed in basic recipe but reduce water from 1½ to 1 c. Combine potatoes, onion and 1 c. water in 2½-qt. glass casserole. Drain clams, reserving liquid. Add clam liquid, salt and pepper to potato mixture. Cover and microwave (high setting) 9 minutes, stirring once. Add asparagus. Cover and microwave 8 minutes. Add clams. Slowly stir milk into flour. Add to clam-vegetable mixture along with butter. Microwave 3 minutes. Stir and continue microwaving 3 more minutes or until hot and slightly thickened.

SALMON SUPPER SOUP

Garnish soup with minced fresh parsley for a special touch of color and flavor.

BASIC RECIPE — MAKES 7 CUPS.

1 c. chopped onion	1 tblsp. vinegar
2 tblsp. butter or regular margarine	1 tsp. paprika
1 c. thinly sliced carrots	1 tsp. sugar
1 c. cubed, pared potatoes	½ tsp. salt
2 (13¾ oz.) cans chicken broth	¼ tsp. dried dillweed
1 (16 oz.) can stewed tomatoes	1 (16 oz.) can pink salmon
	Dairy sour cream

 Range Top: 29 to 39 minutes cooking time

Cook onion in melted butter in 4-qt. Dutch oven until soft, about 5 minutes. Add remaining ingredients except salmon and sour cream. Bring to a boil. Reduce heat to medium. Cook, covered, 20 to 30 minutes or until vegetables are tender. Add salmon with its liquid, breaking salmon into chunks. Simmer 4 minutes. Serve in bowls. Pass sour cream to spoon on top.

 Pressure Cooker: 6 to 7 minutes cooking time

Use ingredients listed in basic recipe. Combine all of them except salmon and sour cream in 4-qt. pressure cooker. Close cover securely. Place over high heat. Bring to 15 lbs. pressure, according to manufacturer's directions for your pressure cooker. When pressure is reached (control will begin to jiggle), reduce heat immediately and cook 3 minutes. Remove from heat. Reduce pressure instantly by placing cooker under cold running water. Add salmon with its liquid, breaking salmon into chunks. Simmer, uncovered, 3 to 4 minutes or until salmon is hot. Serve in bowls. Pass sour cream to spoon on top. Makes about 8½ cups.

BEAN SOUP

Instead of soaking the beans overnight in the slow cooker, they are simmered on low 12 hours. This is added to cooking time.

BASIC RECIPE — MAKES 9 CUPS.

1 c. dried navy beans	1 (8 oz.) can tomatoes, cut up
1 qt. water	2 (13¾ oz.) cans chicken broth
1 lb. cross-cut smoked pork	1 tsp. salt
hocks	⅛ tsp. pepper
1 c. chopped onion	1 c. shredded Cheddar cheese
½ c. chopped celery	(4 oz.)
1 clove garlic, minced	1 tblsp. parsley flakes

 Range Top: 2 hours 5 minutes to 2 hours 35 minutes cooking time

Place beans and 1 qt. water in Dutch oven. Bring to boiling, boil 2 minutes. Cover, remove from heat and let beans stand for 1 hour. (Or soak beans overnight.) Add smoked pork hocks, onion, celery, garlic, tomatoes, chicken broth, salt and pepper. Bring to boiling. Reduce heat and simmer, covered, 2 to 2½ hours or until meat and beans are tender. Remove meat from soup. Cut in bite-size pieces and return to soup. Add cheese and parsley. Stir over heat until cheese is melted, about 3 minutes.

Pressure Cooker: 41 minutes cooking time

Use ingredients listed in basic recipe, but increase water to 6 c., increase salt to 1½ tsp. and add 2 tblsp. cooking oil. Combine beans, 2 c. of the water, 1½ tsp. salt and 2 tblsp. cooking oil in 6-qt. pressure cooker. Cover and soak overnight. Drain well. Add smoked pork hocks, 1 qt. water, onion, celery, garlic, tomatoes, chicken broth and pepper to beans. Close cover securely. Place over high heat. Bring to 15 lbs. pressure, according to manufacturer's directions for your pressure cooker. When pressure is reached (control will begin to jiggle),

reduce heat immediately and cook 40 minutes. Remove from heat. Let
pressure drop of its own accord. Remove meat; cut in bite-size pieces
and return to soup. Add cheese and parsley. Stir over medium heat
until cheese is melted, about 1 minute. Makes 2½ quarts.

 Slow Cooker: 21 hours 5 minutes cooking time
Use ingredients listed in basic recipe. Place beans and 1 qt. water in
cooker. Cover and cook on low overnight or 12 hours. Add pork hocks,
onion, celery, garlic, tomatoes, chicken broth, salt and pepper. Cover
and cook on low 9 hours. Remove meat from soup. Cut in bite-size
pieces and return to soup. Add cheese and parsley. Stir until cheese is
melted, about 5 minutes. Makes 2½ quarts.

EASY BEAN-SAUSAGE SOUP

*This bean soup requires little cooking time because canned navy beans
are used instead of dried ones.*

BASIC RECIPE — MAKES ABOUT 9 CUPS.

½ lb. Polish sausage, cut in ½"
  slices
1 (15 oz.) can navy beans,
  drained
1 c. chopped onion
½ c. chopped celery
½ c. sliced carrot
1 clove garlic, minced
1 (16 oz.) can tomatoes, cut
  up

3 c. water
3 beef bouillon cubes
¾ tsp. salt
½ tsp. dried basil leaves
¼ tsp. pepper
2 small zucchini, cut in ¼"
  slices (1 c.)

 Range Top: 50 minutes cooking time
Combine all ingredients in Dutch oven except zucchini. Bring to a
boil. Reduce heat and simmer, covered, until vegetables are tender,
about 40 minutes. Add zucchini and continue simmering 10 minutes.

Pressure Cooker: 3 minutes cooking time

Use ingredients listed in basic recipe, but reduce water from 3 to 2½ c. and cut zucchini in thicker slices. Combine all ingredients in 6-qt. pressure cooker. Close cover securely. Place over high heat. Bring to 15 lbs. pressure, according to manufacturer's directions for your pressure cooker. When pressure is reached (control will begin to jiggle), reduce heat immediately and cook 3 minutes. Remove from heat. Reduce pressure instantly by placing cooker under cold running water. Makes about 2 quarts.

HERBED TOMATO SOUP

Since this soup recipe makes only 1 quart, it is well suited to microwave cookery as well as to top of the range.

BASIC RECIPE — MAKES 1 QUART.

½ c. chopped onion
½ c. chopped celery
2 tblsp. butter or regular
  margarine
1 (16 oz.) can tomatoes, cut
  up
1 (13¾ oz.) can chicken broth

½ tsp. dried basil leaves
½ tsp. paprika
½ tsp. salt
¼ tsp. pepper
1 bay leaf
2 tblsp. chopped fresh parsley

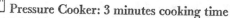 Range Top: 23 minutes cooking time

Cook onion and celery in butter in large saucepan until soft, about 5 minutes. Add remaining ingredients, except parsley. Bring to a boil. Reduce heat and simmer, covered, 15 minutes. Remove bay leaf. Pour half of soup into blender; whirl until smooth. Repeat with remaining half. Return to saucepan; heat to simmering, about 3 minutes. Serve garnished with parsley.

Microwave Oven (high setting): 14½ to 16½ minutes cooking time

Use ingredients listed in basic recipe. Place onion, celery and butter in
3-qt. glass casserole. Cover and microwave 5 to 7 minutes or until
onion and celery are soft, stirring once. Add remaining ingredients except parsley. Cover and microwave 8 minutes or until mixtures comes
to a boil, stirring once. Remove bay leaf. Pour half of soup into
blender; whirl until smooth. Repeat with remaining half. Return to
casserole. Cover and microwave 1½ minutes or until mixture just
comes to a boil. Serve garnished with parsley.

CREAMY CAULIFLOWER SOUP

*More liquid evaporates during range top cooking, so the yield is 7 cups
as compared to 2 quarts in the other two appliances.*

BASIC RECIPE — MAKES ABOUT 7 CUPS.

1 medium head cauliflower, cut in flowerets (6 c.)	½ c. water
1 c. chopped onion	1 tsp. salt
½ c. chopped celery	⅛ tsp. pepper
2 (13¾ oz.) cans chicken broth	½ tsp. Worcestershire sauce
	1½ c. light cream

 Range Top: 12 to 17 minutes cooking time

Combine all ingredients except light cream in Dutch oven. Bring to
boiling. Cook, covered, 10 to 15 minutes or until vegetables are tender.
Purée hot mixture in blender. Return to Dutch oven. Add cream and
bring to boiling; let boil about 2 minutes.

 Pressure Cooker: 4 minutes cooking time

Use ingredients listed in basic recipe, but reduce light cream to 1 cup.
Combine all ingredients except light cream in 6-qt. pressure pan. Close
cover securely. Place over high heat. Bring to 15 lbs. pressure, accord-

ing to manufacturer's directions for your pressure cooker. When pressure is reached (control will start to jiggle), reduce heat immediately and cook 2 minutes. Remove from heat. Reduce pressure instantly by placing cooker under cold running water. Purée hot mixture in blender. Return to pressure pan. Add cream and bring to boiling; let boil about 2 minutes. Makes 2 quarts.

Slow Cooker: 6¼ to 8¼ hours cooking time

Use ingredients listed in basic recipe, but reduce light cream to 1 c. Cut cauliflower into small flowerets. Combine all ingredients except light cream in cooker. Cook, covered, on low 6 to 8 hours. Purée hot mixture in blender. Return to cooker. Add cream and cook, covered, on high 15 minutes or until hot. Makes about 2 quarts.

SPLIT PEA SOUP

We tested this soup in three different appliances. Use the one that fits your time schedule.

BASIC RECIPE — MAKES ABOUT 3 QUARTS.

1 lb. dried green split peas, rinsed and drained	½ c. thinly sliced celery
1 lb. meaty, smoked pork hocks	2 qts. water
1 c. chopped onion	2 tsp. salt
1 c. thinly sliced carrots	½ tsp. dried marjoram leaves
	¼ tsp. pepper

Range Top: 1½ to 2 hours cooking time

Combine ingredients in 5-qt. Dutch oven. Bring to boiling; reduce heat to very low and simmer, covered, 1½ to 2 hours, stirring occasionally. Remove pork hocks; cut meat in bite-size pieces and return to soup. Stir before serving.

Microwave Oven (high setting): 1 hour 20 minutes cooking time

Use ingredients listed in basic recipe. Combine all ingredients in 5-qt. glass casserole. Cover and microwave (high setting) 50 minutes, stirring every 10 minutes. Remove pork hocks. Cut meat in bite-size pieces and return to soup. Cover and microwave 30 minutes, stirring twice. Makes 9 cups.

 Slow Cooker: 10 to 12 hours cooking time

Use ingredients listed in basic recipe. Combine all ingredients in cooker. Cover and cook on low 10 to 12 hours. Remove pork hocks. Cut meat into bite-size pieces and return to soup. Stir well before serving.

CANADIAN CHEESE SOUP

You save time if you cook this soup on the range top rather than the microwave—makes about 2 quarts.

BASIC RECIPE — MAKES ABOUT 2 QUARTS.

½ c. finely chopped onion	1 qt. milk
½ c. finely chopped carrot	¼ c. flour
½ c. finely chopped celery	1 c. grated Cheddar cheese
¼ c. butter or regular margarine	1 tsp. salt
	⅛ tsp. pepper
2 (13¾ oz.) cans chicken broth	1 tblsp. parsley flakes

 Range Top: 19 to 25 minutes cooking time

Cook onion, carrot and celery in melted butter in Dutch oven 5 minutes or until onion is soft. Add chicken broth and cook 7 to 10 minutes or until vegetables are tender. Blend a little milk into flour; stir in remaining milk. Stir into soup and cook over medium heat, stirring constantly, 12 to 15 minutes or until mixture comes to a boil. Add remaining ingredients. Cook just until cheese is melted, stirring constantly.

 Microwave Oven (high setting): 33½ to 34½ minutes cooking time

Use ingredients listed in basic recipe. Microwave (high setting) butter in 3-qt. glass casserole 30 seconds or until melted. Add onion, carrots and celery. Cover and microwave 12 minutes or until vegetables are tender, stirring 3 times. Blend in flour. Blend in a little chicken broth, then remaining broth and milk. Cover and microwave 18 to 19 minutes or until mixture comes to a boil, stirring twice. Add cheese, salt, pepper and parsley. Cook until cheese is melted, about 3 minutes, stirring once.

SUCH GOOD BORSCHT

This hearty soup is best served with a loaf of rye bread and lots of soft butter.

BASIC RECIPE — MAKES 11 CUPS.

2 lbs. stewing beef, cut in 1" cubes
6 c. water
1 tblsp. instant beef bouillon granules
2 tsp. salt
¼ tsp. pepper
¼ tsp. dried dillweed
4 c. shredded cabbage

1 c. chopped onion
1 c. sliced carrots
1 c. sliced celery
1 (6 oz.) can tomato juice
1 (16 oz.) can julienne beets, undrained
2 tblsp. lemon juice
1 c. dairy sour cream

Range Top: 2 hours 30 minutes cooking time

Combine beef, water, beef bouillon granules, salt, pepper and dillweed in Dutch oven. Bring to boiling. Reduce heat and simmer, covered, 2 hours or until beef is tender. Add cabbage, onions, carrots, celery and tomato juice. Simmer 30 minutes or until vegetables are tender. Add beets and lemon juice. Heat thoroughly. Serve in soup bowls topped with sour cream.

 Slow Cooker: 8 hours 15 minutes to 10 hours 15 minutes cooking time

Use same ingredients as listed in basic recipe, but thinly slice carrots, reduce celery from 1 to ½ c. and thinly slice it. Use 3 c. water instead of 6 cups. Combine all ingredients in cooker except beets, lemon juice and sour cream. Cover and cook on low 8 to 10 hours. Stir in beets and lemon juice. Cover and cook on high 15 minutes. Serve in soup bowls topped with sour cream.

SOPA DE MEXICO

Shredded Cheddar or longhorn cheese makes a nutritious garnish for this soup. Adds a bit of color, too.

BASIC RECIPE — MAKES ABOUT 3 QUARTS.

1½ lbs. boneless pork, cut in 1" cubes	1 (6 oz.) can tomato juice
1 c. chopped onion	3 c. water
1 clove garlic, minced	1 (13¾ oz.) can chicken broth
2 tsp. salt	2 c. sliced carrots
1 tsp. chili powder	1 (15 oz.) can red kidney beans, drained
½ tsp. dried oregano leaves	2 ears fresh or thawed frozen corn-on-cob, cut in 1" slices
¼ tsp. pepper	

 Range Top: 2 hours 5 minutes cooking time

Trim excess fat from pork. Place pork, onion, garlic, salt, chili powder, oregano, pepper, tomato juice, water and chicken broth in Dutch oven. Place over medium-high heat and bring to a boil. Reduce heat and simmer 1 hour 30 minutes or until pork is tender. Add carrots and beans and cook 20 more minutes. Add corn and simmer 15 minutes or until tender.

Slow Cooker: 8½ to 10½ hours cooking time

Use ingredients listed in basic recipe, but thinly slice carrots. Place all ingredients except corn in slow cooker. Cover and cook on low 8 to 10 hours. Turn cooker on high. Add corn and cook 30 minutes.

CHAPTER FOUR

Adaptable Main Dishes

Meal planning starts with main dishes. They are the hub around which most of us build menus. Once selected, the other foods, such as vegetables, salads and desserts, usually fall into place. Main dishes also assume responsibility for delivering all-important protein to meals. That's why they make up the largest chapter in this cookbook.

Main dish recipes take more kindly to adjustments for cooking with a variety of appliances than other types of food. Chili con Queso and Family Meat Loaf, for example, are five-way performers. They are so adaptable you can cook them successfully with five appliances. And you will find a sizable number of four-way main dishes on the following pages. Among them are fork-tender Dutch Pork Chops that cook atop a tasty combination of sauerkraut and applesauce; expertly seasoned Stuffed Beef Rolls, and Lamb Stew with Mashed Potatoes. The fluffy potatoes, laced with sour cream, make a perfect topping for the meat-vegetable stew.

Most of the recipes in this chapter are three-way. What a fine variety they offer! Orange-Glazed Ham is a special occasion choice. Brunswick Stew combines chicken and a garden patch of vegetables, such as tomatoes, lima beans, corn, okra, potatoes and onions, in a pleasing, hearty dish. Tasty Marin County Chicken, a California delight, features chicken breasts, vegetables and cashews.

Several recipes on the following pages are two-way; they make such marvelous dishes that it seems wise to include them. And many of them fill a special need. For example, Reuben-Style Meat Loaf, which cooks to perfection in both conventional and microwave ovens, produces pinwheels pretty and delicious enough to star on special occasions. Substantial Rancher's Beef Stew and Wisconsin Beef Stew, each of which can be cooked in a Dutch oven on range top or in the slow cooker, make meals that busy women and hungry men both appreciate. They require little watching while cooking. The slow cooker version takes care of itself when the cook is away from the kitchen for many hours at a time.

Be sure to try some of the fish recipes. Nine-Minute Oriental Tuna provides a quick way, 9 minutes, to cook fish and vegetables and Salmon Loaf with Dill Sauce is a splendid four-way main dish. Both of these use canned fish. Most of the main dish fish recipes are two-way; they usually are cooked with the conventional range and microwave oven. Fresh and frozen fish is tender and delicate and will not stand up in the high heat of the pressure cooker or long cooking of the slow cooker.

If you have trouble deciding what to get for a meal, turn the pages of this chapter. You will find many tempters to use as the spring-board for menu planning.

DOWN-HOME POT ROAST

Onion soup mix adds flavor and color to the gravy—especially important in slow cooker method because meat is not browned.
BASIC RECIPE — MAKES 6 SERVINGS.

3 lb. beef pot roast	1 c. water
Flour	6 small potatoes, pared
2 tblsp. cooking oil	6 carrots, cut in 1" pieces
¾ tsp. salt	¼ c. flour
¼ tsp. pepper	½ c. water
2 tblsp. onion soup mix	

Range Top: 2 hours 58 minutes cooking time

Coat pot roast with flour. Slowly brown beef on both sides in hot oil in Dutch oven, about 10 minutes. Sprinkle with salt, pepper and onion soup mix. Add 1 c. water. Bring to boiling. Reduce heat and simmer, covered, 2 hours. Add potatoes and carrots; continue simmering until vegetables are tender, about 45 minutes. Remove meat and vegetables to hot platter; keep warm. Blend together ¼ c. flour and ½ c. water. Add to pan juices. Cook, stirring constantly, until thickened and bubbly, about 3 minutes. Serve gravy with meat and potatoes.

Electric Frypan: 2 hours 58 minutes cooking time

Use ingredients listed in basic recipe, but make sure pot roast is 2½″ thick and increase cooking oil to 3 tablsp. and flour to 5 tblsp. Coat pot roast with flour. Slowly brown on both sides in 3 tblsp. hot oil in electric frypan (350°), about 10 minutes. Sprinkle with salt, pepper and onion soup mix. Add 1 c. water. Cover and simmer at 220°, with vent closed, 2 hours or until tender. Add potatoes and carrots; continue simmering until vegetables are tender, about 45 minutes. Remove meat and vegetables to a warm platter. Blend together 5 tblsp. flour and ½ c. water. Add to pan juices. Cook, stirring constantly, until thickened and bubbly, about 3 minutes. Serve with meat and potatoes.

Slow Cooker: 9 hours 3 minutes cooking time

Use ingredients listed in basic recipe, but use 2½ lb. pot roast. Also use 6 medium potatoes cut in eighths, 2 c. thinly sliced carrots and 5 tblsp. flour. Place potatoes and carrots in cooker. Sprinkle with salt and pepper. Trim all visible fat from pot roast and if necessary, cut meat to fit into cooker. Place on top of vegetables. Sprinkle with onion soup mix; add 1 c. water. Cover and cook on low 9 hours. Remove vegetables and meat to warm platter. Keep warm. Pour juices from cooker into saucepan. Blend together 5 tblsp. flour and ½ c. water. Add to juices. Heat, stirring constantly, until thickened and bubbly, about 3 minutes. Serve with meat and potatoes.

ITALIAN POT ROAST

You'll have plenty of gravy with this pot roast to spoon over potatoes or noodles no matter which appliance is used.

BASIC RECIPE — MAKES 6 TO 8 SERVINGS.

2 tblsp. cooking oil	2 tsp. salt
3½ lb. rolled beef rump roast	⅛ tsp. pepper
1 c. chopped onion	1 (6 oz.) can tomato paste
½ c. chopped celery	1 (14 oz.) can beef broth
½ c. chopped carrot	2 tblsp. flour
1 (4 oz.) can mushroom stems	¼ c. water
and pieces, drained	Hot cooked rice
1 clove garlic, minced	

 Range Top: 2 hours 43 minutes cooking time

Heat cooking oil in Dutch oven; add meat and brown on all sides, about 10 minutes. Add onion, celery, carrot, mushrooms, garlic, salt and pepper. Blend together tomato paste and broth; pour over pot roast and vegetables. Simmer, covered, 2 hours 30 minutes or until tender. Remove meat and keep warm. Blend together flour and water; add to hot mixture. Cook, stirring constantly, until mixture thickens and bubbles, about 3 minutes. Serve gravy with sliced meat and rice.

Pressure Cooker: 48 minutes cooking time

Use ingredients listed in basic recipe. Heat cooking oil in 4-qt. pressure pan; add meat and brown on all sides, about 10 minutes. Add onion, celery, carrot, mushrooms, garlic, salt and pepper. Blend together tomato paste and broth; pour over meat and vegetables. Close cover securely. Place over high heat. Bring to 15 lbs. pressure, according to manufacturer's directions for your pressure cooker. When pressure is reached (control will begin to jiggle), reduce heat immediately and cook 35 minutes. Remove from heat. Let pressure drop of its own accord. Remove meat and keep warm. Blend together flour and water; add to broth and vegetable mixture. Cook, stirring constantly, until mixture thickens and bubbles, about 3 minutes. Serve gravy with sliced meat and hot rice.

Slow Cooker: 9 hours 3 minutes cooking time
Use ingredients listed in basic recipe, but omit oil and water and increase flour to ½ c. Place onion, celery, carrot, mushrooms and garlic in cooker. Blend together tomato paste and 1 c. of the beef broth. Stir into vegetables along with salt and pepper. Add meat; spoon sauce in cooker over it. Cover. Cook on low 9 hours. Remove meat to warm platter. Pour sauce and vegetables into saucepan. Blend together ½ c. flour and remaining beef broth. Blend into sauce and vegetable mixture. Cook and stir until mixture boils, about 3 minutes. Serve with meat and hot rice. (There is more liquid than when cooking pot roast on Range Top or in Pressure Pan.)

PARTY POT ROAST

You'll need a 6-qt. pressure cooker for this 4 lb. pot roast since it will not fit in the 4-qt. cooker.
BASIC RECIPE — MAKES 6 TO 8 SERVINGS.

1 (4 lb.) boneless beef chuck roast
2 tblsp. cooking oil
1 c. dry red wine
½ c. chopped green pepper
½ c. chopped onion
1 clove garlic, minced
1 tsp. salt
¼ tsp. dried thyme leaves
¼ tsp. dried marjoram leaves
¼ tsp. pepper
2 tblsp. cornstarch
½ c. water
Hot cooked rice

Range Top: 2 hours 50 minutes cooking time

Brown roast on both sides in hot oil in Dutch oven or large skillet, about 15 minutes. Combine wine, green pepper, onion, garlic, salt, thyme, marjoram and pepper. Pour over roast. Cover and cook slowly over low heat 2 hours 30 minutes or until tender. Remove roast to warm platter. Blend cornstarch and water. Stir into pan juices. Cook and stir until thickened and bubbly, about 5 minutes. Serve with hot cooked rice and sliced pot roast.

 Electric Frypan: 2 hours 50 minutes cooking time

Use ingredients listed in basic recipe but increase water to 1 cup. Preheat electric frypan to 350°. Brown roast on both sides in hot oil, about 15 minutes. Combine wine, green pepper, onion, garlic, salt, thyme, marjoram and pepper. Pour over roast. Reduce heat to 220°. Cover and simmer, with vent closed, 2 hours 30 minutes. Remove roast to warm platter. Blend cornstarch and 1 c. water. Stir into pan juices. Cook and stir until thickened and bubbly, about 5 minutes. Serve with hot cooked rice and sliced pot roast.

 Pressure Cooker: 55 minutes cooking time

Use ingredients listed in basic recipe. Brown roast on both sides in hot oil in 6-qt. pressure pan, about 15 minutes. Combine wine, green pepper, onion, garlic, salt, thyme, marjoram and pepper. Pour over roast. Close cover securely. Place over high heat. Bring to 15 lbs. pressure, according to manufacturer's directions for your pressure cooker. When pressure is reached (control will begin to jiggle), reduce heat immediately and cook 35 minutes. Remove from heat. Let pressure drop of its own accord. Remove roast to warm platter. Thicken pan juices as for Range Top, about 5 minutes. Serve with hot cooked rice and sliced pot roast.

SPICY POT ROAST

The subtle blend of seasonings give this pot roast a Southwestern taste —best served with cooked rice.

BASIC RECIPE — MAKES 8 SERVINGS.

1 (3 to 4 lbs.) rolled rump roast	1 tsp. ground cumin
¼ c. flour	1 tsp. salt
2 tblsp. cooking oil	½ tsp. pepper
1 c. chopped onion	1 (8 oz.) can tomato sauce
2 cloves garlic, minced	½ c. water
1 tsp. beef bouillon granules	¼ c. flour
1 tsp. celery seeds	½ c. water
	Hot cooked rice

Range Top: 3 hours 18 minutes cooking time

Coat roast on all sides with ¼ c. flour. Brown on all sides in heavy Dutch oven in hot oil, about 15 minutes. Add onion, garlic, beef bouillon granules, celery seeds, cumin, salt, pepper, tomato sauce and ½ c. water. Cover and cook over low heat 3 hours or until tender. Remove meat and keep warm. Measure pan juices. Add water, if necessary, to make 2½ c. Blend together ¼ c. flour and ½ c. water. Stir into pan juices; cook and stir until thickened about 3 minutes. Serve over sliced meat and rice.

Pressure Cooker: 1 hour 3 minutes cooking time

Use ingredients listed in basic recipe, increasing water as directed. Coat roast on all sides with ¼ c. flour. Brown on all sides in 4-qt. pressure cooker in hot oil, about 15 minutes. Add onion, garlic, beef bouillon granules, celery seeds, cumin, salt, pepper, tomato sauce and 2 c. water. Close cover securely. Place over high heat. Bring to 15 lbs. pressure, according to manufacturer's directions for your pressure cooker.

When pressure is reached (control will begin to jiggle), reduce heat immediately and cook 45 minutes. Remove from heat. Let pressure drop of its own accord. Remove roast and keep warm. Measure pan juices. Add water, if necessary, to make 2½ cups. Return to pressure cooker. Blend together ¼ c. flour and ½ c. water. Add to pan juices in pressure cooker. Cook and stir until thickened, about 3 minutes. Serve gravy over sliced meat and rice.

 Slow Cooker: 9 to 10 hours cooking time

Use ingredients listed in basic recipe, but omit ¼ c. flour, cooking oil and ½ c. water. Place meat in slow cooker. Add onion, garlic, beef bouillon granules, celery seeds, cumin, salt, pepper and tomato sauce. Cover and cook on low for 9 to 10 hours. Remove roast and keep warm. Measure pan juices. Add water, if necessary, to make 2½ c. Pour into saucepan. Blend together ¼ c. flour and ½ c. cold water. Add to pan juices. Cook, stirring constantly, until mixture thickens. Serve over sliced meat and rice.

FAMILY SWISS STEAK

Beef cooked in the pressure cooker tends to be more stringy than when cooked in other appliances, but only takes 28 minutes.

BASIC RECIPE — MAKES 6 SERVINGS.

2 lbs. round steak, ½" thick	¼ tsp. pepper
¼ c. flour	1 (16 oz.) can tomatoes, cut
3 tblsp. cooking oil	up
1 c. chopped onion	2 tblsp. flour
½ c. chopped celery	¼ c. water
1 tsp. salt	

Range Top: 2 hours 13 minutes cooking time

Cut steak in serving pieces; dredge in ¼ c. flour. Brown steak on both sides in hot oil in large, heavy skillet, about 10 minutes. Top with onion, celery, salt, pepper and tomatoes. Cover and simmer 2 hours or until tender. Remove meat to warm platter. Keep warm. Blend 2 tblsp. flour with ¼ c. water. Stir into pan juices and cook, stirring constantly, until mixture thickens and boils, about 3 minutes. Serve with steak.

 Pressure Cooker: 28 minutes cooking time

Use ingredients listed in basic recipe, but decrease cooking oil to 2 tblsp.; decrease flour to 1 tblsp. and water to 2 tblsp. to thicken pan juices. Cut steak in serving pieces; dredge in ¼ c. flour. Brown steak on both sides in 2 tblsp. hot oil in 4-qt. pressure pan, about 10 minutes. Combine steak with onion, celery, salt, pepper and tomatoes. Close cover securely. Place over high heat. Bring to 15 lbs. pressure, according to manufacturer's directions for your pressure cooker. When pressure is reached (control will begin to jiggle), reduce heat immediately and cook 15 minutes. Remove from heat. Let pressure drop of its own accord. Remove meat to warm platter. Keep warm. Blend 1 tblsp. flour with 2 tblsp. water. Stir into pan juices and cook, stirring constantly, until mixture comes to a boil, about 3 minutes. Serve with steak.

 Slow Cooker: 9 hours 25 minutes cooking time

Use ingredients as listed in basic recipe, but increase flour to ¼ c. and water to ½ c. to thicken pan juices. Finely chop onion and celery. Cut steak in serving pieces; dredge in ¼ c. flour. Brown on both sides in hot oil in large, heavy skillet, about 10 minutes. Meanwhile, place onion and celery in bottom of cooker. Top with steak. Sprinkle with salt and pepper; pour on tomatoes. Cover and cook on low 9 hours. Remove meat to warm platter. Keep warm. Turn heat to high. Blend ¼ c. flour with ½ c. water. Stir into pan juices. Cover and cook 15 minutes. Serve with steak.

SWISS STEAK ELEGANTE

If your family likes lots of gravy, prepare the steak in the slow cooker.
BASIC RECIPE — MAKES 6 SERVINGS.

2 lbs. round steak,
  ½″ thick
¼ c. flour
1 tblsp. paprika
1 tsp. salt
¼ tsp. pepper
3 tblsp. cooking oil
¼ c. chopped onion

1 (4 oz.) can mushroom stems
  and pieces, drained
1 clove garlic, minced
½ c. water
1 tblsp. flour
2 tblsp. water
½ c. dairy sour cream

 Range Top: 1 hour cooking time

Cut beef into 6 serving pieces; pound on both sides with meat mallet.
Dredge steak in combined ¼ c. flour, paprika, salt and pepper, coating
well. Heat oil in skillet; add meat and brown on both sides, about 10
minutes. Pour off excess oil. Add onion, mushrooms, garlic and ½ c.
water. Simmer, covered, 45 minutes or until meat is tender. Remove
meat to warm platter. Blend together 1 tblsp. flour and 2 tblsp. water.
Stir into mixture in skillet. Cook, stirring, until mixture comes to a boil,
about 3 minutes. Blend in sour cream. Heat, but do not let boil, about
2 minutes. Pour over steak. Serve with mashed or boiled potatoes, if
you wish.

 Pressure Cooker: 37 minutes cooking time

Use ingredients listed in basic recipe, but omit 1 tblsp. flour and 2
tblsp. water for thickening gravy. Prepare steak as for Range Top. Add
oil to 4-qt. pressure pan. Heat, add meat and brown on both sides,
about 20 minutes. Add onion, mushrooms, garlic and water. Close
cover securely. Place over high heat. Bring to 15 lbs. pressure, accord-

ing to manufacturer's directions for your pressure cooker. When pressure is reached (control will begin to jiggle), reduce heat immediately and cook 15 minutes. Remove from heat. Let pressure drop of its own accord. Remove meat to warm platter. Blend sour cream into drippings. Heat, but do not let boil, about 2 minutes. Pour over steak. (There is less gravy than with steak cooked on Range Top or in Slow Cooker.)

 Slow Cooker: 6¼ to 8¼ hours cooking time

Use ingredients listed in basic recipe, but increase flour to 2 tblsp. and water to ¼ c. for thickening gravy. Trim fat from meat. Prepare meat as for Range Top. Heat oil in skillet, add steak and brown, about 10 minutes. Transfer meat to cooker. Add onion, garlic and ½ c. water. Cover and cook on low 6 to 8 hours. Add mushrooms 30 minutes before serving. Remove meat to warm platter. Pour juices from cooker into saucepan. Blend together 2 tblsp. flour and ¼ c. water. Stir into juices. Cook, stirring constantly, until mixture comes to a boil, about 3 minutes. Blend in sour cream. Heat, but do not let boil, about 2 minutes. Serve over steak. There is more gravy than when beef is cooked on Range Top or in Pressure Cooker.

BEEF BURGUNDY

The pressure cooker saves time, but the flavors have less time to develop in this appliance.

BASIC RECIPE — MAKES 6 SERVINGS.

4 slices bacon, cut up	¼ tsp. pepper
2 lbs. round steak, ½"thick	1 c. chopped onion
¼ c. flour	1 clove garlic, minced
1½ tsp. salt	1 beef bouillon cube
¼ tsp. dried marjoram leaves	1½ c. Burgundy wine
¼ tsp. dried thyme leaves	8 oz. fresh mushrooms, sliced

 Range Top: 1 hour 56 minutes cooking time

Cook bacon in Dutch oven until crisp, about 6 minutes. Remove bacon. Cut round steak in 1″ squares. Shake in plastic bag with flour to coat. Brown in bacon drippings, about 10 minutes. Add bacon, salt, marjoram, thyme, pepper, onion, garlic, bouillon cube and wine. Bring to a boil. Reduce heat and simmer, covered, 1 hour 30 minutes. Add mushrooms; continue simmering, covered, 10 minutes.

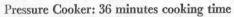 Pressure Cooker: 36 minutes cooking time

Use ingredients listed in basic recipe, but substitute 1 (4 oz.) can mushroom stems and pieces, drained, for fresh mushrooms and add 2 tblsp. cornstarch and ¼ c. water for thickening sauce. Cook bacon in 4-qt. pressure pan until crisp, about 6 minutes. Remove bacon. Brown floured steak squares in bacon drippings, about 10 minutes. Combine bacon, round steak, salt, marjoram, thyme, pepper, onion, garlic, bouillon cube, wine and mushrooms. Close cover securely. Place over high heat. Bring to 15 lbs. pressure, according to manufacturer's directions for your pressure cooker. When pressure is reached (control will begin to jiggle), reduce heat immediately and cook 15 minutes. Remove from heat. Reduce pressure immediately under cold running water. Blend together 2 tblsp. cornstarch and ¼ c. water. Stir into mixture in pressure pan. Cook, stirring constantly, until mixture is thickened and bubbly, about 5 minutes.

Slow Cooker: 9 hours 31 minutes cooking time

Use ingredients listed in basic recipe, but add 2 tblsp. cornstarch and ¼ c. water for thickening sauce and finely chop onions. Cook bacon in large skillet until crisp, about 6 minutes. Remove bacon. Cut round steak in 1″ squares and dredge in flour mixture as for Range Top. Brown steak in bacon drippings, about 10 minutes. Combine bacon, round steak, salt, marjoram, thyme, pepper, onion, garlic, bouillon cube and wine in cooker. Cover and cook on low 9 hours. Turn control to high and add sliced mushrooms. Blend together 2 tblsp. cornstarch and ¼ c. water. Stir into mixture in cooker. Cook, covered, 15 minutes.

BEEF BARBECUE SANDWICHES

Beef pot roast is thinly sliced after cooking and served in this delicious tomato-based sauce. Make ahead and simply reheat.

BASIC RECIPE — MAKES 16 SERVINGS.

1 (15 oz.) can tomato sauce
½ c. water
1 c. chopped onion
¼ c. chopped green pepper
2 tblsp. brown sugar, packed
2 tblsp. Worcestershire sauce
2 tsp. dry mustard
1 tsp. salt

¼ tsp. pepper
Few drops bottled hot pepper
　sauce
2½ lbs. boned chuck beef roast
2 tblsp. flour
¼ c. water
16 hamburger buns, split and
　buttered

 Oven: 2 hours 15 minutes cooking time

Combine first 10 ingredients in Dutch oven. Place meat in Dutch oven and spoon tomato sauce mixture over it. Bake, covered, in 325° oven 2 hours. Cool meat slightly and slice across the grain. Blend flour and ¼ c. water. Stir into tomato sauce mixture. On range top, cook over medium heat stirring constantly, until sauce thickens and is bubbly, about 5 minutes. Add meat; heat thoroughly, about 10 minutes. Serve in split buns.

Pressure Cooker: 45 minutes cooking time

Use ingredients listed in basic recipe, but increase flour to ¼ c. and water to ½ c. for thickening. Combine first 10 ingredients in a 4-qt. pressure cooker. Cut meat to fit, if necessary. Place meat in sauce mixture. Close cover securely. Place over high heat. Bring to 15 lbs. pressure, according to manufacturer's directions for your pressure cooker. When pressure is reached (control will begin to jiggle), reduce heat immediately and cook 40 minutes. Remove from heat. Let pressure drop of its own accord. Cool meat slightly and slice across grain. Blend ¼ c. flour with ½ c. water. Stir into tomato sauce mixture. Cook over medium heat and stir until sauce thickens and is bubbly, about 5 minutes. Add meat; heat thoroughly. Serve in split buns.

 Slow Cooker: 9 hours 15 minutes cooking time

Use ingredients listed in basic recipe, but omit ½ c. water and finely chop onion and green pepper. Cut meat to fit cooker. Combine tomato sauce, onion, green pepper, brown sugar, Worcestershire sauce, mustard, salt, pepper and hot pepper sauce. Pour over meat in cooker. Cover and cook on low 9 hours or until meat is very tender. Lift meat from cooker. Cool pot roast slightly and slice across grain. Turn cooker on high. Skin off fat in cooker. When mixture in cooker is bubbling, stir in flour blended with ¼ c. water. Return meat to cooker and heat, covered, 15 minutes. Serve in split buns.

STUFFED BEEF ROLLS

The tomato sauce adds color so you don't notice the meat rolls are not browned in the microwave version.

BASIC RECIPE — MAKES 6 SERVINGS.

1½ c. herb-seasoned bread
   stuffing
2 tblsp. butter or regular
   margarine, melted
½ c. hot water
6 cube steaks (about 2 lbs.)
2 tblsp. cooking oil

1 (1½ oz.) pkg. seasoning mix
   for sloppy joes
1 (8 oz.) can tomato sauce
1 c. water
1 tblsp. flour
¼ c. water

Range Top: 53 minutes cooking time

Combine stuffing mix, butter and ½ c. hot water. Spread stuffing evenly over center of each cube steak. Roll steak over stuffing; fasten with toothpicks or skewers. Brown three rolls on all sides in hot oil in skillet, about 10 minutes. Remove, set aside and repeat with remaining rolls, about 10 minutes. Return beef rolls to skillet. Combine seasoning mix, tomato sauce and 1 c. water. Pour over meat rolls in skillet. Cover and simmer over low heat 30 minutes. Transfer meat to warm platter; keep warm. Blend flour with ¼ c. water. Stir into sauce in skillet. Cook and stir until thickened and bubbly, about 3 minutes.

Electric Frypan: 43 minutes cooking time

Use ingredients listed in basic recipe. Prepare beef rolls as for Range Top. Preheat electric frypan to 350°. Add oil and brown rolls on all sides, about 10 minutes. Reduce heat to 220°. Combine seasoning mix, tomato sauce and 1 c. water. Pour over meat in frypan. Cover and simmer with vent closed, 30 minutes. Remove rolls to warm platter; keep warm. Blend flour and ¼ c. water. Stir into sauce in frypan; cook and stir until thickened and bubbly, about 3 minutes.

Microwave Oven (high setting): 21 minutes cooking time

Use ingredients listed in basic recipe, but omit cooking oil and flour and reduce water as indicated. Combine butter with ½ c. water in glass measuring cup. Microwave (high setting) 1 minute. Combine stuffing and butter-water mixture. Prepare beef rolls as for Range Top. Place meat rolls in 12×8×2″ glass baking dish (2-qt.). Combine seasoning mix, tomato sauce and ½ c. water. Pour over meat. Cover with waxed paper. Microwave 10 minutes. Uncover, spoon sauce over meat and give dish a half turn. Microwave, uncovered, 10 minutes longer. Spoon sauce over meat once during cooking and again before serving.

Pressure Cooker: 28 minutes cooking time

Use ingredients listed in basic recipe. Prepare beef rolls as for Range Top. Brown rolls on all sides in hot oil in 4-qt. pressure pan, about 20 minutes. Combine seasoning mix, tomato sauce and 1 c. water. Pour over meat. Close cover securely. Place over high heat. Bring to 15 lbs. pressure, according to manufacturer's directions for your pressure cooker. When pressure is reached (control will begin to jiggle), reduce heat immediately and cook 5 minutes. Remove from heat. Let pressure drop of its own accord. Transfer rolls to warm platter; keep warm. Blend flour and ¼ c. water. Stir into sauce. Cook and stir until thickened and bubbly, about 3 minutes.

RANCHER'S BEEF STEW

Cook this stew in the slow cooker if you plan to be out of the kitchen most of the day—it requires no pot-watching.

BASIC RECIPE — MAKES 8 SERVINGS.

2 lbs. beef stew meat, cut in 1½" cubes	2 beef bouillon cubes
½ c. flour	6 medium carrots, sliced
3 tblsp. cooking oil	5 medium potatoes, pared and cut in eighths
2 tsp. salt	1 c. chopped onion
¼ tsp. pepper	1 c. chopped celery
1 tblsp. Worcestershire sauce	¼ c. flour
3 c. water	½ c. water

 Range Top: 2 hours 15 minutes cooking time

Shake meat cubes, a few at a time, in plastic bag with ½ c. flour. Brown beef in Dutch oven in hot oil, about 10 minutes. Add salt, pepper, Worcestershire sauce, 3 c. water and bouillon cubes. Bring to boiling. Reduce heat and cover. Simmer 1 hour 30 minutes or until meat is tender. Add carrots, potatoes, onion and celery and continue simmering until tender, 30 minutes. Blend together ¼ c. flour and ½ c. water. Stir into stew and cook, stirring constantly, until mixture comes to a boil, about 5 minutes.

Slow Cooker: 9 hours 50 minutes cooking time
Use ingredients listed in basic recipe. Flour meat and brown in hot oil in skillet as for Range Top, about 10 minutes. Combine browned beef, carrots, potatoes, onion and celery. Add salt, pepper and Worcestershire sauce in cooker. Pour excess fat from skillet; add 3 c. water and bouillon cubes. Bring to boiling, stirring and scraping brown bits from bottom of skillet. When bouillon cubes are dissolved, pour over meat and vegetables in cooker. Cover and cook on low 9 hours. Turn control to high. Blend together ¼ c. flour and ½ c. water. Stir into stew. Cover and cook 40 minutes.

BELGIAN BEEF

Even though the slow cooker is simmered for over 9 hours, less liquid evaporates in this method so you add less during cooking.
BASIC RECIPE — MAKES 8 SERVINGS.

2 to 3 lbs. boneless beef chuck, cut in 1" cubes	½ tsp. dried thyme leaves
	¼ tsp. pepper
2 tblsp. cooking oil	1 (12 oz.) can beer (1½ c.)
2 c. chopped onion	¼ c. flour
1 clove garlic, minced	½ c. water
2 tsp. salt	

Range Top: 2 hours 43 minutes cooking time
Brown beef cubes in Dutch oven in hot oil, about 10 minutes. Add remaining ingredients except flour and water. Cover and simmer 2 hours 30 minutes. Blend together flour and water. Add to mixture in Dutch oven. Cook, stirring constantly, until mixture comes to a boil and is thickened, about 3 minutes. Delicious served with mashed potatoes.

Pressure Cooker: 33 minutes cooking time
Use ingredients listed in basic recipe, but use 5 tblsp. flour instead of ¼ c. Brown beef cubes in 4-qt. pressure pan in hot oil, about 10 min-

utes. Add remaining ingredients except flour and water. Close cover securely. Place over high heat. Bring to 15 lbs. pressure, according to manufacturer's directions for your pressure cooker. When pressure is reached (control will begin to jiggle), reduce heat immediately and cook 20 minutes. Remove from heat. Let pressure drop of its own accord. Blend together 5 tblsp. flour and water. Add to mixture in pan. Cook, stirring constantly, until mixture boils and thickens, about 3 minutes. Delicious served with mashed potatoes.

Slow Cooker: 9 hours 15 minutes cooking time

Use ingredients listed in basic recipe, but omit cooking oil and use 1 c. beer instead of 1½ c., 3 tblsp. cornstarch instead of flour and ¼ c. water instead of ½ c. Combine beef cubes, onions, garlic, salt, thyme, pepper and 1 c. beer in slow cooker. Cover and cook on low 9 hours. Turn control to high. Blend together 3 tblsp. cornstarch and ¼ c. water. Add to mixture in cooker. Cook, covered, until thickened, about 15 minutes. Delicious served with mashed potatoes.

WISCONSIN BEEF STEW

Brown sugar enhances the flavor of this beef stew. Be sure to thinly slice and chop vegetables in slow cooker method.

BASIC RECIPE — MAKES 8 SERVINGS.

2 lbs. beef stew meat, cut in 1″
    cubes
¼ c. flour
2 tsp. salt
¼ tsp. pepper
2 tblsp. cooking oil
1 c. chopped onion
½ c. ketchup
1 c. water

2 c. sliced carrots
1 c. sliced celery
2 tblsp. brown sugar, packed
⅓ c. vinegar
1 c. frozen peas
2 tblsp. flour
¼ c. water
Hot cooked noodles

Range Top: 2 hours 30 minutes cooking time

Dredge stew meat with combined ¼ c. flour, salt and pepper. Brown in hot oil in Dutch oven, about 10 minutes. Add onion, ketchup and 1 c. water to meat. Bring to a boil, stirring frequently. Reduce heat and simmer, covered, 1 hour 30 minutes. Add carrots, celery, brown sugar and vinegar. Cover and simmer 35 minutes. Add peas; continue cooking 10 minutes or until vegetables are tender. Blend 2 tblsp. flour with ¼ c. water. Add to stew and cook and stir until bubbly and thickened, about 5 minutes. Serve over hot noodles.

Slow Cooker: 9 hours 40 minutes cooking time

Use ingredients listed in basic recipe, but omit oil and reduce water and flour as indicated. Also, cut carrots in thin slices and finely chop celery and onions. Combine stew meat, carrots, onion, celery, salt, pepper, ketchup and ½ c. water in slow cooker. Cover and cook on low 9 hours. Turn cooker to high, stir in peas and brown sugar. Blend vinegar and 2 tblsp. water with ¼ c. flour. Stir into stew. Cover and cook 40 minutes or until vegetables are tender. Serve over hot noodles.

TEXAS BEANS WITH BEEF

Instead of soaking beans overnight in the slow cooker, they are cooked on low for 12 hours and then mixed with other ingredients.

BASIC RECIPE — MAKES ABOUT 3 QUARTS.

1 lb. dried pinto beans (2 c.)
6 c. water
1 lb. chuck beef, cut in 1"
  cubes
½ c. chopped onion
2 cloves garlic, minced

1 (6 oz.) can tomato paste
1 tblsp. salt
2 tsp. chili powder
1 tsp. ground cumin
½ tsp. crushed red pepper

Range Top: 2 hours cooking time

Soak beans in water overnight in Dutch oven. Add remaining ingredients to undrained beans. Bring to boiling. Reduce heat and simmer,
covered, 2 hours or until beans are tender.

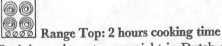 Pressure Cooker: 25 minutes cooking time

Use ingredients listed in basic recipe, but add ¼ c. cooking oil. Also
increase salt to 2 tblsp. and water to 12 c. Place beans, 1 tblsp. salt, ¼
c. cooking oil and 6 c. water in 6-qt. pressure pan. Let stand overnight.
Drain well. Add remaining 6 c. water, 1 tblsp. salt and remaining ingredients to beans; mix well. Close cover securely. Place over high
heat. Bring to 15 lbs. pressure, according to manufacturer's directions
for your pressure cooker. When pressure is reached (control will begin
to jiggle), reduce heat immediately and cook 25 minutes. Remove
from heat. Let pressure drop of its own accord.

 Slow Cooker: 20 to 21 hours cooking time

Use ingredients listed in basic recipe. Combine beans and 6 c. water in
cooker; cover and let cook on low 12 hours or overnight. Stir in
remaining ingredients. Cover and cook on low 8 to 9 hours.

MIDWESTERN STROGANOFF

*You have a choice of four different appliances for this recipe—choose
the one that fits your time schedule.*

BASIC RECIPE — MAKES 6 SERVINGS.

2 lbs. round steak, ½″ thick	1 tblsp. ketchup
2 tblsp. cooking oil	8 oz. fresh mushrooms, sliced
1½ tsp. salt	⅓ c. flour
⅛ tsp. pepper	½ c. water
1 c. chopped onion	1 c. dairy sour cream
1 (14 oz.) can beef broth	Hot, cooked noodles or rice
1 tblsp. Worcestershire sauce	

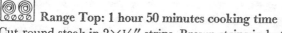 **Range Top: 1 hour 50 minutes cooking time**

Cut round steak in 2×½" strips. Brown strips in hot oil in 4-qt. Dutch oven, about 5 minutes. Add salt, pepper, onion, beef broth, Worcestershire sauce and ketchup. Bring to boiling. Reduce heat; cover and simmer 1 hour 30 minutes or until meat is tender. Add mushrooms; cover and continue simmering 10 more minutes. Blend together flour and water. Stir into hot meat mixture. Cook, stirring constantly, until mixture is thickened, about 3 minutes. Add a small amount of hot gravy to sour cream, blending thoroughly. Return sour cream mixture to Dutch oven. Heat, but do not boil, about 2 minutes. Serve at once over hot noodles or rice.

Electric Frypan: 1 hour 50 minutes cooking time

Use ingredients listed in basic recipe, but increase cooking oil from 2 tblsp. to 3 tblsp. and decrease flour from ⅓ c. to ¼ c. Cut round steak in 2×½" strips. Heat electric frypan to 350°. Add 3 tblsp. oil and heat. Brown beef strips in hot oil, about 5 minutes. Add salt, pepper, onion, beef broth, Worcestershire sauce and ketchup. Bring to boiling. Reduce heat to 220°; cover and simmer, with vent closed, 1 hour 30 minutes or until meat is tender. Add mushrooms; cover and simmer 10 more minutes. Blend together ¼ c. flour and water. Stir into hot mixture. Cook, stirring constantly, until mixture is thickened, about 3 minutes. Add a small amount of hot gravy to sour cream, blending thoroughly. Return sour cream mixture to electric frypan. Heat, but do not boil, about 2 minutes. Serve at once over hot noodles or rice.

Pressure Cooker: 25 minutes cooking time

Use ingredients as listed in basic recipe. Cut round steak in 2×½" strips. Brown beef strips in hot oil in 4-qt. pressure cooker, about 10 minutes. Add salt, pepper, onion, beef broth, Worcestershire sauce, ketchup and mushrooms. Close cover securely. Place over high heat. Bring to 15 lbs. pressure, according to manufacturer's directions for your pressure cooker. When pressure is reached (control will begin to jiggle), reduce heat immediately and cook 10 minutes. Remove from heat. Reduce pressure instantly by placing cooker under cold running water. Blend together flour and water. Stir into hot mixture. Cook, stirring constantly, until mixture is thickened, about 3 minutes. Add a small amount of hot gravy to sour cream, blending thoroughly. Return sour cream mixture to pressure pan. Heat, but do not boil, about 2 minutes. Serve at once over hot noodles or rice.

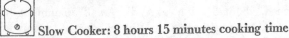 Slow Cooker: 8 hours 15 minutes cooking time

Use ingredients as listed in basic recipe, but omit cooking oil. Cut round steak in 2×½" strips. Place beef strips in cooker. Stir in salt, pepper, onion, beef broth, Worcestershire sauce and ketchup. Cover and cook on low 8 hours or until beef is tender. Turn control to high. Stir in mushrooms. Blend together flour and water. Stir into hot mixture. Cook 15 minutes or until slightly thickened. Add some of the hot gravy to sour cream, blending thoroughly. Return sour cream mixture to cooker. Serve at once over hot noodles or rice.

CHINESE BEEF WITH VEGETABLES

An excellent choice for the first-time user of the microwave oven. It cooks quickly and the vegetables stay tender-crisp.

BASIC RECIPE — MAKES 6 SERVINGS.

1 lb. flank steak	3 tblsp. soy sauce
3 tblsp. cooking oil	½ tsp. beef bouillon granules
8 oz. fresh mushrooms, sliced	1 (6 oz.) pkg. frozen pea pods
1 onion, sliced and separated	(snow peas)
into rings	1 pt. cherry tomatoes
½ c. bias-cut celery, ¼" slices	1 tblsp. cornstarch
1 clove garlic, minced	2 tblsp. water
½ c. water	Hot cooked rice

Range Top: 17 minutes cooking time

Cut and assemble all ingredients before starting to cook. Cut flank steak lengthwise in strips 2″ wide; then slice meat across the grain in thin slices. Brown meat in hot oil in a large heavy skillet over high heat, about 7 minutes. Stir frequently. Add mushrooms, onion, celery, garlic, ½ c. water, soy sauce and bouillon granules. Bring to boiling. Reduce heat and simmer, covered, 5 minutes. Add pea pods and tomatoes. Cover and bring to boiling; cook 3 minutes. Dissolve cornstarch in 2 tblsp. water; stir into meat mixture. Cook and stir until mixture thickens and bubbles, about 2 minutes. Serve over hot cooked rice.

 Microwave Oven (high setting): 13 to 15 minutes cooking time

Use ingredients listed in basic recipe, but omit cooking oil, use only 1 tblsp. water and increase cornstarch to 1½ tblsp. Cut and assemble all ingredients. Place onion, celery and 1 tblsp. water in a 3-qt. glass casserole; cover and microwave (high setting) 3 minutes. Add beef, mushrooms, garlic, bouillon granules, 1½ tblsp. cornstarch and soy sauce; mix lightly. Cover and microwave 8 to 10 minutes or until meat loses its pink color. Stir twice during cooking. Add pea pods. Cover and microwave 2 minutes. Add tomatoes; stir lightly to mix. Microwave, uncovered, 2½ minutes or until tomatoes are heated. Drain juices into a glass cup or dish. Microwave juices, uncovered, 1½ to 2 minutes or until mixture bubbles and thickens. Stir once during cooking. Stir juices into meat mixture. Serve over hot cooked rice.

 Electric Wok: 15 minutes cooking time

Use ingredients listed in basic recipe but reduce oil from 3 to 2 tblsp. and increase cornstarch to 2 tblsp. Cut and assemble all ingredients. Heat electric wok to 375°. Add oil and heat. Add beef; cook and stir until meat loses its pink color, about 5 minutes. Add onion, garlic and celery; cook and stir 3 minutes. Add mushrooms; cook and stir 1 minute. Mix ½ c. water, soy sauce and bouillon granules; add to wok, cover, reduce heat to 300° and cook 3 minutes. Add pea pods and tomatoes; cover and continue cooking 3 minutes. Dissolve 2 tblsp. cornstarch in 2 tblsp. water; stir into meat mixture. Cook and stir until mixture bubbles and thickens. Serve over hot cooked rice.

MONTE VISTA TAMALE PIE

You can make wise use of your conventional oven if you plan to bake dessert while the main dish is in the oven.

BASIC RECIPE — MAKES 6 SERVINGS.

1 c. cold water	1 clove garlic, minced
1 c. cornmeal	1 (16 oz.) can tomatoes, cut
1 tsp. salt	up
6 tsp. chili powder	1 (6 oz.) can tomato paste
2 c. boiling water	½ c. sliced ripe olives
1 lb. ground beef	½ tsp. salt
½ c. chopped onion	1 c. shredded sharp Cheddar
¼ c. chopped green pepper	cheese (4 oz.)

Oven: 1 hour 3 minutes cooking time

Blend together cold water and cornmeal in saucepan. Add 1 tsp. salt, 2 tsp. of the chili powder and boiling water. Cook and stir over medium heat 5 minutes or until mixture is thickened. Spread in greased 13×9×2" baking pan. Cook ground beef, onion, green pepper and garlic in skillet until meat is browned, about 10 minutes. Pour off excess fat. Add tomatoes, tomato paste, olives, ½ tsp. salt and remaining 4 tsp. chili powder. Cover and simmer 15 minutes. Spread over cornmeal mixture. Bake in 350° oven 30 minutes. Sprinkle with cheese. Return to oven just until cheese is melted, 3 minutes.

 Microwave Oven (high setting): 27 to 31 minutes cooking time

Use ingredients listed in basic recipe, but use 3 c. cold water. Combine cornmeal, 2 tsp. of the chili powder, 1 tsp. salt and 3 c. cold water in

12×8×2″ glass baking dish (2-qt.). Microwave (high setting) 8 to 10 minutes or until thickened, stirring three times. Combine beef, onion, green pepper and garlic in 1½-qt. glass bowl. Microwave 6 to 8 minutes, stirring three times to separate meat. Spoon off fat. Add tomatoes, tomato paste, olives, remaining 4 tsp. chili powder and ½ tsp. salt. Spread over cornmeal mixture. Microwave 12 minutes, giving dish a quarter turn twice. Top with cheese; microwave 1 minute or until cheese is melted.

PORCUPINE MEATBALLS

A real time-saver because the meatballs aren't browned in this recipe no matter which appliance you use.

BASIC RECIPE — MAKES 4 SERVINGS.

1 lb. ground beef	1 egg
¼ c. raw regular rice	1 (10½ oz.) can condensed
¼ c. finely chopped onion	tomato soup
1 tsp. salt	½ c. water
⅛ tsp. pepper	1 tsp. Worcestershire sauce

 Range Top: 45 minutes cooking time

Combine ground beef, rice, onion, salt, pepper and egg. Mix lightly, but well. Form mixture into 24 (1″) meatballs. Blend together soup, water and Worcestershire sauce in skillet. Bring to simmering. Add meatballs to hot soup mixture, spooning sauce over all. Simmer, covered, 45 minutes, turning meatballs once or twice.

 Electric Frypan: 45 minutes cooking time

Use ingredients listed in basic recipe, but increase water from ½ c. to ¾ c. Prepare meatballs as for Oven. Combine soup, ¾ c. water and Worcestershire sauce in electric frypan and heat to 220°. Add meatballs to simmering sauce, spooning sauce over all. Continue simmering, covered, with vent closed, 45 minutes, turning meatballs once or twice.

 Microwave Oven (high setting): 30 minutes cooking time
Use ingredients listed in basic recipe. Prepare meatballs as for Oven. Place in 1½-qt. glass casserole. Top with combined soup, water and Worcestershire sauce. Cover and microwave (high setting) 30 minutes, giving casserole a quarter turn twice.

Pressure Cooker: 10 minutes cooking time
Use ingredients listed in basic recipe. Prepare meatballs as for Oven. Blend together soup, water and Worcestershire sauce in 4-qt. pressure pan. Bring to simmering. Add meatballs, spooning sauce over all. Close cover securely. Place over high heat. Bring to 15 lbs. pressure, according to manufacturer's directions for your pressure cooker. When pressure is reached (control will begin to jiggle), reduce heat immediately and cook 10 minutes. Remove from heat. Let pressure drop of its own accord.

BASIC SPAGHETTI SAUCE

The pressure cooker and the microwave oven save cooking time, but the flavor develops more fully in the other appliances.

BASIC RECIPE — MAKES 6 SERVINGS.

1 lb. ground beef	1 tsp. salt
2 c. chopped onion	1 tsp. dried oregano leaves
½ c. chopped green pepper	½ tsp. dried basil leaves
1 clove garlic, minced	¼ tsp. pepper
1 (15 oz.) can tomato sauce	1 (16 oz.) pkg. spaghetti,
1 (6 oz.) can tomato paste	cooked
½ c. water	

Range Top: 1 hour 10 minutes cooking time

Cook ground beef in Dutch oven until browned, about 10 minutes. Add remaining ingredients, except spaghetti. Bring to boiling. Reduce heat and simmer, covered, 1 hour, stirring several times. Serve on hot spaghetti.

 Microwave Oven (high setting): 34 minutes cooking time

Use ingredients listed in basic recipe. Combine onion, green pepper and garlic in 2-qt. glass casserole. Cover and microwave (high setting) 6 minutes. Crumble ground beef into onion mixture. Microwave, covered, until meat is separated and onion is soft, about 8 minutes, stirring every 2 minutes to break up meat. Pour off fat. Stir in tomato sauce, tomato paste, water, salt, oregano, basil and pepper. Microwave, covered, 20 minutes, stirring once. Serve on hot spaghetti.

 Pressure Cooker: 22 minutes cooking time

Use ingredients listed in basic recipe, but omit water and substitute 1 (16 oz.) can tomatoes, cut up, for tomato sauce. Brown ground beef in 4-qt. pressure pan, about 10 minutes. Add remaining ingredients, except spaghetti. Close cover securely. Place over high heat. Bring to 15 lbs. pressure, according to manufacturer's directions for your pressure cooker. When pressure is reached (control will begin to jiggle), reduce heat immediately and cook 12 minutes. Remove from heat. Reduce pressure instantly by placing cooker under cold running water. Serve on hot spaghetti.

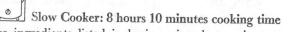 Slow Cooker: 8 hours 10 minutes cooking time

Use ingredients listed in basic recipe, but omit water. Cook ground beef and onion in skillet until meat is browned, about 10 minutes. Pour off fat. Combine meat mixture, green pepper, garlic, tomato sauce, tomato paste, salt, oregano, basil and pepper in cooker. Cover and cook on low to 8 hours. Serve on hot spaghetti.

BEEF-STUFFED PEPPERS

Even though the microwave doesn't brown the beef, you won't notice because it's topped with tomato sauce.

BASIC RECIPE — MAKES 4 SERVINGS.

4 medium green peppers	⅛ tsp. pepper
1 lb. ground beef	2 (8 oz.) cans tomato sauce
2 tblsp. chopped onion	1 (8¾ oz.) can whole kernel
½ c. raw quick-cooking rice	corn, drained
1 tsp. salt	

Oven: 40 to 45 minutes cooking time

Cut green peppers in half lengthwise; remove seeds and membranes. Cook peppers, covered, in 1″ boiling water in skillet 5 minutes. Drain well. Place peppers in 13×9×2″ baking pan. Brown ground beef and onion in same skillet, about 10 minutes. Add rice, salt, pepper, 1 can tomato sauce and corn to beef mixture. Bring to boiling. Cover and remove from heat. Let stand 5 minutes. Fill pepper shells with meat mixture. Spoon remaining 1 can tomato sauce over meat mixture. Bake in 350° oven 25 to 30 minutes or until hot.

Electric Frypan: 40 minutes cooking time

Use ingredients listed in basic recipe, but omit 1 can tomato sauce and add 4 tblsp. ketchup. Cut tops off green peppers and remove seeds and membranes. Bring 1″ water to boiling in electric frypan set at 350°. Add peppers, cut side down. Cover, with vent closed, and cook 5 minutes. Remove peppers from skillet and drain. Pour off water from skillet. Brown ground beef and onion in electric frypan set at 400°, about 5 minutes. Add rice, salt, pepper, corn and 1 can tomato sauce. Bring mixture to boiling. Stuff green peppers with meat mixture. Rinse out skillet. Add stuffed peppers and spoon 1 tblsp.

ketchup over meat mixture in each pepper. Add ½″ water to frypan set at 350°. Bring to boiling. Reduce heat and cover. Simmer with vent closed, 30 minutes.

Microwave Oven (high setting): 18 minutes cooking time
Use ingredients listed in basic recipe, but add 1 egg. Cut peppers in half lengthwise; remove seeds and membrane. Place cut side up in 12×8×2″ glass baking dish (2-qt.). Cover with waxed paper. Microwave (high setting) 4 minutes. Combine ground beef with 1 egg in mixing bowl. Stir in rice, onion, salt, pepper, 1 can tomato sauce and corn. Stuff into pepper shells. Spoon remaining 1 can tomato sauce over meat mixture. Cover with waxed paper. Microwave 14 minutes.

MONTEREY CHILI CON CARNE

The ingredients in the basic recipe were increased for the electric frypan because its surface area is larger than the Dutch oven.
BASIC RECIPE — MAKES 4 SERVINGS.

1 lb. ground beef	2 tsp. chili powder
1 c. chopped onion	1 tsp. ground cumin
1 clove garlic, minced	1 tsp. salt
1 (16 oz.) can tomatoes, cut up	½ c. water
1 (15 oz.) can kidney beans	½ c. cubed Monterey Jack cheese (¼″)

Range Top: 1 hour 5 minutes cooking time
Cook ground beef, onion and garlic in Dutch oven until meat is browned, about 5 minutes. Drain off fat. Add tomatoes, kidney beans, chili powder, cumin, salt and water. Simmer, covered, 1 hour. Serve sprinkled with cheese.

Electric Frypan: 1 hour 5 minutes cooking time
Use ingredients listed in basic recipe, but omit water and use 1 (28 oz.) can tomatoes, 2 (15 oz.) cans kidney beans, ¾ c. cubed Monterey Jack cheese, 3 tsp. chili powder and 1½ tsp. salt. Cook ground beef, onion and garlic in electric frypan at 400° or until meat is browned, about 5 minutes. Drain off fat. Add 1 (28 oz.) can tomatoes, 2 (15 oz.) cans kidney beans, 3 tsp. chili powder, cumin and 1½ tsp. salt. Bring to boiling. Reduce heat to 220°. Cover and simmer, with vent closed, 1 hour. Serve sprinkled with ¾ c. cheese. Makes 6 servings.

 Microwave Oven (high setting): 22 minutes cooking time
Use ingredients listed in basic recipe, but omit water. Combine ground beef, onion and garlic in 2-qt. glass casserole. Microwave (high setting) 6 minutes, stirring twice. Drain off fat. Add tomatoes, kidney beans, chili powder, cumin and salt. Microwave, covered, 16 minutes, stirring three times. Let stand 5 minutes. Serve sprinkled with cheese.

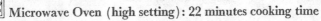

Pressure Cooker: 25 minutes cooking time
Use ingredients listed in basic recipe, but omit water. Cook ground beef, onion and garlic in 4-qt. pressure pan until meat is browned, about 10 minutes. Drain off fat. Add tomatoes, kidney beans, chili powder, cumin and salt. Close cover securely. Place over high heat. Bring to 15 lbs. pressure, according to manufacturer's directions for your pressure cooker. When pressure is reached (control will begin to jiggle), reduce heat immediately and cook 15 minutes. Remove from heat. Let pressure drop of its own accord. Serve sprinkled with cheese.

 Slow Cooker: 9 hours 10 minutes cooking time
Use ingredients listed in basic recipe, but omit water and use 1 (28 oz.) can tomatoes, 2 (15 oz.) cans kidney beans, 3 tsp. chili powder, 1½ tsp. salt and ¾ c. cheese. Cook ground beef, onion and garlic in

skillet until meat is browned, about 10 minutes. Drain off fat. Combine meat mixture, 1 (28 oz.) can tomatoes, 2 (15 oz.) cans kidney beans, 3 tsp. chili powder, 1½ tsp. salt and cumin in slow cooker. Cover and cook on low 9 hours. Serve sprinkled with cheese. Makes 6 servings.

ENCHILADA CASSEROLE

Save time by softening the tortillas in the microwave. Just wrap in plastic wrap and microwave on high 30 seconds.

BASIC RECIPE — MAKES 4 SERVINGS.

3 tblsp. cooking oil
8 corn tortillas
1 lb. ground beef
¼ c. chopped onion
1 (16 oz.) can refried beans
¼ c. hot taco sauce

½ tsp. salt
Dash garlic powder
⅓ c. sliced pitted ripe olives
1 (10 oz.) can enchilada sauce
1½ c. shredded Cheddar cheese

Oven: 37 to 38 minutes cooking time

Heat oil in medium skillet. Dip tortillas in hot oil on both sides to soften; set aside. Cook ground beef and onion in same skillet until meat is browned, about 5 minutes. Remove from heat; drain off fat. Stir refried beans, taco sauce, salt, garlic powder and olives into beef mixture. Place a generous ⅓ c. ground beef mixture on each tortilla and roll up. Pour enchilada sauce into 12×8×2″ glass baking dish (2-qt.). Roll filled tortillas in sauce to moisten all surfaces. Place seam side down in sauce. Cover with aluminum foil. Bake in 350° oven 30 minutes or until hot. Sprinkle with cheese and bake, uncovered, 2 or 3 minutes or until cheese is melted.

Electric Frypan: 12 minutes cooking time

Use ingredients listed in basic recipe. Preheat electric frypan to 220° and add oil. Dip tortillas in hot oil on both sides to soften; set aside.

Increase heat to 350°. Cook beef and onion in the frypan until beef is browned, about 5 minutes. Transfer mixture to medium bowl. Turn off control. Drain fat from frypan. Add refried beans, taco sauce, salt and garlic powder to meat mixture. Mix well and stir in olives. Fill tortillas with meat mixture as for oven. Pour enchilada sauce in electric frypan. Roll filled tortillas in sauce to moisten all surfaces. Place seam side down in sauce. Cover and set control at 220°. When temperature reaches 220°, cover and cook 5 minutes, with vent closed, or until hot. Spoon sauce over tortillas. Sprinkle with cheese and cook, covered, 2 minutes more or until cheese is melted.

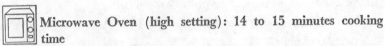 **Microwave Oven (high setting): 14 to 15 minutes cooking time**

Use ingredients listed in basic recipe, but omit 3 tblsp. oil. Combine beef and onion in medium glass bowl. Microwave (high setting), uncovered, 3 minutes, stirring twice to separate meat. Drain off fat. Stir in refried beans, taco sauce, salt and garlic powder. Mix well and stir in olives. Pour enchilada sauce into 12×8×2″ glass baking dish (2-qt.). To soften tortillas, wrap in plastic wrap and microwave 30 seconds. Fill tortillas with meat mixture as for cooking in oven. Roll filled tortillas in enchilada sauce to moisten all surfaces. Place seam side down in sauce. Cover with waxed paper. Microwave 9 to 10 minutes. Spoon sauce over to moisten surfaces once during cooking and give the dish a half turn once. Sprinkle with cheese. Cover and microwave 1 minute 15 seconds or until cheese is melted.

FOUR-WAY MEATBALLS

Prepare Four-way Meatballs and freeze ahead if you wish. You can use them in any of the four meatball dishes that follow.

BASIC RECIPE — MAKES 16 MEATBALLS.

1 lb. ground beef	½ c. soft bread crumbs
1 egg	¼ c. chopped onion (1 small)
¼ c. milk	1 tsp. salt
1 tsp. Worcestershire sauce	¼ tsp. pepper

Oven: 25 to 30 minutes baking time

Thoroughly combine all ingredients in bowl. Mix lightly, but well. Shape into 16 (1½″) meatballs. Place in 8″ square baking pan. Bake meatballs in 375° oven 25 to 30 minutes or until done.

 Electric Frypan: 15 minutes cooking time

Use ingredients listed in the basic recipe, but add 2 tblsp. cooking oil. Prepare and shape meatballs as for Oven. Preheat electric skillet to 350°. Add oil. Brown meatballs on all sides in hot oil, about 15 minutes.

 Microwave Oven (high setting): 8 to 10 minutes cooking time

Use ingredients listed in basic recipe. Prepare and shape meatballs as for Oven. Place in 8″ square glass baking dish. Microwave (high setting) 8 to 10 minutes, turning and rearranging meatballs once during cooking.

 Toaster-Oven: 25 to 30 minutes cooking time

Use ingredients listed in basic recipe. Prepare and shape meatballs as for Oven. Place in 8″ square baking pan. Bake at 375° for 25 to 30 minutes.

BARBECUED MEATBALLS

*If Four-way Meatballs are frozen, thaw before using in this recipe.
Then heat in the easy-to-make barbecue sauce.*

BASIC RECIPE — MAKES 4 SERVINGS.

½ c. ketchup
2 tblsp. brown sugar, packed
2 tblsp. water
2 tblsp. vinegar

1 tsp. Worcestershire sauce
1 recipe Four-way Meatballs
(see Index)

 Range Top: 10 to 15 minutes cooking time
Combine ketchup, brown sugar, water, vinegar and Worcestershire
sauce in medium saucepan. Bring to boiling; add meatballs. Simmer, covered, 10 to 15 minutes, stirring once or twice.

Electric Frypan: 20 to 25 minutes cooking time
Use ingredients listed in basic recipe, but increase water from 2 tblsp.
to ¼ c. Combine ketchup, brown sugar, ¼ c. water, vinegar and
Worcestershire sauce in electric skillet. Bring to simmering 220°.
Add meatballs. Cover and simmer, with vent closed, 20 to 25 minutes,
stirring once or twice during cooking.

Microwave Oven (high setting): 6 to 7 minutes cooking time
Use ingredients listed in basic recipe, but omit water. Combine
ketchup, brown sugar, vinegar and Worcestershire sauce in 1-qt. glass
casserole. Stir in meatballs. Cover and microwave (high setting) 6 to 7
minutes, stirring once.

SWEDISH MEATBALLS

Quick-fix sauce takes little cooking time on range top. Delicious served with hot cooked rice.

BASIC RECIPE — MAKES 4 SERVINGS.

1 (10¾ oz.) can condensed   ¼ tsp. ground nutmeg
  cream of chicken soup   1 recipe Four-way Meatballs
½ c. milk   (see Index)
1 tsp. parsley flakes   ½ c. dairy sour cream

Range Top: 11 to 17 minutes cooking time
Combine soup, milk, parsley and nutmeg in medium saucepan. Heat to boiling. Add meatballs and simmer, covered, 10 to 15 minutes, stirring once or twice. Stir a small amount of hot sauce into sour cream. Return sour cream mixture to saucepan; mix well. Cook on low heat 1 to 2 minutes or until heated.

Electric Frypan: 22 to 27 minutes cooking time
Use ingredients listed in basic recipe, but increase ½ c. milk to 1 c. Combine soup, 1 c. milk, parsley flakes and nutmeg in electric frypan. Bring to simmering set at 220°. Stir in meatballs. Cover and simmer, with vent closed, 20 to 25 minutes, stirring once or twice. Stir in sour cream as for Range Top. Simmer 2 more minutes or until heated.

Microwave Oven (high setting): 7 to 8 minutes cooking time
Use ingredients listed in basic recipe. Combine soup, milk, parsley and nutmeg in 1½-qt. glass casserole; blend well. Add meatballs. Cover and microwave (high setting) 6 to 7 minutes, stirring once. Stir in sour cream as for Range Top. Microwave 1 minute, stirring once.

SPAGHETTI AND MEATBALLS

If you keep a jar of spaghetti sauce in your cupboard, you can serve this meal in 30 minutes.

BASIC RECIPE — MAKES 4 SERVINGS.

½ lb. bulk pork sausage, crumbled

1 (32 oz.) jar spaghetti sauce with mushrooms

1 tblsp. parsley flakes

1 recipe Four-way Meatballs (see Index)

1 lb. spaghetti, cooked

Grated Parmesan cheese

 Range Top: 15 to 20 minutes cooking time

Cook pork sausage in 2-qt. saucepan until lightly browned, about 5 minutes. Stir once or twice to separate meat pieces. Drain off fat. Stir in spaghetti sauce and parsley; mix well. Add meatballs and bring to boiling. Reduce heat and cover. Simmer 10 to 15 minutes to blend flavors, stirring once or twice. Serve over hot spaghetti with Parmesan cheese.

 Electric Frypan: 25 to 30 minutes cooking time

Use ingredients listed in basic recipe. Cook sausage in electric skillet at 350° until lightly browned, about 5 minutes. Stir once or twice to separate meat. Drain off fat; reduce heat to 220°. Stir in spaghetti sauce and parsley. Add meatballs and cover. Simmer, with vent closed, for 20 to 25 minutes. Stir once or twice. Serve over hot spaghetti with Parmesan cheese.

 Microwave Oven (high setting): 10 to 11 minutes cooking time

Use ingredients listed in basic recipe. Place sausage in 1½-qt. glass casserole. Microwave (high setting) 4 minutes or until thoroughly cooked, stirring once or twice to separate meat. Drain off fat. Stir in spaghetti sauce and parsley; mix well. Add meatballs. Cover and microwave 10 minutes or until hot, stirring once. Serve over hot spaghetti with Parmesan cheese.

MEATBALL STROGANOFF

Four-way Meatballs are used in this stroganoff instead of the more expensive steak—a delicious quick meal.

BASIC RECIPE — MAKES 4 SERVINGS.

1 (10¾ oz.) can condensed
   cream of mushroom soup
¼ c. milk
2 tblsp. ketchup
1 recipe Four-way Meatballs
   (see Index)

½ c. dairy sour cream
8 oz. noodles, cooked and
   drained

Range Top: 12 to 17 minutes cooking time

Combine soup, milk and ketchup in medium saucepan. Bring to boiling and add meatballs. Simmer, covered, 10 to 15 minutes, stirring once or twice. Stir a small amount of hot sauce into sour cream. Return sour cream mixture to saucepan; mix well. Cook 2 minutes or just until heated through. Serve over hot noodles.

Electric Frypan: 22 to 27 minutes cooking time

Use ingredients listed in basic recipe, but increase milk from ¼ to ½ c. Combine soup, ½ c. milk and ketchup in electric frypan; blend well. Place meatballs in frypan and stir to coat with sauce. Cover and cook 220°, with vent closed, 20 to 25 minutes or until meat is done. Stir a small amount of hot sauce into sour cream. Return sour cream mixture to skillet; mix well. Cover and cook 2 minutes more until just heated through. Serve over hot noodles.

Microwave Oven (high setting): 7 to 8 minutes cooking time
Use ingredients listed in basic recipe. Combine soup, milk and ketchup in 1½-qt. glass casserole; blend well. Place meatballs in sauce and stir to mix. Cover and microwave (high setting) 6 to 7 minutes, stirring once. Stir a small amount of hot sauce into sour cream. Add sour cream mixture to casserole; mix well. Microwave 1 minute, stirring once. Serve over hot noodles.

HAMBURGER/POTATO SKILLET

This recipe is identical whether it's cooked on the range top or in the electric frypan and the cooking time is the same.

BASIC RECIPE — MAKES 6 SERVINGS.

1½ lbs. ground beef
½ c. chopped onion
½ c. chopped celery
1 tsp. Worcestershire sauce
1½ tsp. salt
¼ tsp. pepper
2 (¾ oz.) pkgs. brown gravy
    mix

2 c. water
2 c. frozen mixed vegetables
Instant mashed potatoes for 6
    servings
½ c. shredded process American
    cheese

 Range Top: 23 to 28 minutes cooking time
Cook ground beef, onion and celery in 12″ skillet until beef is browned, about 10 minutes. Add Worcestershire sauce, salt, pepper, gravy mix, water and mixed vegetables. Bring to a boil. Reduce heat and cover. Simmer 10 to 15 minutes or until vegetables are tender. Meanwhile, prepare mashed potatoes as directed on package. Drop 6 spoonfuls of potatoes over meat mixture. Sprinkle potatoes with cheese. Cover and continue simmering until cheese is melted, about 3 minutes.

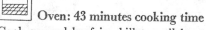 Electric Frypan: 23 to 28 minutes cooking time

Use ingredients listed in basic recipe. Cook ground beef, onion and celery in electric frypan at 350° until browned, about 10 minutes. Add Worcestershire sauce, salt, pepper, brown gravy mix, water and mixed vegetables. Bring mixture to a boil. Reduce heat to simmering (220°) and cover. Cook, with vent closed, 10 to 15 minutes or until vegetables are tender. Meanwhile, prepare mashed potatoes as directed on package. Drop 6 spoonfuls of potatoes over meat mixture. Sprinkle potatoes with cheese. Cover and continue simmering until cheese is melted, about 3 minutes.

SOUTHWESTERN CHILI CASSEROLE

The cheese and corn chip garnish make this casserole equally attractive whether cooked conventionally or microwaved.

BASIC RECIPE — MAKES 6 SERVINGS.

1 lb. ground beef
1 (15 oz.) can kidney beans, drained
1 (10 oz.) can hot enchilada sauce
1 (8 oz.) can tomato sauce

1½ c. shredded sharp process American cheese
1 tblsp. instant minced onion
1 (6 oz.) pkg. corn chips
1 c. dairy sour cream

Oven: 43 minutes cooking time

Cook ground beef in skillet until brown, about 10 minutes. Drain off excess fat. Add kidney beans, enchilada sauce, tomato sauce, 1 c. of the cheese and onion. Reserve 1 c. corn chips; crush the remainder. Stir crushed chips into beef mixture. Turn into 2-qt. casserole. Bake in 375° oven 30 minutes. Gently spread sour cream over top with fork. Sprinkle with remaining ½ c. cheese. Arrange remaining 1 c. corn chips around casserole edge. Bake until cheese is melted, about 3 minutes.

Microwave Oven (high setting): 27 to 28 minutes cooking time

Use ingredients listed in basic recipe. Crumble ground beef into 2-qt. glass casserole. Microwave (high setting) 7 to 8 minutes, stirring three times to separate meat. Drain off fat. Add kidney beans, enchilada sauce, tomato sauce, 1 c. cheese and onion. Reserve 1 c. corn chips; crush the remainder and stir into casserole. Cover and microwave 18 minutes, stirring once. Spread sour cream on top. Sprinkle with remaining cheese and garnish with corn chips as for Oven. Microwave 2 minutes or until cheese is melted.

SUMMERTIME GARDENER'S LASAGNE

Zucchini substitutes for the pasta in this Italian-inspired dish. For a special touch, sprinkle with grated Romano cheese.

BASIC RECIPE — MAKES 4 TO 5 SERVINGS.

6 c. sliced zucchini (about 1¾ lbs.)
½ lb. ground beef
1 small clove garlic, minced
1 (8 oz.) can tomato sauce
1 tsp. salt
¼ tsp. dried oregano leaves

¼ tsp. dried basil leaves
1 c. small-curd cottage cheese
1 egg, beaten
1 tblsp. parsley flakes
¼ c. dry bread crumbs
1 c. shredded mozzarella cheese (4 oz.)

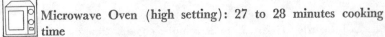 Oven: 38 minutes cooking time

Cook zucchini in boiling water in saucepan until tender-crisp, about 5 minutes. Drain. Cook ground beef and garlic in skillet until beef is browned, about 5 minutes. Stir tomato sauce, salt, oregano and basil into beef mixture. Stir together cottage cheese, egg and parsley. Place half of zucchini in greased 8″ square baking pan. Sprinkle with half of bread crumbs. Spread with half of the cottage cheese mixture, then with half of beef mixture and half of mozzarella cheese. Repeat layers, but reserve remaining mozzarella cheese. Bake in 350° oven 25 minutes. Sprinkle with reserved cheese. Return to oven just long enough to melt cheese, about 3 minutes.

Toaster-Oven: 38 minutes cooking time

Use ingredients listed in basic recipe. Prepare as for Oven. Bake at 350° for 25 minutes. Sprinkle with remaining half of mozzarella cheese. Return to toaster-oven just long enough to melt cheese, about 3 minutes.

Microwave Oven (high setting): 21 to 25 minutes cooking time

Use ingredients listed in basic recipe. Place zucchini in an 8" square glass baking dish. Cover with waxed paper. Microwave (high setting) 7 to 8 minutes or until tender-crisp. Drain and reserve. Crumble beef into 1-qt. glass casserole; add garlic. Microwave, uncovered, 2 to 3 minutes or until meat is cooked. Stir to break up pieces; drain. Stir in tomato sauce, salt, oregano and basil. Mix together cottage cheese, egg and parsley. Remove half of zucchini from baking dish. Arrange remaining slices evenly in baking dish. Sprinkle with half of bread crumbs. Spread with half of cottage cheese mixture and then with half of meat mixture. Sprinkle with half of mozzarella cheese. Repeat layers but reserve the mozzarella cheese. Microwave until mixture is hot in center, 10 to 12 minutes. Sprinkle with reserved cheese. Microwave just long enough to melt cheese, about 2 minutes.

BEEF-EGGPLANT SKILLET

This is a take-off of Eggplant Parmesan, but you can cook it in the electric frypan, microwave oven or on the range top.

BASIC RECIPE — MAKES 6 SERVINGS.

1½ lbs. ground beef	⅛ tsp. pepper
1 c. chopped onion	1 lb. eggplant, pared and cubed
1 clove garlic, minced	(about 4½ c.)
1 (16 oz.) can tomatoes, cut up	1 c. water
2 tsp. salt	1 c. quick-cooking rice
1 tsp. dried oregano leaves	½ c. shredded mozzarella cheese

Range Top: 38 to 40 minutes cooking time

Cook ground beef, onion and garlic in large skillet until meat is browned, about 10 minutes. Drain off excess fat. Stir in tomatoes, salt, oregano, pepper, eggplant and water. Bring to boiling. Stir in rice. Reduce heat and simmer, covered, 25 minutes. Stir occasionally. Sprinkle with cheese. Cover and continue cooking 3 to 5 minutes or until cheese is melted.

 Electric Frypan: 43 to 45 minutes cooking time

Use ingredients listed in basic recipe. Cook ground beef, onion and garlic in frypan set at 350° until meat is browned, about 10 minutes. Drain off excess fat. Stir in tomatoes, salt, oregano, pepper, eggplant and water. Bring to boiling and add rice. Cover and simmer at 220°, with vent closed, 30 minutes or until eggplant is cooked and rice is tender. Stir occasionally while cooking. Sprinkle with cheese. Cover and cook until cheese is melted, 3 to 5 minutes.

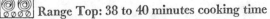 **Microwave Oven (high setting): 34 to 37 minutes cooking time**

Use ingredients listed in basic recipe, but decrease water to ¾ cup. Crumble ground beef into 3-qt. glass casserole. Stir in onion and garlic. Cover and microwave (high setting) 8 minutes or until browned. Stir every 2 minutes to break up ground beef. Add tomatoes, ¾ c. water, salt, oregano and pepper. Microwave, covered, 10 to 12 minutes or until boiling. Stir in eggplant and rice. Microwave, covered, 15 minutes or until eggplant and rice are tender. Stir every 5 minutes. Sprinkle with cheese. Return to oven and microwave until cheese is melted, 1 to 2 minutes. Let stand, covered, 5 minutes.

ITALIAN ZUCCHINI SUPPER

Very little difference in cooking time or final product in any of these appliances.

BASIC RECIPE — MAKES 6 SERVINGS.

1 lb. ground beef
1 c. chopped onion
½ c. chopped green pepper
1 (16 oz.) can tomatoes, cut up
1 pkg. spaghetti sauce mix
1 c. water

½ tsp. salt
⅛ tsp. pepper
1 c. raw quick-cooking rice
1 qt. sliced, unpared zucchini (about 1 lb.)
Grated Parmesan cheese

Range Top: 30 to 35 minutes cooking time
Cook ground beef, onion and green pepper in skillet until meat is browned, about 10 minutes. Stir in tomatoes, sauce mix, water, salt and pepper. Bring to boiling. Stir in rice and zucchini. Reduce heat and simmer, covered, 20 to 25 minutes or until zucchini and rice are tender. Sprinkle with Parmesan cheese.

Electric Frypan: 30 to 35 minutes cooking time
Use ingredients listed in basic recipe. Cook ground beef, onion and green pepper in frypan set at 350° until meat is browned, about 5 minutes. Stir in tomatoes, sauce mix, water, salt and pepper. Bring to boiling. Stir in rice and zucchini. Reduce heat to 220°. Cover and simmer, with vent closed, 25 to 30 minutes or until zucchini and rice are tender. Sprinkle with Parmesan cheese.

Microwave Oven (high setting): 36 to 37 minutes cooking time.
Use ingredients listed in basic recipe, but reduce water from 1 c. to ¾ c. Crumble ground beef into 3-qt. glass casserole. Stir in onion and green pepper. Cover and microwave (high setting) 8 minutes or until meat is cooked, stirring every 2 minutes to separate meat. Stir in tomatoes, sauce mix, ¾ c. water, salt and pepper. Microwave, covered, 8 or 9 minutes or until boiling, stirring twice. Stir in rice and zucchini. Microwave, covered, 20 minutes or until rice and zucchini are tender. Stir every 5 minutes. Let stand 5 minutes. Sprinkle with Parmesan cheese.

HAMBURGER STIR-FRY

Fast-cook main dish based on the Chinese method of stir-frying. Only we substituted ground beef for steak strips.

BASIC RECIPE — MAKES 6 SERVINGS.

1 lb. ground beef
4 tblsp. cooking oil
1 c. chopped onion
1 c. bias-sliced celery, ⅛" thick
1 clove garlic, minced
½ c. chopped green pepper
1 (4 oz.) can mushroom stems
    and pieces, drained

2 c. cooked regular rice
1 c. frozen peas, thawed
12 cherry tomatoes, halved
2 tsp. seasoned salt
1 tsp. beef bouillon granules
2 tblsp. water

Range Top: 14 minutes cooking time
Cut and assemble ingredients before starting to cook. Brown ground beef in 12" skillet over medium-high heat, 5 minutes. Push to one side of skillet. Add 1 tblsp. of the oil to the other side. Add onion, celery and garlic. Stir and fry 2 minutes. Cover and steam 1 minute. Add green pepper and mushrooms. Stir and fry 2 minutes. Push vegetables to other side of skillet. Add remaining 3 tblsp. oil in center. Stir in rice. Cook and stir 2 minutes. Add remaining ingredients. Cook and stir vigorously, until tomatoes and peas are hot, about 2 minutes.

Electric Frypan: 14 minutes cooking time

Use ingredients listed in basic recipe. Brown ground beef in electric frypan at 375°. Follow directions for cooking on Range Top.

 Electric Wok: 13 minutes cooking time

Use ingredients listed in basic recipe, but reduce oil from 4 to 3 tblsp. and omit water. Preheat wok to 375°. Crumble beef into wok. Cook and stir until lightly browned, about 3 minutes. Push meat up the sides. Add 1 tblsp. oil in center. Add onion, celery and garlic. Stir and fry 2 minutes. Cover and steam 1 minute. Add green pepper and mushrooms. Stir and fry 2 minutes. Push vegetables up sides of wok. Add 2 tblsp. oil in center. Stir in rice. Cook and stir 3 minutes. Add remaining ingredients. Stir all of the ingredients together and continue stirring until tomatoes and peas are hot, about 2 minutes.

REUBEN-STYLE MEAT LOAF

A very interesting meat loaf recipe fashioned after the Reuben sandwich. Takes only 24 minutes in microwave.

BASIC RECIPE — MAKES 8 SERVINGS.

1 (11 oz.) can condensed
    tomato bisque soup
1 lb. ground beef
1 (12 oz.) can corned beef,
    crumbled
2½ c. soft bread crumbs
2 eggs

1 (8 oz.) can sauerkraut,
    drained
1 c. shredded Swiss cheese
½ tsp. caraway seeds
2 tsp. prepared horseradish
2 slices Swiss cheese, cut in 8
    triangles (about 2 oz.)

 Oven: 1 hour 12 minutes baking time

Thoroughly mix ¼ c. of the soup, ground beef, corned beef, bread crumbs and eggs. Pat meat mixture on waxed paper into 15×10″ rectangle. Stir together sauerkraut, shredded cheese and caraway seeds. Press evenly into meat to within 1″ of edges. Roll meat tightly jelly roll fashion with waxed paper starting at narrow edge. Seal edges and seam. Place loaf, seam side down, in 12×8×2″ glass baking dish (2-qt.). Bake in 350° oven 1 hour. Meanwhile, combine remaining soup and horseradish. Spoon over loaf and bake 10 minutes. Top with cheese triangles and bake 2 more minutes or until cheese melts.

Microwave Oven (high setting): 24 minutes cooking time
Use ingredients listed in basic recipe. Prepare loaf as for Oven. Place loaf, seam side down, in 12×8×2″ glass baking dish (2-qt.). Cover with waxed paper. Microwave (high setting) 20 minutes or until done, giving dish one half turn. Meanwhile, combine remaining soup and horseradish. Spoon over loaf. Microwave, uncovered, 3 minutes. Arrange cheese triangles over top of loaf. Microwave until cheese melts, about 1 minute.

FAMILY MEAT LOAF

You can "bake" this meat loaf in the electric frypan as well as in the slow cooker and three other ways.
BASIC RECIPE — MAKES 6 SERVINGS.

1 egg, beaten	¼ c. ketchup
1 tsp. salt	1 tsp. Worcestershire sauce
⅛ tsp. pepper	2 c. soft bread cubes
⅛ tsp. rubbed sage	2 tblsp. instant minced onion
½ c. milk	1½ lbs. ground beef

Oven: 1 hour 10 minutes baking time
Combine egg, salt, pepper, sage, milk, 2 tblsp. ketchup, Worcestershire sauce, bread cubes and onions. Add ground beef and combine thoroughly. Press into 8½×4½×2½″ loaf pan. Bake in 350° oven 1

hour. Spread with remaining 2 tblsp. ketchup. Continue baking 10 minutes.

Electric Frypan: 1 hour 15 minutes cooking time
Use ingredients listed in basic recipe. Prepare as for Oven. Press mixture into 8½×4½×2½″ loaf pan. Spread with remaining 2 tblsp. ketchup before baking. Preheat frypan to 420°. Place pan on rack in frypan. Cover and bake, with vent closed, for 1 hour. Open vent and bake 15 minutes more.

Microwave Oven (high setting): 18 minutes cooking time
Use ingredients listed in basic recipe. Prepare as for Oven. Press meat mixture into 1½-qt. glass loaf dish. Spread with remaining 2 tblsp. ketchup. Cover with waxed paper. Microwave (high setting) 18 minutes, giving dish a quarter turn every 6 minutes. Let stand 5 minutes.

Slow Cooker: 6 to 8 hours cooking time
Use ingredients listed in basic recipe, but use 2 eggs instead of 1 egg. Prepare as for Oven. Cut two strips of heavy-duty aluminum foil 15×2″ (or double thickness of regular foil). Cross strips in bottom of cooker and let them come up sides. Shape mixture into a round loaf and place on top of crossed strips. Meat loaf should not touch sides of cooker. Cover and cook on low 6 to 8 hours. Lift foil strips to remove loaf. Spread remaining 2 tblsp. ketchup on loaf and serve.

Toaster-Oven: 1 hour 10 minutes baking time
Use ingredients listed in basic recipe. Prepare as for Oven. Bake as directed in Oven method.

CALIFORNIA MEAT LOAF

Your toaster-oven is handy when you only want to bake one food at a time—no need to heat the large oven.

BASIC RECIPE — MAKES 8 SERVINGS.

1½ lbs. ground beef	⅛ tsp. pepper
2 eggs, beaten	⅓ c. saltine cracker crumbs
1 c. saltine cracker crumbs	1 c. cream-style cottage cheese
1 (8 oz.) can tomato sauce	1 egg, beaten
½ c. chopped onion	2 tblsp. chopped fresh parsley
¼ c. chopped green pepper	½ tsp. dried oregano leaves
½ tsp. garlic salt	¼ c. grated Parmesan cheese
½ tsp. salt	

 Oven: 1 hour baking time

Combine ground beef, 2 eggs, 1 c. cracker crumbs, tomato sauce, onion, green pepper, garlic salt, salt and pepper in bowl. Mix lightly, but well. Pat one half of mixture into bottom of 8″ square baking pan. Combine remaining ingredients. Spread evenly over meat. On a piece of waxed paper, pat remaining meat mixture in 8″ square. Invert over cheese. Peel off paper. Bake at 350° 1 hour. Let stand 10 minutes before serving.

Electric Frypan: 1 hour 15 minutes cooking time

Use ingredients listed in basic recipe but add 2 tblsp. ketchup. Prepare meat loaf and pack into 8″ square baking pan as for Oven. Preheat frypan to 420°. Place pan on rack in skillet. Bake, covered, with vent closed, 1 hour. Pour off juices. Spread 2 tblsp. ketchup over top of meat. Continue cooking with vent open 15 minutes. Let stand 10 minutes before serving.

Microwave Oven (high setting): 31 minutes cooking time
Use ingredients listed in basic recipe, but add 2 tblsp. water and 2 tblsp. ketchup. Combine onion, green pepper and 2 tblsp. water in glass mixing bowl. Cover with waxed paper. Microwave (high setting) 4 minutes or until tender. Drain. Add ground beef, 1 c. cracker crumbs, tomato sauce, 2 eggs, garlic salt, salt and pepper; mix to blend. Pat mixture into 8″ square baking dish as for Oven. Complete meat loaf as for Oven. Spread top with 2 tblsp. ketchup. Cover with waxed paper. Microwave 27 minutes. Give dish a quarter turn two times. Let stand 10 minutes before serving.

Toaster-Oven: 1 hour baking time
Use ingredients listed in basic recipe. Prepare meat loaf and pack into 8″ square baking pan as for Oven. Bake at 350° for 1 hour. Let stand 10 minutes before serving.

HEARTY HASH

You save a lot of time because you don't need to peel potatoes for this hash recipe—you use frozen hashed browns.

BASIC RECIPE — MAKES 6 SERVINGS.

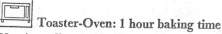

1 c. chopped onion	1 (¾ oz.) pkg. brown gravy
¼ c. butter or regular margarine	mix
	1 c. water
3 c. finely cubed cooked beef	1½ tsp. salt
2 (12 oz.) pkgs. frozen hashed brown potatoes, thawed	½ tsp. pepper
	Paprika

Oven: 53 minutes cooking time
Cook onion in melted butter in skillet until soft, about 8 minutes. Thoroughly combine beef and potatoes in large mixing bowl, crum-

bling potatoes to break them apart. Add onion mixture. Prepare gravy
with water according to package directions. Stir into meat mixture
along with salt and pepper. Spread in greased 13×9×2″ baking pan.
Sprinkle with paprika. Bake in 350° oven 45 minutes.

 Microwave Oven (high setting): 25 minutes cooking time
Use ingredients listed in basic recipe. Place butter in 1-qt. glass casserole. Microwave (high setting) 1 minute or until melted. Stir in
onions. Microwave, covered, 8 minutes or until tender, stirring once.
Blend gravy mix and water in 2-c. glass measure. Microwave 1 minute; stir. Continue microwaving 1 minute or until mixture bubbles,
stirring every 30 seconds. Thoroughly combine beef and potatoes in
large mixing bowl crumbling potatoes to break them apart. Add onion
mixture, gravy, salt and pepper; mix thoroughly. Spread in 12×8×2″
glass baking dish (2-qt.). Sprinkle with paprika. Cover with waxed
paper and microwave 8 minutes. Give a half turn and microwave
another 7 minutes.

Slow Cooker: 7 to 9 hours cooking time
Use ingredients listed in basic recipe, but omit paprika and finely chop
onion. Place beef and finely chopped onion in slow cooker. Crumble
potatoes to break them apart and mix with beef and onion. Prepare
gravy with water as directed on package. Pour over meat mixture;
add butter, salt and pepper; mix thoroughly. Cover and cook on low
7 to 9 hours.

NEW ENGLAND BOILED DINNER

This corned beef dinner is especially suited to the long simmering in a slow cooker—perfect for busy days.

BASIC RECIPE — MAKES 6 SERVINGS.

1 (3 to 4 lb.) corned beef brisket
1 clove garlic, minced
1 bay leaf
6 medium potatoes, pared

3 carrots, cut in halves
2 small onions, cut in quarters
1 small head cabbage, cut in sixths

Range Top: 3 hours 35 minutes cooking time

Place corned beef in Dutch oven; barely cover beef with water. Add garlic and bay leaf. Bring to boiling; reduce heat and simmer, covered, 3 hours or until meat is tender when pricked with a fork. Remove meat from broth and keep warm. Add potatoes, carrots and onions to broth; cover and cook 10 minutes. Add cabbage and continue cooking, covered, 20 minutes. Remove bay leaf. Slice corned beef and heat with vegetables, about 5 minutes.

Pressure Cooker: 1 hour 11 minutes cooking time

Use ingredients listed in basic recipe. Place corned beef on rack in 6-qt. pressure cooker. Add 2 c. water, garlic and bay leaf. Close cover securely. Place over high heat. Bring to 15 lbs. pressure, according to manufacturer's directions for your pressure cooker. When pressure is reached (control will begin to jiggle), reduce heat immediately and cook 1 hour. Remove from heat. Let pressure drop of its own accord. Remove meat from broth and keep warm. Remove rack. Add potatoes, carrots, onions and cabbage to broth in pressure cooker. Close cover securely. Place over high heat. Bring to 15 lbs. pressure, according to manufacturer's directions for your pressure cooker. When pressure is reached (control will begin to jiggle), reduce heat immediately and cook 6 minutes. Remove from heat. Reduce pressure instantly by placing cooker under cold running water. Remove bay leaf. Slice corned beef and heat with vegetables, about 5 minutes.

 Slow Cooker: 12 hours 45 minutes cooking time

Use ingredients listed in basic recipe, but substitute 1 c. thinly sliced carrots for carrot halves and cut potatoes in quarters. Place potatoes, onions, carrots, garlic and bay leaf in slow cooker. Trim excess fat from corned beef and place meat on vegetables in cooker. (Cut meat to fit, if necessary.) Add 1½ c. water. Cover and cook on low 12 hours. Thirty minutes before mealtime, remove 1 c. liquid from cooker. Pour 1 c. liquid into a skillet, add cabbage wedges, cover and cook 30 minutes or until cabbage is tender. Remove bay leaf. Slice corned beef and heat with vegetables, about 15 minutes.

LIVER WITH STUFFING

Chopped fresh parsley and paprika are added for color in the microwaved version of this unusual liver recipe.

BASIC RECIPE — MAKES 8 SERVINGS.

2 lbs. sliced beef liver	¼ c. instant minced onion
1 tsp. salt	3 c. herb-seasoned stuffing mix
¼ tsp. pepper	6 slices bacon, chopped
1¾ c. hot water	2 (4 oz.) cans mushroom stems
1 tblsp. beef bouillon granules	and pieces, drained

 Oven: 45 minutes cooking time

Line bottom of greased 12×8×2″ glass baking dish (2-qt.) with liver. Sprinkle with salt and pepper. Combine hot water, bouillon granules and instant onion in bowl. Let stand a few minutes. Combine stuffing mix, bacon and mushrooms. Stir bouillon mixture into stuffing. Spread evenly over liver. Bake in 350° oven 45 minutes.

 Microwave Oven (high setting): 21 to 23 minutes cooking time

Use ingredients listed in basic recipe, but in different amounts. Substitute onion rings for instant minced onion and add parsley and paprika. Place half of 2 lbs. sliced beef liver in 12×8×2″ glass baking dish (2-qt.). Sprinkle with ½ tsp. salt and ⅛ tsp. pepper. Top with 1 large onion, sliced and separated into rings, then with 1½ c. stuffing mix combined with 1 (4 oz.) can mushroom stems and pieces, drained, and 3 slices bacon, chopped. Cover with remaining liver slices. Combine ½ c. hot water and 1 tsp. beef bouillon granules; pour over liver. Sprinkle with remaining salt and pepper, 1 tsp. chopped fresh parsley and ¼ tsp. paprika. Cover with waxed paper. Microwave (high setting) 21 to 23 minutes, giving dish a half turn twice. Let stand 10 minutes.

PEPPY LIVER WITH BACON

The bacon and other seasonings turn liver into something different— makes liver more appealing.

BASIC RECIPE — MAKES 4 SERVINGS.

6 slices bacon
¼ c. chopped onion
1 lb. beef liver, cut in 2×½″ strips
¼ c. water

2 tblsp. ketchup
1 tblsp. vinegar
2 tsp. prepared mustard
1 tsp. Worcestershire sauce
½ tsp. salt

 Range Top: 19 minutes cooking time

Cook bacon in skillet until crisp, about 6 minutes. Drain bacon on paper toweling; crumble and set aside. Stir onion and liver into pan drippings in skillet. Add water. Simmer, covered, 10 minutes. Pour off all the liquid. Meanwhile, combine remaining ingredients except bacon. Stir into liver mixture; heat, about 3 minutes. Serve liver sprinkled with bacon.

 Microwave Oven (high setting): 13 to 15½ minutes cooking time

Use ingredients listed in basic recipe, but omit water. Place 6 bacon slices in 12×8×2″ glass baking dish (2-qt.). Microwave (high setting) 5 to 6 minutes, giving dish one quarter turn. Remove bacon; drain on paper towels. Pour off bacon drippings, but leave 2 tblsp. in dish. Crumble bacon and set aside. Add onion to bacon drippings in dish. Cover with waxed paper. Microwave 3 minutes or until tender. Add liver strips and stir to coat with bacon drippings. Cover and microwave 4 to 5 minutes or until center of liver is barely pink. Stir twice during cooking. Meanwhile, combine remaining ingredients, except bacon. Drain juices from liver and discard. Add ketchup mixture to liver, stirring to coat. Microwave, covered, 1 minute. Sprinkle with crumbled bacon. Microwave, uncovered, 30 seconds.

CHINESE PORK WITH VEGETABLES

One pound of pork steak stretches to serve six, making this a very economical dish. Serve with lots of cooked rice.

BASIC RECIPE — MAKES 6 SERVINGS.

1 lb. pork steak, cut in ⅛″ strips

3 tblsp. soy sauce

¼ tsp. ground ginger

5 tblsp. cooking oil

1½ c. bias-sliced carrots, ⅛″ thick

3 tblsp. water

1 (4 oz.) can mushroom stems and pieces

2 tblsp. cornstarch

1 tsp. chicken bouillon granules

1 (6 oz.) pkg. frozen pea pods

1½ c. thinly sliced cauliflower

6 green onions and tops, cut in ½″ lengths

Hot cooked rice

Range Top: 11 minutes cooking time

Cut and measure all ingredients before starting to cook. Combine pork, soy sauce and ginger in bowl; let stand while preparing other ingredients. Heat 12″ skillet over high heat. Add 3 tblsp. of the oil; heat. Add meat mixture; stir and fry until all pink is gone, about 2 minutes. Push to one side of skillet. Add carrots; stir and fry 2 minutes. Stir meat and carrots together. Add water; cover and steam 2 minutes. Remove from skillet. Drain mushrooms, reserving liquid. Add enough water to reserved liquid to make ½ c. Blend in cornstarch and bouillon granules. Add remaining 2 tblsp. oil to skillet. Stir in frozen pea pods, cauliflower, green onions and mushrooms. Stir and fry 3 minutes. Return meat and carrots to skillet. Stir in cornstarch mixture. Cook and stir until mixture thickens and bubbles, about 2 minutes. Serve over rice.

 Electric Frypan: 11 minutes cooking time

Use ingredients listed in basic recipe. Preheat skillet to 375°. Cook as for Range Top.

 Electric Wok: 11 minutes cooking time

Use ingredients listed in basic recipe, but reduce cooking oil from 5 to 3 tblsp. Cut and measure all ingredients before starting to cook. Combine pork, soy sauce and ginger in bowl; let stand while preparing other ingredients. Heat electric wok to 375°. Add 2 tblsp. of the oil; heat. Add meat mixture; stir and fry until all pink is gone, about 2 minutes. Push to one side of wok. Add carrots; stir and fry 2 minutes. Stir meat and carrots together. Add water; cover and steam 2 minutes. Remove from wok. Drain mushrooms, reserving liquid. Add enough water to reserved liquid to make ½ c. Blend in cornstarch and bouillon granules. Add remaining 1 tblsp. oil to wok. Stir in frozen pea pods, cauliflower, green onions and mushrooms. Stir and fry 3 minutes. Return meat and carrots to wok. Stir in cornstarch mixture. Cook and stir until mixture thickens and bubbles, about 2 minutes. Serve with rice.

CURRIED PORK

*Here's a handy tip. Partially freeze the pork steak before cutting it in
⅛″ strips—so much easier to cut up.*
BASIC RECIPE — MAKES 4 SERVINGS.

1 lb. boneless pork steak, ½″
    thick
5 tblsp. butter or regular
    margarine
2 c. chopped onion
1 large Golden Delicious apple,
    cored and thinly sliced

1¼ c. apple juice
1 tblsp. cornstarch
1½ tsp. curry powder
1 tsp. salt
2 tblsp. sweet pickle relish
Hot cooked rice
½ c. coarsely chopped peanuts

Range Top: 18 minutes cooking time

Cut and prepare all ingredients before starting to cook. Cut pork into
⅛″ thick strips across grain. Melt 4 tblsp. of the butter in 12″ skillet
over medium high heat, about 1 minute. Add pork; cook and stir 5
minutes. Remove from skillet and reserve. Reduce heat to medium.
Melt remaining 1 tblsp. butter in skillet; add onion. Cook, stirring
frequently, 3 minutes. Add apple. Cook, stirring frequently, 2 minutes. Blend together apple juice, cornstarch, curry powder and salt.
Add cornstarch mixture to skillet. Cook and stir until bubbly and
thickened, about 2 minutes. Stir in pork and pickle relish. Cover, reduce heat and simmer 5 minutes. Serve over hot cooked rice; sprinkle
with peanuts.

Electric Frypan: 18 minutes cooking time

Use ingredients listed in basic recipe, but increase apple juice from 1¼
to 1½ c. Cut and assemble ingredients before starting to cook. Cut ingredients as for Range Top. Melt 4 tblsp. of the butter in electric
frypan at 350°, about 1 minute. Add pork; cook and stir 5 minutes.
Remove from skillet and reserve. Reduce heat to 300°. Melt remaining

1 tblsp. butter in skillet. Add onion; cook and stir 3 minutes. Add apple; cook and stir 2 minutes. Blend together 1½ c. apple juice, cornstarch, curry powder and salt. Add cornstarch mixture to skillet. Cook and stir until bubbly and thickened, about 2 minutes. Stir in pork and pickle relish. Cover, reduce heat to 220°. Simmer, with vent closed, 5 minutes. Serve over hot cooked rice; sprinkle with peanuts.

 Electric Wok: 19 minutes cooking time

Use ingredients listed in basic recipe but use only 4 tblsp. butter. Cut and assemble all ingredients before starting to cook. Cut ingredients as for Range Top. Melt 3 tblsp. of the butter in wok at 350°, about 1 minute. Add pork; cook and stir 6 minutes. Remove from wok and reserve. Reduce heat to 300°. Melt remaining butter in wok. Add onion. Cook and stir 3 minutes. Add apple; cook and stir 2 minutes. Blend together apple juice, cornstarch, curry powder and salt. Add cornstarch mixture to skillet. Cook and stir until bubbly and thickened, about 2 minutes. Stir in pork and pickle relish. Cover and cook 5 minutes, stirring once. Serve over hot cooked rice; sprinkle with peanuts.

SWEET-SOUR PORK

If pineapple slices aren't available in your supermarket, use pineapple chunks and cut in two. Or use pineapple tidbits.

BASIC RECIPE — MAKES 4 SERVINGS.

¾ lb. lean pork
1 (15¼ oz.) can sliced
    pineapple
¼ c. brown sugar, packed
2 tblsp. cornstarch
½ tsp. salt
¼ c. vinegar

3 tblsp. cooking oil
1 green pepper, cut in long
    strips
12 green onions, cut in 1"
    lengths
⅓ c. mixed sweet pickles, sliced
Hot cooked rice

Range Top: 11 minutes cooking time

Cut and assemble ingredients before cooking. Cut pork in ⅛" wide strips across grain. Drain pineapple, reserving juice. Add water to pineapple juice to make 1 c. Cut pineapple slices into eighths. Blend together brown sugar, cornstarch and salt. Blend in pineapple juice and vinegar. Heat 12" skillet over high heat. Add oil and heat. Add pork; cook and stir 3 minutes. Add green pepper; cook and stir 1 minute. Add onions; cook and stir 2 minutes. Add pineapple juice mixture. Cook and stir until mixture bubbles and thickens, about 2 minutes. Add pineapple and pickles. Reduce heat to low. Cover and simmer 3 minutes. Serve over hot rice.

 Electric Frypan: 13 minutes cooking time

Use ingredients listed in basic recipe. Cut and assemble ingredients before cooking. Prepare them as for Range Top. Heat electric frypan to 375°. Add oil and heat. Add pork; cook and stir 3 minutes. Add green pepper; cook and stir 1 minute. Add onions; cook and stir 2 minutes. Add pineapple juice mixture. Cook and stir until mixture bubbles and thickens, about 2 minutes. Add pineapple and pickles. Reduce heat to simmer (220°). Cover and simmer, with vent closed, until vegetables are heated through and green pepper and onion are tender-crisp, 5 minutes. Serve over hot cooked rice.

 Electric Wok: 11 minutes cooking time

Use ingredients listed in basic recipe, but reduce cooking oil from 3 to 2 tblsp. Cut and assemble all ingredients before cooking. Prepare them as for Range Top. Heat wok to 375°. Add oil; heat. Add pork; cook and stir 3 minutes. Add green pepper; cook and stir 1 minute. Add onions; cook and stir 2 minutes. Add pineapple juice mixture. Cook and stir until mixture bubbles and thickens, about 2 minutes. Add pineapple and pickles. Cover; reduce heat to 250°. Simmer 3 minutes. Serve over hot cooked rice.

DUTCH PORK CHOPS

It's amazing that pork can be cooked to doneness in so little time. Although not browned in microwave, the chops are moist and flavorful.
BASIC RECIPE — MAKES 4 SERVINGS.

4 loin pork chops, ½" thick
Salt
Pepper
2 tblsp. cooking oil
1 (16 oz.) can sauerkraut,
   drained

1 (8 oz.) can applesauce
2 tblsp. brown sugar, packed
½ tsp. caraway seeds

Range Top: 45 to 50 minutes cooking time
Season pork chops with salt and pepper. Brown pork chops in hot oil in 10" skillet on both sides, about 15 minutes. Remove chops from skillet; drain off fat from skillet. Combine remaining ingredients in skillet. Top with pork chops. Cover and simmer 30 to 35 minutes or until chops are tender.

Electric Frypan: 50 to 55 minutes cooking time
Use ingredients listed in basic recipe. Set electric frypan at 300°. Season pork chops with salt and pepper. Brown chops in hot oil in frypan on both sides, about 15 minutes. Remove chops; drain off fat from skillet. Combine remaining ingredients in electric frypan. Top with pork chops. Reduce to 220° and cover. Simmer, with vent closed, 35 to 40 minutes or until chops are tender.

Microwave Oven (high setting): 10 to 12 minutes cooking time
Use ingredients listed in basic recipe, but omit cooking oil and add a sprinkling of paprika. Combine sauerkraut, brown sugar, caraway

seeds and applesauce in 8″ square glass baking dish. Season pork chops with salt, pepper and paprika. Place on top of sauerkraut mixture. Cover with waxed paper. Microwave (high setting) 10 to 12 minutes. Give dish a half turn once during cooking.

BARBECUED COUNTRY-STYLE RIBS

These ribs are pre-cooked in oven for the slow cooker method. Some of the fat is cooked off and you get better results in the cooker.
BASIC RECIPE — MAKES 6 SERVINGS.

3 to 4 lbs. country-style ribs
¾ c. ketchup
2 tblsp. chopped onion
2 tblsp. brown sugar, packed

½ tsp. salt
1 tblsp. Worcestershire sauce
1 tblsp. vinegar
1 tblsp. prepared mustard

Oven: 1 hour and 20 minutes cooking time
Cut meat in single rib pieces. Place in Dutch oven and cover with water. Bring to boiling. Reduce heat and simmer, covered, 1 hour. Meanwhile, combine remaining ingredients in saucepan. Bring to boiling. Drain ribs; place in 12×8×2″ glass baking dish (2-qt.). Pour boiling sauce over ribs. Bake in 350° oven 20 minutes, basting occasionally.

Microwave Oven (high setting): 24 to 28 minutes cooking time
Use ingredients listed in basic recipe. Cut meat in single rib pieces. Place in 12×8×2″ glass baking dish (2-qt.). Cover with waxed paper Microwave (high setting) 16 to 18 minutes or until meat is no longer pink. Rearrange ribs in dish once while cooking. Drain off fat. Meanwhile, combine remaining ingredients. Spoon over ribs. Cover with waxed paper. Microwave 8 to 10 minutes.

Slow Cooker: 7 hours 30 minutes cooking time

Use ingredients listed in basic recipe. Place meat, cut in single rib pieces, on rack in broiler pan. Bake in 400° oven 15 minutes. Turn and continue baking 15 more minutes. Place ribs in the slow cooker. Meanwhile, combine remaining ingredients. Pour over ribs. Cover and cook on low 7 hours.

PORK POTATO STEW

A great choice for the slow cooker. Flavors mingle and develop during the long cooking process.

BASIC RECIPE — MAKES 6 SERVINGS.

2 lbs. boneless pork, cut in 1½" cubes	1½ c. water
⅓ c. flour	2 chicken bouillon cubes
2 tsp. salt	½ tsp. dried tarragon leaves
¼ tsp. pepper	1 bay leaf
2 tblsp. cooking oil	6 medium potatoes, pared and quartered
1 c. chopped onion	2 tblsp. flour
½ c. chopped celery	½ c. water

Range Top: 1 hour 32 minutes cooking time

Shake pork cubes in mixture of ⅓ c. flour, salt and pepper in plastic bag. Brown pork cubes on all sides in hot cooking oil in Dutch oven, about 10 minutes. Drain off excess fat. Add onion, celery, 1½ c. water, chicken bouillon cubes, tarragon and bay leaf. Bring to boiling. Reduce heat and simmer, covered, 50 minutes or until almost tender. Add potatoes and continue simmering until tender, about 30 minutes. Remove bay leaf. Blend together remaining 2 tblsp. flour and ½ c. water. Add to stew. Cook and stir until bubbly, about 2 minutes.

Slow Cooker: 7 hours 25 minutes cooking time

Use ingredients listed in basic recipe but reduce 1½ c. water to 1 c. Shake pork cubes in mixture of ⅓ c. flour, salt and pepper in plastic bag. Brown on all sides in hot cooking oil in skillet, about 10 minutes. Remove pork to slow cooker. Add onion, celery, 1 c. water and bouillon cubes to drippings in skillet. Bring to boiling, stirring to loosen crusty, brown food that adheres to bottom of skillet. Stir into meat mixture along with tarragon, bay leaf and potatoes. Cover and cook on low 7 hours. Skim off fat. Blend together 2 tblsp. flour and ½ c. water. Stir into pork mixture. Turn to high setting and cook 15 minutes. Remove bay leaf.

HUNGARIAN PORK WITH SAUERKRAUT

If you can find Hungarian paprika in an herb or spice shop, try it when you prepare this dish—it has more zip and flavor.

BASIC RECIPE — MAKES 6 SERVINGS.

2 lbs. boneless pork, cut in 1″ cubes
2 tblsp. cooking oil
2 (16 oz.) cans sauerkraut, drained and rinsed
½ c. chopped onions

1 clove garlic, minced
2 tsp. paprika
2 tsp. chicken bouillon granules
½ tsp. dried dillweed
1 c. water
½ c. dairy sour cream

 Range Top: 1 hour 28 minutes cooking time

Trim excess fat from pork. Heat oil in Dutch oven and brown meat on all sides, about 10 minutes. Stir in remaining ingredients except sour cream. Simmer, covered, about 1 hour 15 minutes or until pork is tender. Remove from heat. Stir some of hot mixture into sour cream. Add sour cream to pork mixture. Heat about 3 minutes (do not boil).

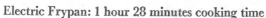 Electric Frypan: 1 hour 28 minutes cooking time

Use ingredients listed in basic recipe, but increase water from 1 c. to 1¼ c. Trim excess fat from pork. Heat oil in electric frypan set at 350°. Brown meat on all sides in hot oil, about 10 minutes. Stir in remaining ingredients except sour cream. When mixture bubbles, reduce heat to 220°. Cover and simmer, with vent closed, 1 hour 15 minutes or until pork is tender. Stir some of hot mixture into sour cream. Blend sour cream mixture into pork mixture. Heat about 3 minutes (do not boil).

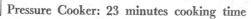 Pressure Cooker: 23 minutes cooking time

Use ingredients listed in basic recipe, but reduce water to ¾ c. Trim excess fat from pork. Heat oil in 4-qt. pressure cooker. Brown pork on all sides in hot oil, about 10 minutes. Stir in remaining ingredients except sour cream. Close cover securely. Place over high heat. Bring to 15 lbs. pressure, according to manufacturer's directions for your pressure cooker. When pressure is reached (control will begin to jiggle), reduce heat immediately and cook 10 minutes. Remove from heat. Let pressure drop of its own accord. Stir in some of hot mixture into sour cream. Add sour cream mixture to pork mixture. Heat about 3 minutes (do not boil).

Slow Cooker: 8 hours 3 minutes cooking time

Use ingredients listed in basic recipe, but omit cooking oil and use ¾ c. *boiling* water instead of 1 c. water. Trim excess fat from pork. Combine pork cubes, sauerkraut, onions, garlic, paprika, bouillon granules, dillweed and ¾ c. boiling water in the slow cooker. Cover and cook on low 8 hours. Stir some of hot mixture into sour cream. Stir sour cream mixture into pork mixture. Heat about 3 minutes (do not boil).

PORK CHOPS WITH STUFFING

The pork chops cooked by all three ways are equally moist and succulent. The dish is covered with foil in the oven method.

BASIC RECIPE — MAKES 6 SERVINGS.

½ c. butter or regular
    margarine
1 c. chopped onion
1 c. chopped celery
10 c. soft bread cubes
2 tblsp. parsley flakes
½ tsp. salt
½ tsp. rubbed sage

½ tsp. pepper
½ c. hot water
6 pork chops, ½" thick
Salt
Pepper
1 (10½ oz.) can condensed
    cream of chicken soup

 Oven: 1 hour 7 minutes baking time

Melt butter in skillet, about 2 minutes. Cook onion and celery in butter until soft, about 5 minutes. Combine with bread cubes, parsley, ½ tsp. salt, sage, ½ tsp. pepper and water in bowl; mix lightly. Spread in greased 13×9×2" baking pan. Season pork chops with salt and pepper. Place pork chops on stuffing. Spoon soup over chops. Cover with aluminum foil. Bake in 350° oven 1 hour or until chops are tender.

 Electric Frypan: 1 hour 17 minutes cooking time

Use ingredients listed in basic recipe, but add 3 tblsp. cooking oil and ½ c. water. Set electric frypan at 350°. Season pork chops with salt and pepper. Heat 3 tblsp. cooking oil in frypan. Brown pork chops on both sides in hot oil, about 10 minutes. Meanwhile, prepare stuffing as for Oven. Form stuffing into 6 mounds. Place on top of chops. Blend together soup and ½ c. water. Pour over stuffing and chops. Reduce heat to 220° and simmer, covered, with vent closed, 1 hour or until chops are tender.

Microwave Oven (high setting): 37 minutes cooking time
Use ingredients listed in basic recipe. Place onion, celery and butter in glass bowl; cover with waxed paper. Microwave (high setting) 7 minutes. Combine with bread cubes, parsley, ½ tsp. salt, sage, ½ tsp. pepper and water. Spread in greased 12×8×2″ glass baking dish (2-qt.). Season pork chops with salt and pepper. Arrange pork chops on stuffing. Spoon soup over chops. Cover with waxed paper and microwave 30 minutes, giving dish a quarter turn once.

PORK CHOP DINNER

If you want to speed up time in the pressure cooker, brown the four pork chops at one time in a large skillet.

BASIC RECIPE — MAKES 4 SERVINGS.

4 pork chops, ½″ thick	¼ c. chopped onion
2 tblsp. cooking oil	¼ c. chopped celery
1 tsp. chicken bouillon granules	1 tsp. salt
1 c. boiling water	⅛ tsp. pepper
4 small potatoes, pared and halved lengthwise	2 tblsp. flour
4 carrots, thickly sliced (2 c.)	½ c. water

Range Top: 42 to 47 minutes cooking time
Brown pork chops in hot oil in 10″ skillet over medium heat, about 15 minutes. Drain off excess fat. Dissolve bouillon granules in 1 c. boiling water; pour over chops. Top with potatoes, carrots, onion, celery, salt and pepper. Cover and simmer over low heat 25 to 30 minutes or until vegetables are tender. Remove vegetables and chops to warm platter; keep warm. Combine flour with ½ c. water. Stir into pan juices in

skillet. Cook, stirring constantly, until mixture is thickened and bubbly, about 2 minutes. Pass gravy.

 Electric Frypan: 1 hour 7 minutes to 1 hour 17 minutes cooking time
Use ingredients listed in the basic recipe. Set electric frypan at 300°. Brown pork chops on both sides in hot oil, about 15 minutes. Drain off excess fat. Dissolve bouillon granules in 1 c. boiling water; pour over chops. Top with potatoes, carrots, onion, celery, salt and pepper. Cover and simmer at 220°, with vent closed, 50 to 60 minutes or until vegetables are tender. Turn potatoes once during cooking to ensure even doneness. Remove meat and vegetables to warm platter; keep warm. Make gravy as for Range Top. Pass gravy.

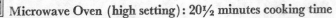

 Microwave Oven (high setting): 20½ minutes cooking time
Use ingredients listed in basic recipe, but omit oil, add a sprinkling of paprika and decrease water from ½ c. to ¼ c. when making gravy. Arrange potatoes around outside edges of 12×8×2″ glass baking dish (2-qt.). Place carrots in center; sprinkle onion and celery over all. Place 1 c. water in glass bowl and microwave (high setting) to boiling about 2½ minutes. Add bouillon granules and stir to dissolve; pour over vegetables. Arrange pork chops in center of dish. Sprinkle with salt, pepper and paprika. Cover; microwave 15 minutes or until tender, giving dish a half turn once. Remove chops and vegetables to serving platter; keep warm. Pour juices from baking dish into 2-c. glass measuring cup. Combine flour and ¼ c. water. Stir into juices. Microwave 3 minutes, stirring after each minute. Add a little browning for gravy if deeper color is desired.

Pressure Cooker: 42 minutes cooking time
Use ingredients listed in basic recipe, but use ½ c. boiling water. Brown pork chops on both sides in hot oil in 4-qt. pressure cooker, two at a time, about 30 minutes. Dissolve bouillon granules in ½ c. boiling water; pour over pork chops. Top with potatoes, carrots, onion, celery, salt and pepper. Close cover securely. Place over high heat. Bring to 15 lbs.

pressure, according to manufacturer's directions for your pressure cooker. When pressure is reached (control will begin to jiggle), reduce heat immediately and cook 10 minutes. Remove from heat. Reduce pressure instantly by placing cooker under cold running water. Remove chops and vegetables to warm platter; keep warm. Combine flour and ½ c. water; add to juices in pan. Cook, stirring constantly, until mixture is thickened and bubbly, about 2 minutes. Pass gravy.

SAUCY PORK CHOPS

This recipe cooks in one-third the time in the microwave oven. The sauce helps to make the pork chops appealing.

BASIC RECIPE — MAKES 4 SERVINGS.

4 pork chops, ½″ thick	4 thin onion slices
Salt	½ c. whole cranberry sauce
Pepper	2 tblsp. bottled barbecue sauce
2 tblsp. cooking oil	3 tblsp. water

Range Top: 55 minutes cooking time

Season pork chops with salt and pepper. Brown pork chops in hot oil in 10″ skillet on both sides, about 10 minutes. Top each chop with an onion slice. Blend together cranberry and barbecue sauces. Spoon on top of pork chops. Pour water around chops. Simmer, covered, 45 minutes or until chops are tender.

Microwave Oven (high setting): 15 minutes cooking time

Use ingredients listed in basic recipe, but omit cooking oil and reduce water from 3 to 1 tblsp. Season pork chops with salt and pepper. Arrange pork chops in 8″ square glass baking dish. Top each chop with an onion slice. Blend together cranberry and barbecue sauces with 1 tblsp. water. Pour over chops. Cover with waxed paper. Microwave (high setting) 15 minutes or until done. Give dish a quarter turn twice during cooking.

ORANGE-GLAZED HAM

This recipe has been adjusted for the electric frypan. Glaze is only spread on top of ham because it would burn on skillet bottom.
BASIC RECIPE — MAKES 10 TO 12 SERVINGS.

½ c. orange marmalade	⅛ tsp. ground cloves
2 tblsp. prepared mustard	3 lb. canned ham

Oven: 1 hour 30 minutes baking time

Combine marmalade, mustard and cloves. Drain ham; place in shallow pan. Spread half of marmalade mixture on top of ham. Bake in 325° oven 1 hour. Turn ham. Top with remaining glaze, brushing some of it on sides of ham. Continue baking 30 minutes.

Electric Frypan: 50 minutes cooking time

Use ingredients listed in basic recipe, but add 2 tblsp. cooking oil and ¼ c. water. Reduce orange marmalade to ¼ c., prepared mustard to 1 tblsp. and ground cloves to a dash. Heat oil in electric frypan at 350°. Add drained ham and brown on all sides, about 10 minutes. Reduce heat to 250°, cover and open vent. Cook 20 minutes. Meanwhile, combine ¼ c. orange marmalade, 1 tblsp. mustard and a dash of cloves. Spread mixture on top of ham. Pour ¼ c. water in skillet around ham. Continue cooking 20 minutes.

Microwave Oven (high setting): 20 minutes cooking time

Use ingredients listed in basic recipe. Combine marmalade, mustard and cloves. Drain ham and place in 9″ glass pie plate. Spread half of marmalade mixture on top and sides of ham. Cover loosely with waxed paper. Microwave (high setting) 12 minutes, giving one quarter turn. Turn ham; top with remaining glaze. Microwave, uncovered, 8 minutes. Cover loosely with aluminum foil. Let stand 5 minutes.

HOOSIER HAM LOAF

A very interesting flavor combination. Ham and pork sausage blend well with ketchup, mustard and onion.

BASIC RECIPE — MAKES 6 SERVINGS.

2 eggs, beaten	1 lb. ground cooked ham
½ c. milk	8 oz. lean bulk pork sausage
1 tblsp. prepared mustard	1 tblsp. brown sugar, packed
1 tsp. grated onion	1 tblsp. ketchup
¾ c. cracker crumbs	2 tblsp. prepared mustard

 Oven: 1 hour baking time

Blend together eggs and milk. Stir in 1 tblsp. mustard, onion, cracker crumbs, ham and sausage. Mix thoroughly. Press ham mixture into 8½×4½×2½" loaf pan. Bake in 350° oven 50 minutes. Pour off excess fat. Spread top with mixture of brown sugar, ketchup and 2 tblsp. mustard. Continue baking 10 minutes.

 Electric Frypan: 1 hour 15 minutes cooking time

Use ingredients listed in basic recipe. Combine them and press in pan as for Oven. Preheat frypan to 400°. Place meat loaf on rack in frypan. Cover and cook, with vent closed, 1 hour. Pour off excess fat. Spread top with mixture of brown sugar, ketchup and remaining 2 tblsp. mustard. Continue cooking, with vent open, 15 minutes.

 Slow Cooker: 7 hours 10 minutes cooking time

Use ingredients listed in basic recipe. Combine them as for Oven. Crisscross 2 (15×2") strips of aluminum foil across bottom and up sides of cooker. (Use heavy duty foil or double thickness of regular foil.) Place ham mixture in cooker on top of foil. Pat to form a round loaf that does not touch the sides of the cooker. Cover and cook on low 7 hours. Blend together brown sugar, ketchup and 2 tblsp. mustard. Spoon over ham loaf. Cook, covered, on high 10 minutes.

Toaster-Oven: 1 hour baking time
Use ingredients listed in basic recipe. Combine ingredients and press in pan as for Oven. Bake in toaster-oven at 350° for 50 minutes. Pour off excess fat. Spread top with mixture of brown sugar, ketchup and 2 tblsp. mustard. Continue baking 10 minutes.

LAMB STEW WITH MASHED POTATOES

You have a choice of four appliances to cook this stew. Use mashed fresh potatoes if your family doesn't care for the instant ones.

BASIC RECIPE — MAKES 6 SERVINGS.

2 lbs. boned lamb shoulder, cut in 1" cubes	6 medium carrots, sliced
3 tblsp. flour	3 onions, sliced
2 tsp. salt	2 celery branches, sliced
1/4 tsp. pepper	2 c. unreconstituted instant mashed potatoes*
2 tblsp. cooking oil	1/2 tsp. salt
1 1/2 c. water	2 c. boiling water
1 tblsp. Worcestershire sauce	1 c. dairy sour cream

Range Top: 1 hour 40 minutes cooking time
Shake lamb cubes, a few at a time, in plastic bag with flour, 2 tsp. salt and pepper. Brown lamb in hot cooking oil in Dutch oven, about 10 minutes. Add 1 1/2 c. water and Worcestershire sauce. Bring to boiling. Reduce heat and simmer, covered, 1 hour or until tender. Add carrots, onion and celery; simmer 30 minutes. Stir together instant mashed potatoes, salt and boiling water; potatoes should be stiff. Beat in sour cream. Serve stew over mashed potatoes.
*Note: If you use instant potato *flakes,* increase to 3 cups.

Microwave Oven (high setting): 47 to 57 minutes cooking time

Use ingredients listed in basic recipe, but omit pepper and cooking oil. Add 1 (1 oz.) pkg. brown gravy mix and change amount of water and salt according to directions that follow. Also use only 1 sliced onion instead of 3, and cut carrots and celery in 1″ pieces. Combine lamb, gravy mix and 1 c. water in 3-qt. glass casserole. Microwave (high setting), uncovered, 5 minutes. Add carrots, celery, onion, Worcestershire sauce and ½ tsp. salt. Cover and microwave 40 to 50 minutes or until meat and vegetables are tender, stirring every 10 minutes. Blend together 3 tblsp. flour and ¾ c. cold water. Stir into stew. Microwave 2 minutes or until boiling. Prepare mashed potatoes as for basic recipe; serve stew over mashed potatoes.

 Pressure Cooker: 25 minutes cooking time

Use ingredients listed in basic recipe, cutting vegetables in bigger pieces and adding extra flour according to directions that follow. Shake lamb cubes, a few at a time, in plastic bag with 3 tblsp. flour, 2 tsp. salt and pepper. Brown lamb on all sides in hot cooking oil in 4-qt. pressure cooker, about 10 minutes. Add carrots, cut in 1″ pieces, sliced onion and celery, cut in 2″ pieces, 1 c. water and Worcestershire sauce. Close cover securely. Place over high heat. Bring to 15 lbs. pressure, according to manufacturer's directions for your pressure cooker. When pressure is reached (control will begin to jiggle), reduce heat immediately and cook 10 minutes. Remove from heat. Reduce pressure immediately under cold running water. Blend 3 tblsp. flour with ½ c. cold water. Stir into stew; cook and stir until bubbly, about 5 minutes. Prepare mashed potatoes as for basic recipe; serve stew over mashed potatoes.

 Slow Cooker: 10 hours 10 minutes cooking time

Use ingredients listed in basic recipe, but use 1½ c. chopped onion instead of sliced onions and thinly sliced carrots and celery. Change amounts of flour and water according to directions that follow. Trim excess fat from lamb. Shake lamb cubes, a few at a time, in plastic bag with 2 tblsp. flour, 2 tsp. salt and pepper. Brown lamb on all sides in hot cooking oil in skillet, about 10 minutes. Combine lamb, carrots, celery, 1½ c. onion, ⅔ c. water and Worcestershire sauce in slow cooker. Cover and cook on low 9 hours. Blend together ¼ c. flour and ½ c. cold water. Turn cooker to high. Stir flour mixture into stew. Cover and cook 1 hour. Prepare potatoes as for basic recipe; serve stew over mashed potatoes.

LENTIL STEW

This is called a stew because it's thicker than soup. If you prefer a soup, just stir in additional water before serving.

BASIC RECIPE — MAKES 6 SERVINGS.

1 lb. boneless lamb, cut in 1" cubes	2 tsp. chicken bouillon granules
2 tblsp. cooking oil	1 tsp. salt
1 c. chopped onion	½ tsp. oregano leaves
1 c. chopped celery	¼ tsp. pepper
2 cloves garlic, minced	1 bay leaf
1 (16 oz.) can tomatoes, cut up	1 c. dried lentils
	2 c. sliced carrots
1 c. water	2½ c. water

Range Top: 2 hours 10 minutes cooking time

Brown lamb in hot oil in 12" skillet about 10 minutes. Pour off excess fat. Add onion, celery, garlic, tomatoes, 1 c. water, chicken bouillon granules, salt, oregano, pepper and bay leaf. Bring to a boil. Reduce heat and simmer, covered, 1 hour. Rinse lentils. Add to meat mixture along with carrots and 2½ c. water. Continue simmering 1 hour, stirring 2 to 3 times. Add more water, if necessary. Remove bay leaf.

Electric Frypan: 2 hours 10 minutes cooking time

Use ingredients listed in basic recipe. Brown lamb in hot oil in electric frypan (350°), about 10 minutes. Pour off excess fat. Add onion, celery, garlic, tomatoes, 1 c. water, chicken bouillon granules, oregano, salt, pepper and bay leaf. Cover, reduce heat to simmering (220°) and cook 1 hour with vent closed. Rinse lentils. Add to meat mixture along with carrots and 2½ c. water. Continue simmering, with vent closed, 1 hour, stirring 2 to 3 times. Add more water if necessary. Remove bay leaf.

Slow Cooker: 10 to 11½ hours cooking time

Use ingredients listed in basic recipe, but soak lentils as follows, use less water and cut vegetables as follows. Soak 1 c. lentils overnight in 1½ c. water. Cut carrots in thin slices; finely chop onion and green pepper. Combine with remaining ingredients in slow cooker. Cover and cook on low 9 to 10 hours. Turn heat to high and cook until vegetables are tender, 1 to 1½ hours. Remove bay leaf.

WESTERN SHEEPHERDER'S STEW

Remember to cut vegetables in larger pieces for the pressure cooker and in smaller pieces for the slow cooker—see directions.

BASIC RECIPE — MAKES 6 SERVINGS.

2 lbs. boneless lamb, cut in 1″ cubes
¼ c. chopped fresh parsley
1 tsp. minced garlic
3 large carrots, sliced
3 medium potatoes, pared and quartered
1 large onion, coarsely chopped

1 large green pepper, cut in lengthwise strips
2 tsp. salt
¼ tsp. pepper
2 slices bacon, cut in thirds
½ c. water
4 tsp. cornstarch
2 tblsp. water

Oven: 2 hours 5 minutes baking time

Place half of meat in bottom of heavy Dutch oven with tight-fitting lid. Sprinkle with half the parsley and garlic. Add half of carrot, potatoes and onion. Arrange half the green pepper strips over top. Sprinkle with half of salt and pepper. Repeat layers. Lay bacon strips over the top. Add ½ c. water. Cover and bake in 350° oven 2 hours or until meat and vegetables are tender. Drain off juices and add water to make 1 c. Blend together cornstarch and 2 tblsp. water. Add along with juices to stew. Cook and stir until bubbly and thick, about 5 minutes.

Electric Frypan: 1 hour 35 minutes cooking time

Use ingredients listed in basic recipe, but cut carrots in half lengthwise and increase amount of water as indicated. Set electric frypan at 400°. Combine lamb, garlic, salt, pepper and 1½ c. water in frypan. Bring to a boil. Reduce heat to 220°. Cover and cook, with vent closed, 1 hour. Add carrots, potatoes, onion, green pepper, parsley, bacon and 1 c. water. Continue simmering, covered, with vent closed, until meat and vegetables are tender, 30 minutes. Turn off heat. Drain off juices and add water to make 1 c. Blend together cornstarch and 2 tblsp. water. Add to stew along with juices. Turn skillet to 400°. Cook and stir gently until bubbly and thick, about 5 minutes.

Pressure Cooker: 15 minutes cooking time

Use ingredients listed in basic recipe, but increase amount of water and use flour instead of cornstarch as directed in recipe. Cut carrots in 3" lengths, onions in eighths and potatoes in halves. Combine meat, garlic, salt, pepper, 1 c. water, carrots, potatoes, onion, green pepper strips, parsley and bacon in 6-qt. pressure cooker. Close cover securely. Place over high heat. Bring to 15 lbs. pressure, according to manufacturer's directions for your pressure cooker. When pressure is reached (control will begin to jiggle), reduce heat immediately and cook 10 minutes. Remove from heat. Let pressure drop of its own accord. Blend together 6 tblsp. flour and ½ c. water. Add to stew. Cook, stirring gently, until bubbly and thick, about 5 minutes.

Slow Cooker: 10 hours 30 minutes cooking time

Use ingredients listed in basic recipe, but omit bacon and use 2 tblsp. cornstarch and add 2 c. thinly sliced carrots, 2 c. cubed, pared potatoes, 1 c. finely chopped onion and ¾ c. finely chopped green pepper. Combine lamb, parsley, garlic, 2 c. thinly sliced carrots, 2 c. cubed potatoes, 1 c. finely chopped onion, ¾ c. finely chopped green pepper, salt, pepper and ½ c. water in cooker. Cover and cook on low 10 hours. Blend together 2 tblsp. cornstarch and 2 tblsp. water. Stir into stew. Turn heat on high and cook until mixture comes to a boil, about 30 minutes.

BARBECUED CHICKEN

Homemade barbecue sauce is so much better than bottled. That's the key to making this chicken so extra-good.

BASIC RECIPE — MAKES 4 SERVINGS.

1 (2½ to 3 lb.) broiler-fryer, cut up	Barbecue Sauce (recipe follows)
¼ c. cooking oil	

Oven: 1 hour baking time

Brown chicken on all sides in hot cooking oil in skillet, about 10 minutes. Place, skin side up, in 13×9×2″ baking pan. Pour Barbecue Sauce over chicken. Bake in 350° oven 50 minutes or until tender, basting occasionally with sauce.

Barbecue Sauce: Combine 1 c. ketchup, ¼ c. vinegar, 2 tblsp. brown sugar, packed, 1 tsp. salt, ⅛ tsp. pepper, ¼ c. chopped onion and 1 tblsp. Worcestershire sauce in small saucepan. Bring to boiling. Reduce heat and simmer, covered, 10 minutes.

Electric Frypan: 50 minutes cooking time

Use ingredients listed in basic recipe. Heat oil in electric frypan at 350°. Brown chicken on all sides in hot oil, about 10 minutes. Reduce heat to 220°. Prepare Barbecue Sauce as for Oven; pour over chicken. Simmer, covered, with vent closed, 40 minutes.

Microwave Oven (high setting): 31 minutes cooking time

Use ingredients listed in basic recipe, but omit oil. Place chicken, skin side up, in 12×8×2″ glass baking dish (2-qt.). Combine ingredients for Barbecue Sauce in glass bowl or 1-qt. glass measuring cup. Microwave (high setting) 6 minutes, stirring once. Pour Barbecue Sauce over chicken. Cover with waxed paper. Microwave 12 minutes. Baste chicken with sauce and give dish a quarter turn. Continue microwaving, covered, 13 more minutes.

BRUNSWICK STEW

This chicken dish takes only 18 minutes in the pressure cooker. A perfect last-minute meal when you don't have time to spare.

BASIC RECIPE — MAKES 3 QUARTS.

1 (3 lb.) broiler-fryer, cut up
1 qt. water
4 tsp. salt
1 (16 oz.) can tomatoes, cut up (2 c.)
1 (10 oz.) pkg. frozen baby lima beans (2 c.)
1 (10 oz.) pkg. frozen corn

1 (10 oz.) pkg. frozen okra, cut in ½″ pieces (2 c.)
2 medium potatoes, pared and diced (2 c.)
1 medium-large onion, sliced
2 tsp. sugar
1 tsp. pepper

Range Top: 1 hour 10 minutes cooking time

Combine chicken, water and salt in large kettle or Dutch oven. Cover and simmer 45 minutes or until tender. Remove chicken and set aside. Add remaining ingredients. Cover and simmer 15 minutes or until vegetables are tender. Meanwhile, bone chicken and cut in cubes. Return to kettle with vegetables and heat thoroughly, about 10 minutes.

Microwave Oven (high setting): 1 hour cooking time

Use ingredients in basic recipe. Combine all ingredients except okra in large (5-qt.) glass casserole. Cover and microwave (high setting) 45 minutes or until chicken is done, stirring twice. Remove chicken. Bone and cut in cubes; set aside. Add okra to casserole. Cover and microwave 10 more minutes. Return chicken to casserole and microwave 5 minutes or until hot and potatoes and lima beans are tender.

Pressure Cooker: 18 minutes cooking time
Use ingredients listed in basic recipe. Combine all ingredients in 6-qt. pressure pan. Close cover securely. Place over high heat. Bring to 15 lbs. pressure, according to manufacturer's directions for your pressure cooker. When pressure is reached (control will begin to jiggle), reduce heat immediately and cook 15 minutes. Remove from heat. Let pressure drop of its own accord. Remove chicken from pressure pan. Bone, cut in cubes and return to vegetable mixture. Heat thoroughly, about 3 minutes.

COQ AU VIN

Although the microwave version takes half the time to cook, the flavors develop better in the other two versions.

BASIC RECIPE — MAKES 4 SERVINGS.

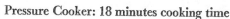

½ c. flour	1 clove garlic, minced
1 tsp. salt	1 c. water
¼ tsp. pepper	1 c. dry red wine
1 (3 lb.) broiler-fryer, cut up	2 tsp. chicken bouillon granules
6 slices bacon	½ tsp. thyme leaves
1 large onion, cut in eighths	1 bay leaf
8 oz. fresh mushrooms, sliced	1 tblsp. chopped fresh parsley
1 c. sliced carrots	

Range Top: 1 hour 8 minutes cooking time
Combine flour, salt and pepper. Dredge chicken with flour mixture. Reserve excess seasoned flour. Cook bacon in 12″ skillet until crisp.

about 6 minutes. Drain and crumble. Brown chicken on all sides in bacon drippings, about 10 minutes. Pour off excess fat. Add bacon, onion, mushrooms, carrots, garlic, ½ c. of the water, wine, bouillon granules, thyme and bay leaf. Stir into skillet. Cover and simmer until chicken and vegetables are tender, about 50 minutes. Blend together reserved seasoned flour and remaining ½ c. water. Stir into chicken mixture. Cook 2 minutes or until bubbly and thickened, stirring gently. Remove bay leaf. Serve garnished with parsley.

 Electric Frypan: 1 hour 8 minutes cooking time
Use ingredients listed in basic recipe. Combine flour, salt and pepper. Dredge chicken with flour mixture. Reserve excess seasoned flour. Cook bacon in electric frypan at 350° until crisp, about 6 minutes. Drain and crumble. Brown chicken on all sides in bacon drippings at 350°, about 10 minutes. Pour off excess fat. Add bacon, onion, mushrooms, carrots, garlic, wine, ½ c. of the water, bouillon granules, thyme and bay leaf. Reduce heat to simmer (220°). Cook, covered, with vent closed, 50 minutes or until chicken and vegetables are tender. Blend together reserved seasoned flour and remaining ½ c. water. Stir into chicken mixture. Cook 2 minutes or until bubbly and thickened, stirring gently. Remove bay leaf. Serve garnished with parsley.

 Microwave Oven (high setting): 37 to 38 minutes cooking time
Use ingredients listed in basic recipe, but reduce bacon to 3 slices and chicken bouillon granules to 1 tsp. and omit water. Cut bacon in 1" pieces. Combine flour, salt and pepper. Dredge chicken in flour mixture. Place bacon in 3-qt. glass casserole; microwave (high setting) 2 to 3 minutes or until almost crisp. Add chicken, reserved seasoned flour, onion, mushrooms, carrots, garlic, 1 tsp. chicken bouillon granules, red wine, thyme leaves, bay leaf and parsley. Cover and microwave 35 minutes, stirring 3 times after the first 15 minutes. Remove bay leaf. Serve garnished with parsley.

SPANISH CHICKEN WITH RICE

Quick-cooking rice must be substituted for the regular rice in the microwave version to get the same results.

BASIC RECIPE — MAKES 6 SERVINGS.

2 lbs. chicken legs and thighs (4 of each)

¼ c. butter or regular margarine

¼ c. chopped onion

¼ c. chopped green pepper

2 c. uncooked regular rice

1 (16 oz.) can tomatoes, cut up

2¼ c. water

1 (8 oz.) pkg. brown-and-serve sausages, cut up

2 tsp. parsley flakes

1½ tsp. salt

⅛ tsp. pepper

⅛ tsp. ground turmeric

Salt

Paprika

1 c. frozen peas, cooked and drained

Oven: 1 hour 2 minutes cooking time

Brown chicken on all sides in melted butter in skillet, about 10 minutes. Remove chicken as it browns. Add onion and green pepper to pan drippings; saute until tender, about 2 minutes. Stir in rice, tomatoes, water, sausages, parsley, 1½ tsp. salt, pepper and turmeric. Bring mixture to boiling. Turn into greased 3-qt. casserole. Top with chicken pieces, skin side up. Sprinkle chicken with salt and paprika. Cover. Bake in 375° oven 50 minutes or until chicken is tender. Garnish with hot cooked peas.

Microwave Oven (high setting): 23 minutes cooking time

Use ingredients listed in basic recipe, but use quick-cooking instead of regular rice and do not cook the peas separately. You will also need to decrease the amount of butter and water as indicated. Combine onion, green pepper and 2 tblsp. butter in 3-qt. glass casserole. Cover. Microwave (high setting) 3 minutes. Stir in 2 c. uncooked quick-cooking rice, tomatoes, ½ c. water, sausages, parsley, 1½ tsp. salt, pepper, turmeric and unthawed frozen peas. Top with chicken pieces, skin side up. Sprinkle chicken with salt and paprika. Cover. Microwave 20 minutes, giving casserole a quarter turn after 10 minutes.

CALORIE-WISE CHICKEN

Do not expect the chicken to be brown and crispy when cooked in the microwave. If you prefer it that way, use the oven method.

BASIC RECIPE — MAKES 4 SERVINGS.

1 tsp. garlic salt	½ tsp. onion salt
1 tsp. dried tarragon leaves	¼ tsp. pepper
1 tsp. paprika	1 (3 lb.) broiler-fryer, cut up

Oven: 1 hour baking time

Combine seasonings. Wash chicken and pat dry. Sprinkle seasonings evenly over chicken pieces. Arrange chicken, skin side up, in 12×8×2″ glass baking dish (2-qt.). Bake, uncovered, in 350° oven 1 hour or until chicken is tender.

Microwave Oven (high setting): 25 to 30 minutes cooking time

Use ingredients listed in basic recipe. Prepare as for Oven. Arrange chicken pieces, skin side up, with thickest pieces to outside edges of 12×8×2″ glass baking dish (2-qt.). Cover with waxed paper. Microwave (high setting) 25 to 30 minutes or until chicken is tender, giving dish a half turn twice.

SMOKY CHICKEN SPECIAL

There is little difference in appearance of cooked dishes whether cooked on range top or in the microwave oven.

BASIC RECIPE — MAKES 6 SERVINGS.

6 slices bacon
3 whole chicken breasts, split,
  boned and skinned
¼ c. water
1 (3 oz.) pkg. sliced smoked
  beef

1 (10½ oz.) can condensed
  cream of onion soup
½ c. dairy sour cream
1 tblsp. flour
Paprika

 Range Top: 24 minutes cooking time

Cook bacon in skillet until crisp, about 6 minutes. Remove, crumble and set aside. Drain bacon drippings from skillet; discard. Place chicken breasts and water in same skillet. Cover and cook 10 minutes or until tender. Drain water from skillet. Roll up one slice of smoked beef and wrap around center of each chicken breast. Return chicken to skillet. Combine soup, sour cream and flour in small bowl. Cut up remaining smoked beef and add to sour cream mixture. Spoon over chicken in skillet. Sprinkle with paprika. Simmer, covered, 8 minutes or until hot. Serve garnished with bacon.

 Microwave Oven (high setting): 19 to 23 minutes cooking time

Use ingredients listed in basic recipe, but omit water. Place bacon between paper towels in 12×8×2″ glass baking dish (2-qt.). Microwave (high setting) 6 to 7 minutes or until crisp. Crumble bacon and set aside. Pour bacon drippings from dish; discard. Place chicken in same baking dish. Cover with waxed paper. Microwave 9 to 10 minutes. Pour off juices. Roll up one slice of smoked beef and wrap around center of each chicken breast. Return to baking dish. Combine soup, sour cream and flour in small bowl. Cut up remaining smoked beef and add to sour cream mixture. Spoon over chicken in baking dish. Sprinkle with paprika. Microwave, covered, 4 to 5 minutes or until hot. Serve garnished with bacon.

CRANBERRY-SAUCED CHICKEN

To conserve oven heat, bake your favorite bread stuffing and acorn squash halves along with the cranberry-topped chicken.

BASIC RECIPE — MAKES 4 SERVINGS.

1 c. whole cranberry sauce
½ c. finely chopped onion
½ c. ketchup
1 tblsp. brown sugar, packed
½ tsp. salt
3 tblsp. vinegar

3 tblsp. water
2 tblsp. prepared mustard
1 tblsp. Worcestershire sauce
4 tsp. cornstarch
1 (3 lb.) broiler-fryer, cut up

Oven: 1 hour 10 minutes cooking time

Combine cranberry sauce, onion, ketchup, brown sugar, salt, vinegar, 1 tblsp. of the water, mustard and Worcestershire sauce in saucepan. Bring to boiling. Reduce heat and simmer, covered, 10 minutes. Blend together cornstarch and remaining 2 tblsp. water. Add to sauce, stirring well. Place chicken, skin side up, in 13×9×2" baking pan. Spoon sauce over chicken. Cover with aluminum foil. Bake in 375° oven 1 hour or until chicken is tender. Place chicken pieces on platter. Skim fat from sauce. Stir sauce and spoon some of it over chicken. Pass remaining sauce.

Electric Frypan: 45 minutes cooking time

Use ingredients listed in basic recipe, but increase water to ½ c. and Combine cornstarch, brown sugar and salt. Stir in cranberry sauce, onion, ketchup, vinegar, mustard, Worcestershire sauce and ½ c.

water; blend well. Pour into frypan. Turn heat to 375°. Heat sauce until bubbling, about 5 minutes. Add chicken, skin side up, spoon cranberry sauce over chicken. Bring to boiling. Reduce to 220° and simmer, covered, with vent closed, 40 minutes or until chicken is tender. Baste once during cooking. Place chicken on platter. Skim excess fat from sauce. Stir sauce and spoon some of it over chicken. Pass remaining sauce.

Microwave Oven (high setting): 28 minutes cooking time
Use ingredients listed in basic recipe, but omit water. Combine all ingredients but chicken in 12×8×2″ glass baking dish (2-qt.). Place chicken pieces, skin side down, in dish. Turn skin side up to coat pieces with sauce. Cover with waxed paper. Microwave (high setting) 28 minutes or until chicken is tender, making a half turn after 14 minutes. Place chicken pieces on platter. Skim excess fat from sauce. Stir sauce and spoon some of it over chicken. Pass remaining sauce.

CHICKEN PARMESAN

Crushed corn flakes help to make the microwaved chicken look more attractive—even though it doesn't brown while cooking.
BASIC RECIPE — MAKES 4 SERVINGS.

½ c. corn flake crumbs
¼ c. grated Parmesan cheese
1 tsp. salt
⅛ tsp. pepper

⅓ c. butter or regular
  margarine
1 (3 lb.) broiler-fryer, cut up

Oven: 1 hour 2 minutes cooking time
Combine corn flake crumbs, cheese, salt and pepper. Melt butter in small skillet, about 2 minutes. Dip chicken pieces in melted butter, then roll in corn flake mixture. Line 15½×10½×1″ jelly roll pan

with aluminum foil. Arrange chicken pieces on foil. Bake in 350° oven 1 hour or until chicken is tender.

Microwave Oven (high setting): 29 minutes cooking time
Use ingredients listed in basic recipe. Place butter in small glass bowl. Microwave (high setting) 1 minute or until melted. Dip chicken pieces in butter and roll in corn flake mixture. Place in 12×8×2″ glass baking dish (2-qt.). Arrange meaty pieces toward outside of dish. Cover with paper towels. Microwave 23 minutes. Uncover. Microwave 5 more minutes or until chicken is tender.

SPECIAL CHICKEN-RICE CASSEROLE

The slow cooker is the perfect choice when you plan to be away from home for most of the day—dinner is ready when you come back.
BASIC RECIPE — MAKES 6 TO 8 SERVINGS.

3 tblsp. butter or regular margarine	1 (13¾ oz.) can chicken broth
8 chicken thighs	Salt
1 (6 oz.) pkg. long grain and wild rice	Pepper
1 (4 oz.) can mushroom stems and pieces	Paprika

Oven: 1 hour 2 minutes cooking time
Melt butter in skillet, about 2 minutes. Add chicken and brown on all sides, about 10 minutes. Remove chicken as it browns. Meanwhile, combine rice with seasoning mix from rice package in greased 13×9×2″ baking pan. Drain mushrooms, reserving ¼ c. liquid. Add mushrooms, ¼ c. mushroom liquid and chicken broth to pan drippings in skillet. Bring to boiling. Stir broth mixture into rice in baking pan. Top with chicken thighs; sprinkle with salt, pepper and paprika. Cover with aluminum foil. Bake in 375° oven 50 minutes or until chicken is tender.

Microwave Oven (high setting): 35 minutes cooking time
Use ingredients listed in basic recipe, but add enough water to reserved mushroom liquid to make ½ c. Combine rice, seasoning mix from rice package and chicken broth in 12×8×2″ glass baking dish (2-qt.). Stir in mushrooms and ½ c. reserved mushroom liquid. Cover with waxed paper. Microwave (high setting) 10 minutes. Add chicken. Sprinkle chicken with salt, pepper and paprika. Cover and microwave 25 minutes, giving dish a quarter turn twice. Let stand 5 minutes before serving.

Slow Cooker: 6 to 7 hours cooking time
Use ingredients listed in basic recipe. Combine rice, seasoning mix from rice package and chicken broth in cooker. Drain mushrooms, reserving ¼ c. liquid. Add mushrooms and ¼ c. reserved mushroom liquid to rice; mix well. Top with chicken; sprinkle chicken with salt, pepper and paprika. Cover and cook on low 6 to 7 hours.

MARIN COUNTY CHICKEN

Stir-fried main dishes are always so colorful and fast-cooking. The vegetables are slightly crisp and taste so good on hot rice.

BASIC RECIPE — MAKES 4 SERVINGS.

2 whole chicken breasts (1½ to 2 lbs.)
¼ c. soy sauce
1 (9 oz.) pkg. frozen French-style green beans, thawed
½ c. water
4 tsp. cornstarch
2 tblsp. chicken bouillon granules

5 tblsp. cooking oil
½ c. roasted cashew nuts
1½ c. bias-cut carrots, ⅛″ slices
1 c. bias-cut celery, ⅛″ slices
½ c. chopped onion
1 clove garlic, minced

Range Top: 10½ to 12½ minutes cooking time

Cut and measure all ingredients before starting to cook. Remove skin and bones from chicken breasts. Cut in 2×⅛″ strips. Stir in soy sauce and let stand while preparing other ingredients. Blot thawed green beans with paper towels. Blend together water, cornstarch and bouillon granules. Add 2 tblsp. of the oil to skillet. Place over high heat. Toast cashews lightly, about 30 seconds (they burn easily); remove. Add 1 more tblsp. oil to skillet. Add chicken mixture. Stir and fry until chicken is opaque, about 1 to 2 minutes. Remove chicken. Add 2 more tblsp. oil to skillet. Stir in carrots. Cover and steam 1 minute. Stir in celery, onion and garlic. Cover and steam 1 minute. Then cook and stir until tender-crisp, 3 to 4 minutes. Return chicken to skillet along with cornstarch mixture. Cook and stir until mixture is thickened and bubbly, about 2 minutes. Add green beans and half of cashews. Cook and stir just until beans are thoroughly heated, about 2 minutes. Serve garnished with remaining cashews.

 Electric Frypan: 10½ to 12½ minutes cooking time

Use ingredients listed in basic recipe. Cut, measure and prepare ingredients as for Range Top. Heat electric frypan to 375°. Cook as for Range Top.

 Electric Wok: 10½ to 12½ minutes cooking time

Use ingredients listed in basic recipe, but reduce cooking oil from 5 to 4 tblsp. Cut, measure and prepare ingredients as for Range Top. Heat wok to 375°. Add 1 tblsp. of the oil and toast cashews lightly, about 30 seconds; remove. Add 1 more tblsp. oil to wok. Add chicken mixture. Cook and stir until chicken is opaque, 1 to 2 minutes; remove. Add 2 more tblsp. oil; then stir in carrots. Cover and steam 1 minute. Add celery, onion and garlic and steam 1 minute. Then cook and stir until tender-crisp, 3 to 4 minutes. Return chicken to wok along with cornstarch mixture. Cook and stir until thickened and bubbly, about 2 minutes. Add green beans and half of cashews. Cook and stir just until beans are heated thoroughly, about 2 minutes. Serve garnished with remaining cashews.

CHICKEN CACCIATORE

Spaghetti sauce seasoning mix adds the special flavor to the tomato sauce. A good choice for the microwave or slow cooker.

BASIC RECIPE — MAKES 4 SERVINGS.

1 (3 lb.) broiler-fryer, cut up	½ tsp. salt
¼ c. cooking oil	⅛ tsp. pepper
1 (1.5 oz.) pkg. spaghetti seasoning mix	8 oz. spaghetti, cooked and drained
1 (15 oz.) can tomato sauce	
1 (4 oz.) can mushroom stems and pieces, drained	

Range Top: 50 minutes cooking time

Brown chicken on all sides in hot oil in skillet, about 10 minutes. Remove chicken and pour off oil. Combine spaghetti mix and tomato sauce in same skillet. Bring to boiling, stirring constantly. Add mushrooms, salt, pepper and chicken. Spoon sauce over chicken. Cover and simmer 40 minutes or until chicken is tender. Serve over hot, cooked spaghetti.

Microwave Oven (high setting): 31 minutes cooking time

Use ingredients listed in basic recipe, but omit cooking oil. Arrange chicken pieces in 12×8×2″ glass baking dish (2-qt.), meaty parts to outside. Top with mushrooms, salt and pepper. Combine spaghetti mix and tomato sauce in 1-qt. glass measuring cup. Microwave (high setting) 6 minutes or until mixture comes to a boil, stirring several times during the last half of cooking. Spoon over chicken. Cover with plastic wrap. Microwave 15 minutes. Rearrange chicken pieces and spoon sauce over them. Continue microwaving 10 more minutes. Let stand 5 minutes before serving. Serve over hot, cooked spaghetti.

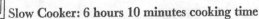

Slow Cooker: 6 hours 10 minutes cooking time

Use ingredients listed in basic recipe. Brown chicken on all sides in hot oil in skillet, about 10 minutes. Remove chicken to cooker. Pour oil from skillet. Combine remaining ingredients, except spaghetti, in same skillet. Heat to a boil, stirring constantly. Pour over chicken. Cover and cook on low 6 hours. Serve over hot, cooked spaghetti.

CHICKEN BREASTS IN SOUR CREAM SAUCE

This recipe is elegant enough for company. Serve with buttered noodles or rice pilaf and tossed green salad.

BASIC RECIPE — MAKES 6 SERVINGS.

¼ c. butter or regular margarine	⅛ tsp. pepper
3 whole chicken breasts, split	1 c. water
Bouquet Garni (recipe follows)	1 chicken bouillon cube
2 tblsp. flour	2 tblsp. flour
2 tsp. paprika	¼ c. water
½ tsp. salt	1 c. dairy sour cream
¼ tsp. rubbed sage	Hot buttered noodles

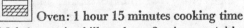

Oven: 1 hour 15 minutes cooking time

Melt butter in skillet, about 2 minutes. Add chicken and brown on all sides, about 10 minutes. Meanwhile, make Bouquet Garni. Arrange chicken in 13×9×2″ baking pan. Place Bouquet Garni in center. Pour drippings from skillet, reserving 2 tblsp. Combine 2 tblsp. flour, paprika, salt, sage and pepper with 2 tblsp. reserved pan drippings in skillet. Slowly stir in 1 c. water. Add bouillon cube and cook, stirring constantly, until mixture is bubbly and bouillon cube is dissolved, about 5 minutes. Pour over chicken. Cover with aluminum foil. Bake in 350° oven 50 minutes or until chicken is tender. Discard Bouquet Garni; place chicken on platter and keep warm. Pour sauce from baking pan into skillet. Blend together remaining 2 tblsp. flour and ¼ c. water. Stir into sauce in skillet and cook, stirring constantly, until mixture boils, about 5 minutes. Remove from heat. Stir a small amount of hot sauce into sour cream. Return all of sour cream mixture to skillet, blending thoroughly. Heat until just hot, but do not let boil, about 3 minutes. Serve chicken with noodles and pass sour cream sauce.

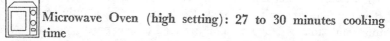 Electric Frypan: 1 hour 15 minutes cooking time

Use ingredients listed in basic recipe. Melt butter in electric frypan set at 350°, about 2 minutes. Add chicken and brown on all sides, about 10 minutes. Meanwhile, make Bouquet Garni. Remove chicken from skillet. Pour off drippings from skillet, reserving 2 tblsp. Place reserved 2 tblsp. pan drippings in skillet; reduce heat to 220°. Blend 2 tblsp. flour, paprika, salt, sage and pepper into pan drippings. Slowly add 1 c. water and bouillon cube. Cook, stirring constantly, until mixture is bubbly and bouillon cube is dissolved, about 5 minutes. Return chicken to skillet; spoon sauce over it. Add Bouquet Garni. Cover and simmer, with vent closed, 50 minutes or until chicken is tender. Remove Bouquet Garni. Place chicken on platter and keep warm. Add sour cream to sauce as for Oven. Serve chicken with noodles and pass sour cream sauce.

Microwave Oven (high setting): 27 to 30 minutes cooking time

Use ingredients listed in basic recipe, but omit 2 tblsp. flour and ¼ c. water. Arrange chicken in 12×8×2″ glass baking dish (2-qt.). Make Bouquet Garni and place in center. Blend together 2 tblsp. flour, paprika, salt, sage and pepper in 2 c. glass measuring cup. Slowly stir in 1 c. water. Add bouillon cube. Microwave (high setting) 1 minute; stir. Microwave 2 to 3 minutes or until thick and bubbly, stirring every 30 seconds. Pour over chicken and microwave 24 minutes, giving dish one quarter turn. Discard Bouquet Garni. Place chicken on platter and keep warm. Stir a little hot sauce into sour cream. Return sour cream mixture to baking dish; blend well. Microwave just until hot, about 45 seconds. Serve chicken with noodles and pass sour cream sauce.

Bouquet Garni: Place 3 or 4 sprigs fresh parsley, ½ bay leaf, ½ tsp. thyme leaves, 1 onion slice and 1 (2″) celery branch in cheesecloth. Tie with string.

PARMESAN SOLE ON TOAST

If you use frozen sole fillets, just cut into four pieces while still partially frozen. Makes it easier to divide in fourths.

BASIC RECIPE — MAKES 4 SERVINGS.

1 lb. fresh or frozen, thawed sole fillets	1¼ c. milk
2 tblsp. butter or regular margarine	¼ c. grated Parmesan cheese
2 tblsp. flour	2 tblsp. parsley flakes
½ tsp. salt	4 slices toasted, buttered French bread
	Paprika

Range Top: 17 minutes cooking time

Cut sole in 4 pieces and place in skillet. Cover with water. Bring to boiling. Reduce heat and simmer, covered, 6 minutes or until fish flakes easily. Meanwhile, melt butter in saucepan, about 1 minute. Blend in flour and salt. Add milk. Cook, stirring constantly, until mixture comes to a boil, about 5 minutes. Add cheese, parsley and fish separated in small pieces. Heat thoroughly, about 5 minutes. Serve fish mixture over toasted French bread. Sprinkle with paprika.

Microwave Oven (high setting): 10 minutes cooking time

Use ingredients listed in basic recipe. Cut sole in 4 pieces and place in 12×8×2″ glass baking dish (2-qt.). Cover and microwave (high setting) 5 minutes or until fish flakes easily. Drain fish. Microwave butter in 1-qt. glass bowl or measuring cup 30 seconds or until melted. Stir in flour and salt. Blend in milk. Microwave, uncovered, 3 minutes or until mixture boils. Stir occasionally during last half of cooking. Stir in Parmesan cheese. Cut fish in small pieces. Add to sauce along with parsley. Microwave 1½ minutes. Serve over toasted French bread. Sprinkle with paprika.

CREAM-TOPPED FISH FILLETS

Freshly grated Romano cheese is a good substitute for the grated Parmesan. It has more flavor.

BASIC RECIPE — MAKES 6 SERVINGS.

2 lbs. frozen fish fillets, thawed	1 tblsp. parsley flakes
1 tsp. salt	1 tsp. instant minced onion
¾ c. dairy sour cream	¼ c. grated Parmesan cheese
¼ c. dry bread crumbs	Paprika

Oven: 20 to 25 minutes baking time

Cut each 1 lb. block of fish fillets in thirds. Place in greased 13×9×2″ baking pan. Sprinkle with salt. Stir together sour cream, bread crumbs, parsley and onion. Spread over fish. Sprinkle with Parmesan cheese, then paprika. Bake in 400° oven 20 to 25 minutes or until fish flakes easily.

Microwave Oven (high setting): 8 to 9 minutes cooking time

Use ingredients listed in basic recipe. Cut each 1 lb. block of fish fillets in thirds. Place in 12×8×2″ glass baking dish (2-qt.). Sprinkle with salt. Stir together sour cream, bread crumbs, parsley and onion. Spread over fish. Sprinkle with Parmesan cheese, then paprika. Microwave (high setting) 8 to 9 minutes or until fish flakes easily, giving dish a half turn once.

FLAVORFUL BAKED FISH

If you keep frozen fish fillets on hand, you can make this dinner in just minutes. So delicious, too.

BASIC RECIPE — MAKES 4 SERVINGS.

2 tblsp. butter or regular margarine

1 lb. frozen fish fillets, thawed and cut in serving size portions

½ c. chopped celery

¼ c. chopped onion

2 tblsp. chopped fresh parsley

¼ c. butter or regular margarine

1 tblsp. lemon juice

Salt

Pepper

Oven: 24 minutes cooking time

Melt 2 tblsp. butter in 13×9×2" baking pan in oven, about 2 minutes. Rotate pan to coat evenly with butter. Sprinkle celery, onion and parsley in baking pan. Lay fish on vegetables. Melt the remaining ¼ c. butter in small saucepan, about 2 minutes. Add lemon juice to melted butter. Drizzle over fish and season fish with salt and pepper. Bake in 350° oven 10 minutes. Turn fish fillets and continue baking 10 minutes or until fish flakes easily.

Microwave Oven (high setting): 8 to 9 minutes cooking time

Use ingredients listed in basic recipe. Place 2 tblsp. butter in 12×8×2" glass baking dish (2-qt.). Microwave (high setting) 30 seconds or until butter is melted. Rotate dish to coat evenly with butter. Sprinkle celery, onion and parsley in baking dish. Lay fish on vegetables in baking dish. Microwave remaining ¼ c. butter and lemon juice in glass measuring cup 30 seconds or until butter is melted. Drizzle over fish and season with salt and pepper. Microwave, uncovered, 7 to 8 minutes or until fish flakes easily. Spoon butter and vegetables over fish once during cooking.

BAKED FISH FILLETS

You can prepare two vegetables and this dish in the microwave by the time this dish would be done when cooked conventionally.

BASIC RECIPE — MAKES 4 SERVINGS.

1 egg, slightly beaten	1 lb. fresh or frozen fish fillets,
1 tblsp. lemon juice	thawed
½ tsp. seasoned salt	¾ c. corn flake crumbs
⅛ tsp. pepper	

Oven: 20 to 25 minutes baking time

Blend together egg, lemon juice, seasoned salt and pepper in shallow bowl. Dip fish into egg mixture and then into corn flake crumbs. Arrange fish in greased 12×8×2″ glass baking dish (2-qt.). Bake in 350° oven 20 to 25 minutes or until fish flakes easily.

Microwave Oven (high setting): 4 to 5 minutes cooking time

Use ingredients listed in basic recipe. Prepare them as for Oven. Arrange in 12×8×2″ glass baking dish (2-qt.). Cover with waxed paper. Microwave (high setting) 4 to 5 minutes or until fish flakes easily.

BAKED FISH WITH STUFFING

Stuffing gives these fish fillets a different touch. Needs no watching when baked in the conventional oven. So good, too.

BASIC RECIPE — MAKES 6 SERVINGS.

¼ c. butter or regular
   margarine
1 c. chopped celery
½ c. chopped onion
½ tsp. salt
¼ tsp. pepper
4 c. soft bread cubes
2 tblsp. lemon juice

2 lbs. fresh or thawed frozen fish
   fillets
½ tsp. salt
1 (10½ oz.) can condensed
   cream of mushroom soup
¼ c. chopped fresh parsley
2 tblsp. chopped pimiento
2 tblsp. water

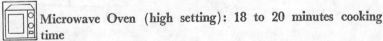

Oven: 41 minutes cooking time

Melt butter in skillet, about 1 minute. Add celery and onion and cook until tender, about 5 minutes. Combine onion mixture, ½ tsp. salt, pepper, bread cubes and lemon juice in bowl; toss lightly to mix. Place half of fish fillets in bottom of greased 13×9×2″ baking pan. Spoon stuffing mixture over fish. Top with remaining fillets. Sprinkle with ½ tsp. salt. Cover pan with foil. Bake in 350° oven 25 minutes. Meanwhile, combine remaining ingredients in small saucepan and heat, about 5 minutes. Spread over fish. Return to oven for 5 minutes.

Microwave Oven (high setting): 18 to 20 minutes cooking time

Use ingredients listed in basic recipe. Place butter, celery and onion in glass mixing bowl. Microwave (high setting) 6 minutes or until vegetables are partially cooked, stirring once. Stir in ½ tsp. salt, pepper, bread cubes and lemon juice; toss lightly to mix. Place half of fish fillets in greased 12×8×2″ glass baking dish (2-qt.). Spoon stuffing mixture over fish. Top with remaining fillets. Sprinkle with ½ tsp. salt.

Cover with waxed paper. Microwave 9 to 11 minutes or until fish flakes easily with a fork. Give dish a half turn once. Let stand covered. Meanwhile, combine remaining ingredients in a 2-c. glass measuring cup. Microwave 3 minutes or until bubbly, stirring once. Spread over fish fillets and serve.

SEAFOOD LUNCHEON SPECIAL

Any leftover cooked fish can be used in this dish. A quick-fix meal when you want to serve supper in a hurry.
BASIC RECIPE — MAKES 5 SERVINGS.

1 (10¾ oz.) can condensed
   cream of shrimp soup
3 tblsp. milk
1 c. diced cooked fish
½ c. frozen peas, thawed
2 hard-cooked eggs, chopped

1 (4 oz.) can mushroom stems
   and pieces, drained
1 tsp. parsley flakes
¼ tsp. salt
1 tsp. lemon juice

Range Top: 5 minutes cooking time
Blend together soup and milk in saucepan. Stir in remaining ingredients. Bring to a boil, stirring frequently. Reduce heat and simmer, covered, 5 minutes or until peas are cooked. Serve over toast, toasted English muffins or rice.

Microwave Oven (high setting): 6 to 8 minutes cooking time
Use ingredients listed in basic recipe, but decrease milk from 3 to 2 tblsp. Blend together soup and 2 tblsp. milk in 1-qt. glass casserole. Stir in remaining ingredients. Cover and microwave (high setting) 6 to 8 minutes or until bubbly, stirring once. Serve over toast, toasted English muffins or rice.

SALMON-VEGETABLE CASSEROLE

Why not keep convenience foods on hand for busy days? You can serve this meal even on days when you're too tired to cook.

BASIC RECIPE — MAKES 6 SERVINGS.

1¼ c. milk
2 tblsp. flour
1 (10 oz.) pkg. frozen Welsh
  rarebit, thawed
1 (16 oz.) can salmon, drained
  and broken in large pieces

1 c. frozen peas and carrots,
  thawed
1 (16 oz.) pkg. frozen fried
  potato nuggets

 Oven: 40 minutes cooking time.

Blend a little milk into flour; then add remaining milk. Stir into rarebit in saucepan. Cook, stirring constantly, until mixture comes to a boil, about 5 minutes. Combine rarebit mixture, salmon, peas and carrots with half of potatoes in greased 2-qt. casserole. Top with remaining potatoes. Bake, uncovered, in 400° oven 35 minutes.

 Oven: 40 minutes cooking time

Use ingredients listed in basic recipe, but use unthawed rarebit. Remove frozen rarebit from foil pan. Place in 2-qt. glass casserole. Microwave (high setting), covered, 5 minutes, stirring once. Blend a little milk into flour; then add remaining milk. Stir into rarebit. Microwave, uncovered, 1½ minutes. Stir. Continue microwaving until thick and bubbly, about 4½ minutes. Stir after each minute. Stir in salmon, peas and carrots and half of potatoes. Microwave, covered, 5 minutes. Stir. Top with remaining potatoes and microwave, uncovered, 8 minutes.

SALMON LOAF WITH DILL SAUCE

The top of the loaf doesn't brown in the microwave oven or in the electric frypan—the dill sauce helps disguise this.

BASIC RECIPE — MAKES 5 TO 6 SERVINGS.

1 (16 oz.) can salmon, drained and flaked	1 tblsp. grated onion
2 eggs	1 tblsp. lemon juice
½ c. milk	2 tsp. parsley flakes
1½ c. soft bread cubes	¼ tsp. salt
¼ c. chopped dill pickle	⅛ tsp. pepper
	Dill Sauce (recipe follows)

 Oven: 55 minutes cooking time

Combine salmon and eggs in mixing bowl; beat with fork. Beat in milk and bread cubes. Stir in remaining ingredients except Dill Sauce. Spread in greased 8½×4½×2½″ loaf pan. Bake in 350° oven 50 minutes. Serve with Dill Sauce.

Dill Sauce: Combine ½ c. dairy sour cream, 2 tblsp. milk, 2 tblsp. finely chopped green onions, ¼ tsp. dried dillweed and ⅛ tsp. salt in small saucepan. Cook, stirring constantly, until sauce is hot, but do not let boil, about 5 minutes. Makes ¾ cup.

Electric Frypan: 55 minutes cooking time

Use ingredients listed in basic recipe. Combine ingredients for loaf and spread in greased 8½×4½×2½″ loaf pan as for Oven. Place rack in electric frypan. Preheat frypan to 420°. Set loaf pan on rack. Cover and bake, with vent closed, for 50 minutes. Prepare Dill Sauce as for Oven and serve with loaf.

Microwave Oven (high setting): 11 minutes cooking time
Use ingredients listed in basic recipe. Combine ingredients as for
Oven. Spread in ungreased 8½×4½×2½" glass loaf dish. Micro-
wave (high setting) 10 minutes, giving dish a quarter turn twice.
Place ingredients for Dill Sauce in glass bowl or measuring cup. Mi-
crowave 30 seconds, stir and microwave 15 more seconds.

Toaster-Oven: 55 minutes cooking time
Use ingredients listed in basic recipe. Combine ingredients as for
Oven. Place in greased 8½×4½×2½" loaf pan. Bake at 350° for 50
minutes. Prepare Dill Sauce as for Oven and serve with loaf.

TUNA-RICE SKILLET

*A high-protein skillet that's terrific for a quick lunch or supper. Chil-
dren especially will like this tuna dish.*
BASIC RECIPE — MAKES 4 TO 5 SERVINGS.

¼ c. chopped onion	1 c. uncooked regular rice
¼ c. chopped celery	1 (12½ oz.) can chunk-style
¼ c. chopped green pepper	tuna, drained
2 tblsp. butter or regular	½ tsp. salt
margarine	⅛ tsp. pepper
1 (4 oz.) can mushroom stems	1 chicken bouillon cube
and pieces	1 (8 oz.) can peas, drained

Range Top: 25 minutes cooking time
Cook onion, celery and green pepper in butter in 10" skillet until soft,
about 5 minutes. Drain mushrooms, reserving liquid. Add water to
mushroom liquid to make 2 c.; pour into skillet. Stir in mushrooms,
rice, tuna, salt, pepper and bouillon cube; mix well. Bring to a boil;
cover and simmer over low heat 20 minutes or until rice is tender, stirring once or twice. Stir in peas.

Microwave Oven (high setting): 23 to 27 minutes cooking time

Use ingredients listed in basic recipe. Combine onion, celery, green pepper and butter in 2-qt. glass casserole. Cover and microwave (high setting) 3 to 4 minutes or until vegetables are soft, stirring once. Drain mushrooms, reserving liquid. Add water to mushroom liquid to make 2 c.; pour into casserole. Stir in mushrooms, rice, tuna, salt, pepper and bouillon cube; mix well. Microwave, covered, 20 to 23 minutes or until rice is tender, stirring every 5 minutes. Stir in peas.

 Pressure Cooker: 20 to 25 minutes cooking time

Use ingredients listed in basic recipe. Cook onion, celery and green pepper in butter in 4-qt. pressure cooker until soft, about 5 minutes. Drain mushrooms, reserving liquid. Add water to mushroom liquid to make 2 c.; pour into pressure cooker. Stir in mushrooms, rice, tuna, salt, pepper and bouillon cube. Close cover securely. Place over high heat. Bring to 15 lbs. pressure, according to manufacturer's directions for your pressure cooker. When pressure is reached (control will begin to jiggle), remove from heat. Let pressure drop of its own accord. Stir in peas before serving.

NINE-MINUTE ORIENTAL TUNA

A stir-fried tuna dish that's ready in only 9 minutes. You can slice vegetables ahead. Measure out other ingredients to save time at end.

BASIC RECIPE — MAKES 5 TO 6 SERVINGS.

2 tblsp. cornstarch	¼ c. sliced green onions
¼ tsp. ground ginger	2 (7 oz.) cans water-pack tuna,
1 (13¾ oz.) can chicken broth	drained and broken in chunks
3 tblsp. soy sauce	1 (16 oz.) can bean sprouts,
3 tblsp. cooking oil	drained
1 c. bias-cut celery, ¼″ thick	1 c. frozen peas, thawed
1 c. bias-cut carrots, ⅛″ thick	Hot cooked rice
1 clove garlic, minced	

Range Top: 9 minutes cooking time

Cut and assemble all ingredients before starting to cook. Blend together cornstarch, ginger, chicken broth and soy sauce. Heat 12″ skillet over high heat. Add cooking oil and heat. Stir in celery, carrots and garlic. Cook and stir 3 minutes. Add onions; cook and stir 1 minute. Stir in cornstarch mixture. Cook and stir until mixture is thickened and bubbly, about 2 minutes. Stir in tuna, bean sprouts and peas. Cover and reduce heat to low. Cook 3 minutes or until thoroughly heated. Serve over hot cooked rice.

 Electric Frypan: 9 minutes cooking time

Use ingredients listed in basic recipe. Cut and assemble ingredients before starting to cook. Blend together cornstarch, ginger, chicken broth and soy sauce. Heat electric frypan to 375°. Add oil and heat. Stir in celery, carrots and garlic. Cook and stir 3 minutes. Add onions; cook and stir 1 minute. Stir in cornstarch mixture. Cook and stir until mixture is thickened and bubbly, about 2 minutes. Stir in tuna, bean sprouts and peas. Cover and reduce heat to 220°. Cook, with vent closed, 3 minutes or until thoroughly heated. Serve over hot cooked rice.

 Electric Wok: 9 minutes cooking time

Use ingredients listed in basic recipe, but reduce cooking oil to 2 tblsp. Cut and assemble all ingredients before starting to cook. Blend together cornstarch, ginger, chicken broth and soy sauce. Heat electric wok to 375°. Add oil and heat. Stir in celery, carrots and garlic. Cook and stir 3 minutes. Add onions; cook and stir 1 minute. Stir in cornstarch mixture. Cook and stir until mixture is thickened and bubbly, about 2 minutes. Stir in tuna, bean sprouts and peas. Cover and reduce heat to 250°. Cook 3 minutes or until thoroughly heated. Serve over hot cooked rice.

VEGETABLE-SHRIMP SCRAMBLE

A good dish for brunch. And you have a choice of three appliances in which to cook it.

BASIC RECIPE — MAKES 4 SERVINGS.

2 tblsp. butter or regular margarine	1 c. small cooked shrimp
2 c. finely chopped zucchini	3 eggs, beaten
¼ c. chopped onion	½ tsp. salt
	¼ tsp. pepper

Range Top: 11 minutes cooking time

Cut and measure all ingredients before starting to cook. Melt butter in 10″ skillet over medium heat, about 1 minute. Stir in zucchini and onion. Cover and steam 2 minutes. Cook and stir until zucchini is tender-crisp, 3 minutes. Add shrimp. Cook and stir 2 minutes. Turn heat to low. Add mixture of eggs, salt and pepper. Gently turn over with spatula until eggs are barely set, about 3 minutes. Serve at once.

Microwave Oven (high setting): 7½ minutes cooking time

Use ingredients listed in basic recipe. Cut and measure them before starting to cook. Place butter in 1-qt. glass casserole. Microwave (high setting) 30 seconds or until butter is melted. Add zucchini and onion, cover and microwave 4 minutes, stirring once. Add shrimp; microwave, covered, 1 minute. Add mixture of eggs, salt and pepper. Cook 2 minutes or until eggs are barely set, stirring after 1 minute.

Electric Wok: 8 to 9 minutes cooking time

Use ingredients listed in basic recipe. Cut and measure all ingredients before starting to cook. Heat wok to 300°. Melt butter, about 1 minute. Stir onion and zucchini into melted butter. Cover and steam 1 minute. Cook and stir until zucchini is tender-crisp, 2 to 3 minutes. Add shrimp and stir 1 minute. Turn heat to 250°. Add mixture of eggs, salt and pepper. Gently turn mixture with spatula until eggs are barely set, about 3 minutes.

HOT SHRIMP SALAD CASSEROLE

A great choice for the microwave because it's ready in minutes. You can cook it after your luncheon guests arrive.

BASIC RECIPE — MAKES 6 SERVINGS.

1 lb. frozen deveined, cooked small shrimp, thawed and drained

2 c. sliced celery

½ c. water chestnuts, drained and sliced

2 hard-cooked eggs, chopped

2 tblsp. grated onion

¾ c. mayonnaise or salad dressing

2 tblsp. lemon juice

½ tsp. salt

½ c. shredded process American cheese (2 oz.)

1 c. crushed potato chips

 Oven: 20 minutes baking time

Combine shrimp, celery, water chestnuts, eggs and onion in bowl. Blend together mayonnaise, lemon juice and salt. Stir into shrimp mixture. Place in 8″ round glass baking dish. Top with cheese, then with potato chips. Bake in 400° oven 20 minutes or until hot.

Microwave Oven (high setting): 6 minutes cooking time

Use ingredients listed in basic recipe. Combine shrimp, celery, water chestnuts, eggs and onion in bowl. Blend together mayonnaise, lemon juice and salt. Stir into shrimp mixture. Place in 8″ round glass baking dish. Cover with waxed paper. Microwave (high setting) 4 minutes, stirring once. Stir again and sprinkle with cheese. Microwave 1 more minute. Top with potato chips. Microwave 1 more minute.

Toaster-Oven: 20 minutes cooking time
Use ingredients listed in basic recipe. Prepare as for Oven. Place in 8"
square baking pan. Bake at 400° for 15 minutes. Top with cheese and
then with potato chips. Continue baking 5 more minutes.

LIMA BEAN/FRANKFURTER BARBECUE

*The cooking time for the slow cooker includes 12 hours of cooking on
low instead of soaking beans overnight as in other two methods.*
BASIC RECIPE — MAKES 6 SERVINGS.

2 c. dried lima beans (1 lb.)	3 c. tomato juice
2 qts. water	¼ c. ketchup
4 slices bacon	1 tblsp. Worcestershire sauce
½ c. chopped onion	½ tsp. salt
¼ c. chopped celery	½ tsp. dried basil
¼ c. chopped green pepper	1 (12 oz.) pkg. frankfurters,
1 clove garlic, minced	cut in 1" lengths (8 to 10)

Range Top: 1 hour 13 minutes cooking time
Wash beans and place in Dutch oven; add water and bring to boiling.
Boil 2 minutes and let stand 1 hour. (Or soak beans in water overnight.) Drain. Cook bacon in small skillet until crisp, about 6 minutes.
Drain on paper towels. Crumble and set aside. Cook onion, celery,
green pepper and garlic in bacon drippings until soft, about 5 minutes.
Combine remaining ingredients, drained beans, crumbled bacon and
onion mixture in Dutch oven; mix well. Bring to boiling; reduce heat
and simmer, covered, 1 hour or until beans are tender.

Pressure Cooker: 36 minutes cooking time
Use ingredients listed in basic recipe, but add ¼ c. cooking oil and 1
tblsp. salt. Place beans in 4-qt. pressure pan, add water, ¼ c. cooking
oil and 1 tblsp. salt. Cover and soak overnight. Drain. Cook bacon in

pressure pan until crisp, about 6 minutes. Drain on paper towels. Crumble and set aside. Cook onion, celery, green pepper and garlic in bacon drippings until soft, about 5 minutes. Add remaining ingredients, drained beans and crumbled bacon to onion mixture. Mix well. Close cover securely. Place over high heat. Bring to 15 lbs. pressure, according to manufacturer's directions for your pressure cooker. When pressure is reached (control will begin to jiggle), reduce heat immediately and cook 25 minutes. Remove from heat. Let pressure drop of its own accord.

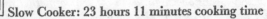 Slow Cooker: 23 hours 11 minutes cooking time

Use ingredients listed in basic recipe. Place beans in cooker; add the water and cook, covered, on low 12 hours or overnight. Drain. Cook bacon in small skillet until crisp, about 6 minutes. Drain on paper towels; crumble and set aside. Cook onion, celery, green pepper and garlic in bacon drippings until soft, about 5 minutes. Add onion mixture to beans along with bacon and remaining ingredients; mix well. Cover and cook on low 11 hours or until beans are tender.

FRANK AND BEAN COMBO

If you can't find smoked frankfurters in your supermarket, the regular ones are just as good in this recipe.

BASIC RECIPE — MAKES 4 TO 6 SERVINGS.

4 slices bacon	1 lb. smoked frankfurters
½ c. chopped onion	Ketchup
2 (16 oz.) cans pork and beans in brown sugar sauce or tomato sauce	Prepared mustard
	Cheddar cheese, cut in thin strips
1 tsp. Worcestershire sauce	

Range Top: 28 minutes cooking time

Cook bacon in 10″ skillet 6 minutes or until crisp. Remove, crumble and reserve. Cook onion in bacon drippings in same skillet 4 minutes or until tender. Drain ½ c. sauce from two cans of beans and discard. Stir beans with remaining sauce, Worcestershire sauce and bacon into onion. Cut frankfurters lengthwise in half, but not quite through. Place on top of beans. Simmer, covered, 15 minutes. Spread frankfurters apart and spread with ketchup and mustard; top with cheese. Cover and cook on low heat until cheese is melted, 3 minutes.

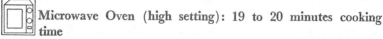

Microwave Oven (high setting): 19 to 20 minutes cooking time

Use ingredients listed in basic recipe. Place bacon in 12×8×2″ glass baking dish (2-qt.). Microwave (high setting) 5 minutes or until crisp. Remove bacon and drain on paper towel. Crumble and reserve. Add onion to bacon drippings and microwave, uncovered, 4 to 5 minutes. Drain ½ c. sauce from two cans of beans and discard. Stir beans with remaining sauce, Worcestershire sauce and bacon into baking dish. Cut frankfurters lengthwise in half, but not quite through, place them on beans. Cover with waxed paper and microwave 6 minutes or until hot. Give dish a half turn once. Spread frankfurters apart and spread with ketchup and mustard. Top with cheese. Continue cooking 4 minutes or until cheese is melted.

SONNY'S POTATO FRANK BAKE

Recipe works successfully in all three cooking appliances. Choose the one that is most convenient for you.

BASIC RECIPE — MAKES 6 SERVINGS.

2 c. water
3 tblsp. butter or regular
  margarine
¾ tsp. garlic salt
½ tsp. salt
½ c. milk
2 c. unreconstituted instant
  mashed potatoes*

½ c. small-curd cottage cheese
6 frankfurters
Prepared mustard
1 c. grated sharp process
  American cheese (4 oz.)

Oven: 23 minutes cooking time

Combine water, butter, garlic salt and salt in saucepan. Bring to a boil. Remove from heat and add milk. Stir in instant potatoes with fork until smooth. Stir in cottage cheese. Spread in greased 8" square baking pan. Cut frankfurters lengthwise almost through; spread apart and spread cut surfaces with mustard. Place mustard side up on potatoes. Bake in 375° oven until thoroughly hot, about 20 minutes. Sprinkle with cheese. Return to oven until cheese is melted, about 3 minutes.

*Note: If instant mashed potato *flakes* are used, increase to 3 c.

 Microwave Oven (high setting): 9 to 10 minutes cooking time

Use ingredients listed in basic recipe. Combine water, butter, garlic salt and salt in 1-qt. glass casserole. Cover and microwave (high setting) 4 to 5 minutes or until boiling. Remove and add milk. Stir in instant potatoes with fork until smooth. Stir in cottage cheese. Spread in 8" square glass baking dish. Cut frankfurters lengthwise almost through, spread apart and spread cut surfaces with mustard. Place mustard side up on potatoes. Sprinkle with cheese. Microwave 5 minutes or until thoroughly hot. Give dish a quarter turn once.

 Toaster-Oven: 23 minutes cooking time

Use ingredients listed in basic recipe. Prepare them as for Oven. Place in greased 8" square baking pan. Bake in toaster-oven at 375° for 15 minutes. Cover with foil and continue baking 5 minutes or until potatoes are hot. Remove foil and sprinkle with cheese. Return to toaster-oven until cheese is melted, about 3 minutes.

THREE-BEAN FRANK SKILLET

A skillet casserole based on the flavor combination of traditional three-bean salad. A great way to serve franks for a change.

BASIC RECIPE — MAKES 6 SERVINGS.

½ c. chopped onion
2 tblsp. butter or regular
   margarine
½ c. bottled barbecue sauce
¼ c. brown sugar, packed
1 (16 oz.) can green lima
   beans, drained

1 (16 oz.) can cut green beans,
   drained
1 (15 oz.) can kidney beans
1 lb. frankfurters, bias-cut in
   1″ pieces

 Range Top: 15 minutes cooking time

Cook onion in melted butter in 10″ skillet 5 minutes or until soft. Add barbecue sauce and brown sugar; mix well. Stir in lima beans, green beans, undrained kidney beans and frankfurters. Bring to a boil. Reduce heat and simmer, covered, 10 minutes. Stir mixture twice during cooking.

 Electric Frypan: 15 minutes cooking time

Use ingredients listed in basic recipe. Cook onion in melted butter in 12″ electric frypan at 300° for 5 minutes or until soft. Add barbecue sauce and brown sugar; mix well. Stir in lima beans, green beans, undrained kidney beans and frankfurters. Bring to a boil. Reduce heat and simmer, covered, 10 minutes. Stir mixture twice during cooking.

 Microwave Oven (high setting): 11 to 12 minutes

Use ingredients listed in basic recipe. Combine onion and butter in 3-qt. glass casserole. Cover and microwave (high setting) 3 to 4 minutes or until soft, stirring once. Stir in barbecue sauce and brown sugar; mix well. Stir in lima beans, green beans, undrained kidney beans and frankfurters. Cover and microwave 8 minutes or until hot, stirring four times.

TORTILLA BEAN STACK-UPS

The tortillas are much crisper when heated in the oven. However, most people won't notice the difference.

BASIC RECIPE — MAKES 8 SERVINGS.

1 (16 oz.) can red kidney beans, drained	8 corn tortillas
1 c. shredded Cheddar cheese (4 oz.)	2 c. finely shredded lettuce
¼ c. bottled taco sauce	2 tomatoes, peeled and chopped
1 tblsp. grated onion	1 (16 oz.) pkg. frozen guacamole, thawed
½ tsp. chili powder	½ c. shredded Cheddar cheese (2 oz.)

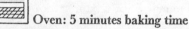 Oven: 5 minutes baking time

Mash beans. Stir in 1 c. cheese, taco sauce, onion and chili powder. Spread bean mixture on each tortilla. Place tortillas on 2 baking sheets. Bake in 450° oven 5 minutes or until cheese melts. Serve tortillas topped with lettuce, tomatoes, guacamole and ½ c. shredded cheese.

Microwave Oven (high setting): 4 minutes cooking time

Use ingredients listed in basic recipe. Prepare bean mixture as for Oven. Spread over tortillas. Place 4 tortillas on paper towels in microwave oven. Microwave, uncovered, 2 minutes or until cheese melts. Repeat with remaining 4 tortillas. Top tortillas with lettuce, tomatoes, guacamole and ½ c. shredded cheese.

CHAPTER FIVE

Vegetable Variety

Recipes in this chapter feature vegetables from A to Z, starting with asparagus and ending with zucchini. No wonder meal planners lean so heavily on gifts from the garden to provide variety to menus. They vary so much in looks, taste and texture.

Contrast Stir-fried Beans, cooked in 8 to 10 minutes in the electric or non-electric skillet, electric wok and by microwaving, with the green beans grandmother simmered with bacon or other cured pork a long time. The speedy cooking retains much of the vegetable's green color and food value; the beans are tender, but somewhat crisp. The old way of cooking destroyed the color and texture of the beans and the flavor of cured meat predominated.

Foods and seasonings that team delightfully with vegetables are numerous. Sometimes fruit enhances them. Ruby Sauced Beets, for instance, owe some of their beauty in looks and taste to the cranberry juice cocktail in which they are cooked. Oranges and raisins impart their appealing flavors to carrots in Carrots in Orange-Raisin Sauce, and practically everyone who tastes Sweet Potato Boats praises the way pineapple enhances the vegetable.

Combining two or more vegetables of contrasting texture, color and flavor in one dish introduces interest and variety to meals. Frozen broccoli, cauliflower and carrots get together in Mixed Vegetable Casserole, an ideal vegetable dish to tote to potluck suppers or serve on your own buffet.

While vegetables traditionally play second fiddle to meats, poultry, fish and other protein foods, some of the recipes in this chapter produce dishes that boost the protein in meals. Mixed Bean Casserole, and a Wisconsin-inspired recipe, Spinach-Cheese Casserole, are two such recipes.

Most people have nostalgic memories of warm vegetable salads which once frequently graced country meals. Since they provide a change from cold salads and are fast to make, a revival of interest in them is occurring. This cookbook has some superior recipes for them. Wilted Leaf Lettuce offers an easy and delicious way to celebrate the arrival of spring and the early garden's contributions. Hot German Potato Salad and Pennsylvania Dutch Cabbage quickly cook with the microwave oven and pressure cooker as well as with the conventional range.

Enthusiasm for vegetable dishes comes easier to many home gardeners, who take pride in what they plant and reap. But tested, updated recipes, like those that follow, also give convenient frozen, canned and market-fresh vegetables an opportunity to gain warm and wide acceptance. Commercial farmers and experts in processing and transporting vegetables have made great progress in recent years. If homemakers keep up with them, they can create exceptionally tasty dishes. So turn the pages and decide which vegetable to cook first. Remember you can cook it your way.

ORANGE-BUTTERED ACORN SQUASH

To make more efficient use of your oven, bake squash along with dessert and your family's favorite meat loaf.
BASIC RECIPE — MAKES 4 SERVINGS.

2 medium acorn squash
Salt
2 tblsp. brown sugar, firmly
  packed

2 tblsp. butter or regular
  margarine
¼ c. orange juice

Oven: 55 to 60 minutes baking time
Halve and seed squash. Place cut side down in 13×9×2″ baking pan. Bake in 350° oven for 40 minutes. Turn cut side up. Sprinkle with salt and add to each half ½ tblsp. brown sugar, ½ tblsp. butter and 1 tblsp. orange juice. Continue baking until tender, 15 to 20 minutes.

Electric Frypan: 35 to 45 minutes cooking time

Use ingredients listed in basic recipe. Place halved and seeded squash cut side down in electric frypan. Add 1 c. water and bring to boiling (350°). Reduce heat to 220° and simmer 20 to 25 minutes with vent open. Turn squash cut side up. Sprinkle with salt and add brown sugar, butter and orange juice to squash halves as in Oven. Cook 15 to 20 minutes, covered, or until tender.

 Microwave Oven (high setting): 17 to 20 minutes cooking time

Use ingredients listed in basic recipe. Wash whole squash and prick in one or two places with skewer. Microwave (high setting) 12 to 15 minutes or until soft, giving squash two quarter turns. Let stand 5 minutes. Carefully cut squash (it is very tender); scoop out seeds. Place cut side up in 12×8×2" glass baking dish (2-qt.). Sprinkle with salt. Add brown sugar, butter and orange juice to squash halves as for Oven. Microwave 5 minutes or until orange juice mixture is bubbly.

 Slow Cooker: 7 to 9 hours cooking time

Use ingredients listed in basic recipe, but use smaller squash. Place whole squash in cooker. Add ¼ c. water. Cover and cook on high 1 hour. Reduce heat to low; cook 6 to 8 hours or until squash is tender. Carefully cut squash in half; scoop out seeds. Sprinkle with salt. Add brown sugar, butter and orange juice to squash as for Oven and serve.

ASPARAGUS IN SHRIMP SAUCE

You don't need to wait for spring to serve this asparagus dish. It's made with frozen asparagus topped with shrimp soup sauce.

BASIC RECIPE — MAKES 6 SERVINGS.

2 (10 oz.) pkgs. frozen
   asparagus spears
1 (3 oz.) pkg. cream cheese,
   softened
1 (10¾ oz.) can condensed
   cream of shrimp soup

2 tblsp. butter or regular
   margarine, melted
½ c. dry bread crumbs
Paprika

 Oven: 35 minutes cooking time

Cook asparagus as directed on package, about 10 minutes. Drain. Meanwhile, beat together cream cheese and about one-third of soup in bowl until smooth. Stir in remaining soup. Toss together butter and bread crumbs. Place asparagus in greased 1½-qt. casserole. Pour soup mixture over asparagus. Top with buttered crumbs. Sprinkle with paprika. Bake in 350° oven 25 minutes or until hot.

Microwave Oven (high setting): 21½ minutes cooking time.

Use ingredients listed in basic recipe. Place butter in small glass bowl; microwave (high setting) 30 seconds or until melted. Add bread crumbs and toss. Set aside. Place asparagus in 10×6×1½″ glass baking dish. Cover with waxed paper. Microwave 5 minutes. Separate spears with fork. Cover and microwave 8 minutes. Drain. Meanwhile, combine soup mixture as for Oven. Pour soup mixture over asparagus in same baking dish. Top with buttered crumbs and sprinkle with paprika. Microwave 8 minutes, giving casserole a quarter turn after cooking 4 minutes.

Toaster-Oven: 25 minutes cooking time

Use ingredients listed in basic recipe. Prepare as for Oven. Place in greased 10×6×1½″ glass baking dish (1½-qt.). Bake at 350° for 25 minutes. Cover with foil the last 5 minutes of baking if necessary to prevent excessive browning. (Do not let foil touch heating elements.)

TENDER-CRISP ASPARAGUS

It's so easy to cook fresh asparagus using the Chinese stir-fry method. We've even adapted it to the microwave oven.

BASIC RECIPE — MAKES 6 SERVINGS.

3 tblsp. cooking oil	½ tsp. salt
2 lbs. asparagus, cut on bias in 2×¼″ slices	¼ c. water

 Range Top: 6 to 8 minutes cooking time

Heat 12″ skillet over high heat. Add oil and heat. Stir in asparagus and salt until asparagus is coated with oil. Add water. Cover and steam 3 minutes. Remove cover; stir and cook until asparagus is tender-crisp, 3 to 5 minutes.

 Electric Frypan: 6 to 8 minutes cooking time

Use ingredients as listed in basic recipe. Heat electric frypan to 375°. Add oil and heat. Stir in asparagus and salt until asparagus is coated with oil. Add water. Cover and steam 3 minutes with vent closed. Remove cover. Stir and cook until asparagus is tender-crisp, 3 to 5 minutes.

Microwave Oven (high setting): 5 to 6 minutes cooking time

Use ingredients listed in basic recipe, but reduce them as follows. Combine 1 lb. asparagus, bias-cut in 2×¼" slices, 1 tblsp. cooking oil, ¼ tsp. salt and 2 tblsp. water in 8" square glass baking dish. Cover with plastic wrap. Microwave (high setting) 2 minutes. Stir. Continue microwaving, covered, until tender-crisp, 3 to 4 minutes. Makes 3 servings.

Electric Wok: 7 to 9 minutes cooking time

Use ingredients listed in basic recipe, but reduce cooking oil from 3 to 2 tblsp. and water from ¼ c. to 1 tblsp. Heat electric wok to 375°. Add 2 tblsp. oil and heat. Stir in asparagus and salt until asparagus is coated with oil. Add 1 tblsp. water. Cover and cook 4 minutes. Remove cover. Stir and cook until asparagus is tender-crisp, 3 to 5 minutes.

MIXED BEAN CASSEROLE

This dish takes only minutes to heat in the microwave oven. However, flavor develops better in the other two appliances.

BASIC RECIPE — MAKES 8 TO 10 SERVINGS.

3 slices bacon, cut up
½ c. chopped onion
1 (31 oz.) can pork and beans in tomato sauce
1 (15 oz.) can kidney beans, drained

1 (15 oz.) can dried lima beans (butter beans), drained
3 tblsp. brown sugar, packed
½ tsp. dry mustard
3 tblsp. ketchup

 Oven: 1 hour 40 minutes cooking time

Cook bacon in skillet 5 minutes or until crisp. Drain on paper towels. Cook onion in bacon drippings 5 minutes or until soft. Combine beans

in greased 2-qt. casserole. Add brown sugar, mustard, ketchup, bacon and onion to beans. Mix thoroughly. Bake in 325° oven 1 hour 30 minutes.

Microwave Oven (high setting): 26 minutes cooking time
Use ingredients listed in basic recipe. Place onion and bacon in 2-qt. glass casserole. Cover with paper towels. Microwave (high setting) 4 minutes, stirring once. Add beans. Stir in brown sugar, mustard and ketchup; mix well. Cover and microwave 22 minutes, giving casserole a quarter turn twice.

Slow Cooker: 7 to 8 hours cooking time
Use ingredients listed in basic recipe, but use 2 tblsp. grated onion instead of chopped onion. Combine all ingredients in cooker. Cover and cook on low 7 to 8 hours.

TRIPLE BEAN MEDLEY

If you like three-bean salad, you'll like this hot vegetable adaptation. It's a popular choice for potluck suppers.

BASIC RECIPE — MAKES 8 SERVINGS.

4 slices bacon, chopped
1 medium onion, sliced and
  separated into rings
½ green pepper, cut in
  lengthwise strips
½ c. sugar
1 tsp. salt
¼ tsp. pepper
⅔ c. vinegar

1 (16 oz.) can green beans,
  drained
1 (16 oz.) can wax beans,
  drained
1 (15 oz.) can kidney beans,
  drained
1 tblsp. cornstarch
¼ c. water

Range Top: 32 minutes cooking time

Cook bacon in 10″ skillet 6 minutes or until crisp. Drain on paper towels and reserve. Cook onion and green pepper in bacon drippings 5 minutes, stirring occasionally. Add sugar, salt, pepper, vinegar and beans. Bring to a boil over high heat. Reduce heat, cover and simmer 20 minutes or until onion and green pepper are tender. Blend together cornstarch and water. Add to bean mixture. Cook and stir 1 minute or until mixture bubbles and thickens. Serve sprinkled with bacon.

Microwave Oven (high setting): 17 to 20 minutes cooking time

Use ingredients listed in basic recipe, but omit water. Place bacon in 2-qt. glass casserole. Cover with paper towels. Microwave (high setting) 4 to 5 minutes or until crisp, stirring once. Remove bacon with slotted spoon and reserve. Stir onion and green pepper into bacon drippings; cover. Microwave 4 to 5 minutes or until tender-crisp, stirring once. Blend together sugar, cornstarch, salt, pepper and vinegar. Stir into onion mixture. Microwave 3 to 4 minutes or until mixture bubbles and thickens. Stir in beans; cover. Microwave 6 minutes, stirring once. Keep covered and let stand 10 minutes to blend flavors. Serve sprinkled with bacon.

CREAMY GREEN BEANS WITH MUSHROOMS

Microwaved green beans retain their bright green color and have a fresher flavor than those cooked on range top.

BASIC RECIPE — MAKES 5 TO 6 SERVINGS.

1 lb. fresh green beans
1 (4 oz.) can mushroom stems
    and pieces, drained

1 c. dairy sour cream
¾ tsp. salt
⅛ tsp. pepper

Range Top: 25 to 35 minutes cooking time

Trim ends from beans; cut in 1″ lengths. Place beans with enough water to cover in saucepan. Cover and cook 20 to 30 minutes or until beans are tender. Drain. Add mushrooms, sour cream, salt and pepper. Heat thoroughly, but do not let boil, about 5 minutes.

 Microwave Oven (high setting): 16 to 18 minutes cooking time

Use ingredients listed in basic recipe, but add 1 tblsp. flour. Prepare beans as for Range Top. Combine with ¼ c. water in 1½-qt. glass casserole. Cover and microwave (high setting) 12 to 14 minutes or until beans are tender. Drain. Add mushrooms. Combine sour cream, 1 tblsp. flour, salt and pepper. Stir into beans. Cover and microwave 4 minutes. Stir and let stand 5 minutes.

STIR-FRIED BEANS

The stir-frying method of cookery is well-suited to garden-fresh vegetables such as green beans.

BASIC RECIPE — MAKES 6 SERVINGS.

3 tblsp. cooking oil
1 lb. green beans (about 4 c. cut)
¼ c. sliced green onions

1 tsp. chicken bouillon granules
½ tsp. salt
½ c. water

 Range Top: 8 to 10 minutes cooking time

Prepare and measure all ingredients before starting to cook. Cut green beans on the bias in 2×⅛″ strips. Heat heavy skillet over high heat. Add oil and heat. Add beans; stir and fry 3 minutes. Add remaining ingredients. Reduce heat to medium, cover and cook until tender-crisp, 5 to 7 minutes.

Electric Frypan: 8 to 10 minutes cooking time

Use ingredients listed in basic recipe, but increase amount of water from ½ to ¾ c. Prepare ingredients as for Range Top and measure before starting to cook. Heat electric skillet set at 375°. Add oil and heat. Add beans; stir and fry 3 minutes. Add onions, bouillon granules, salt and ¾ c. water. Reduce heat to simmer (220°). Cover and cook, with vent closed, 5 to 7 minutes or until beans are tender-crisp.

 Microwave Oven (high setting): 7 to 10 minutes cooking time

Use ingredients listed in basic recipe, but reduce cooking oil from 3 to 1 tblsp. and water from ½ to ¼ c. Prepare ingredients as for Range Top and measure before starting to cook. Combine 1 tblsp. oil and beans in 8″ square glass baking dish. Cover with plastic wrap and microwave (high setting) 2 minutes. Stir in onion, bouillon granules, salt and ¼ c. water. Cover and microwave 5 to 8 minutes or until beans are tender-crisp.

Electric Wok: 8 to 10 minutes cooking time

Use ingredients listed in basic recipe, but decrease cookng oil to 2 tblsp. Prepare ingredients as for Range Top and measure before starting to cook. Heat wok to 375°. Add oil and heat. Add beans; stir and fry 3 minutes. Add remaining ingredients. Turn heat to 300°. Cover and cook until beans are tender-crisp, 5 to 7 minutes.

WINTER GREEN BEANS

Make everyday green beans a little extra-special with this sweet-sour sauce spiked with bacon bits.

BASIC RECIPE — MAKES 6 SERVINGS.

2 (10 oz.) pkgs. frozen French-style green beans	2 tblsp. vinegar
	2 tsp. sugar
4 slices bacon, cut up	¾ tsp. salt
¼ c. chopped onion	⅛ tsp. pepper

Range Top: 16 to 21 minutes cooking time

Cook beans in boiling salted water in 2-qt. saucepan 10 to 15 minutes or until tender. Meanwhile, cook bacon in small skillet until crisp, about 5 minutes. Remove bacon with slotted spoon; reserve. Cook onion in bacon drippings until soft. Drain beans, stir in bacon, onion with drippings, vinegar, sugar, salt and pepper. Simmer 1 minute.

 Microwave Oven (high setting): 18 to 18½ minutes cooking time

Use ingredients listed in basic recipe. Place bacon and onion in 1½-quart glass casserole. Microwave (high setting) 4 to 4½ minutes, stirring once. Stir in vinegar, sugar, salt and pepper. Add green beans. Cover with waxed paper. Microwave 8 minutes. Stir to break beans apart. Microwave 4 minutes. Stir; microwave 2 more minutes.

RUBY-SAUCED BEETS

You can substitute home-grown beets in this recipe. Just cook and drain before adding to thickened sauce.

BASIC RECIPE — MAKES 6 SERVINGS.

2 tblsp. sugar
2 tblsp. cornstarch
¼ tsp. salt

1½ c. cranberry juice cocktail
2 (16 oz.) cans beets, drained

 Range Top: 8 to 9 minutes cooking time

Combine sugar, cornstarch and salt in saucepan. Blend in cranberry juice cocktail. Heat, stirring constantly, 5 minutes or until mixture bubbles, thickens and looks translucent. Add beets and simmer, covered, 3 to 4 minutes or until heated through.

Microwave Oven (high setting): 8 to 9 minutes cooking time
Use ingredients listed in basic recipe. Combine sugar, cornstarch and salt in 2-qt. glass casserole. Stir in cranberry juice cocktail. Microwave (high setting) 2 minutes. Stir. Microwave 2 minutes more or until mixture bubbles, thickens and looks translucent; stir after each minute. Add beets. Microwave 4 to 5 minutes or until heated through, stirring twice.

BROCCOLI WITH CHEESE

Bake this dish in the toaster-oven on hot summer days when you don't want to use your conventional oven.

BASIC RECIPE — MAKES 6 SERVINGS.

2 (10 oz.) pkgs. frozen chopped broccoli	¾ tsp. salt
	1 c. milk
2 tblsp. butter or regular margarine	1 (3 oz.) pkg. cream cheese
	½ c. shredded sharp process
2 tblsp. flour	American cheese

Oven: 45 minutes cooking time
Cook broccoli as directed on package, about 8 minutes. Drain thoroughly in a sieve. Meanwhile, melt butter in saucepan, about 1 minute. Blend in flour and salt. Add milk and cook 5 minutes, stirring constantly, until mixture comes to a boil. Cut cream cheese in small cubes. Add to sauce and stir over low heat 3 minutes or until cheese is blended into sauce. Place broccoli in greased 1½-qt. casserole. Stir in sauce. Bake in 350° oven 25 minutes. Sprinkle with process cheese. Continue baking until cheese is melted, 3 minutes.

Microwave Oven (high setting): 21 minutes cooking time
Use ingredients listed in basic recipe. Microwave (high setting) butter in glass bowl until melted, about 30 seconds. Stir in flour and salt;

blend in milk. Microwave 1 minute; stir. Continue cooking, stirring every 30 seconds, until thickened, 1½ minute. Cut cream cheese in small cubes. Add to sauce and microwave, stirring every minute, until blended, about 3 minutes. Place broccoli in 1½-qt. glass casserole. Cover with waxed paper and microwave 8 minutes. Drain thoroughly in a sieve. Combine broccoli and sauce in the casserole. Microwave 3 minutes, give casserole a quarter turn. Microwave 3 more minutes. Sprinkle with process cheese. Microwave 1 minute or until cheese is melted.

 Toaster-Oven: 42 minutes cooking time

Use ingredients listed in basic recipe. Cook broccoli as directed on package, about 8 minutes. Drain thoroughly in a sieve. Meanwhile, melt butter in saucepan, about 1 minute. Blend in flour and salt. Add milk and cook 5 minutes, stirring constantly, until mixture comes to a boil. Cut cream cheese in small cubes. Add to sauce and stir over low heat until cheese is blended into sauce. Place broccoli in greased 10×6×1½″ glass baking dish (1½-qt.). Stir in sauce. Bake at 350° for 25 minutes. Sprinkle with process cheese. Continue baking until cheese is melted, 3 minutes.

EASY CREAMED BRUSSELS SPROUTS

The cooking time is the same in both methods, but the microwave oven cooks only 3 servings in the time the other cooks 6 servings.
BASIC RECIPE — MAKES 6 SERVINGS.

2 tsp. instant minced onion
2 (8 oz.) pkgs. frozen Brussels
  sprouts
1 c. water

½ tsp. salt
2 (3 oz.) pkgs. cream cheese,
  cut in ¼″ cubes

 Range Top: 5 to 7 minutes cooking time

Place onion, Brussels sprouts, water and salt in a saucepan. Bring to a boil. Reduce heat to medium and simmer, covered, 5 to 7 minutes or

until sprouts are tender. Pour off all but 2 tblsp. cooking liquid. Add
cream cheese. Cover and let stand 3 minutes. Stir until cheese and
liquid are blended.

Microwave Oven (high setting): 5 to 7 minutes cooking time
Use ingredients listed in basic recipe, but cut in half and reduce
amount of water. Place 1 tsp. instant minced onion and 2 tblsp. water
in 1-qt. glass casserole. Let stand 1 minute. Add 1 (8 oz.) pkg. frozen
Brussels sprouts and ¼ tsp. salt. Microwave (high setting), covered, 5
to 7 minutes. Top with 1 (3 oz.) pkg. cream cheese, cut in ¼" cubes.
Cover and let stand 3 minutes. Stir until cheese and liquid are
blended. Makes 3 servings.

CABBAGE WITH CHOPPED HAM

Can you imagine cooking cabbage in only 8 minutes? Just tear into
small pieces and stir-fry in one of the following appliances.
BASIC RECIPE — MAKES 8 SERVINGS.

3 tblsp. cooking oil
1 small head cabbage, about
    2½ lbs.
½ c. chopped cooked ham
¼ c. chopped green onions and
    tops

2 tblsp. chopped fresh parsley
1 garlic clove, minced
2 tsp. chicken bouillon granules
½ tsp. salt
⅓ c. water

Range Top: 7 to 8 minutes cooking time
Cut and assemble all ingredients before starting to cook. Cut cabbage
in quarters; cut core and thickened part of leaves from each piece, saving thickened leaf parts for soup. Break apart other portions of leaves,
tearing them in 1 to 2" pieces. Heat 12" skillet over high heat. Add oil
and heat. Add torn cabbage. Cook and stir 1 minute. Reduce heat to
medium. Add ham, green onions, parsley, garlic, chicken bouillon

granules, salt and water. Cover and steam 5 minutes. Remove lid. If necessary, cook and stir until cabbage is tender-crisp, 1 to 2 minutes.

 Electric Frypan: 7 to 8 minutes cooking time
Use ingredients listed in basic recipe. Prepare as for Range Top. Heat electric frypan to 375°. Add oil and heat. Add cabbage. Cook and stir 1 minute. Reduce heat to simmer (220°). Add ham, green onions, parsley, garlic, chicken bouillon granules, salt and water. Cover and steam 5 minutes with vent closed. Remove lid. If necessary, cook and stir until cabbage is tender-crisp, 1 to 2 minutes.

 Electric Wok: 7 to 8 minutes cooking time
Use ingredients listed in basic recipe, but reduce oil from 3 tblsp. to 2 tblsp. Prepare as for Range Top. Heat electric wok to 375°. Add oil and heat. Add cabbage. Cook and stir 1 minute. Stir in ham, green onions, parsley, garlic, chicken bouillon granules, salt and water. Cover and steam 5 minutes. Remove lid. If necessary, cook and stir until cabbage is tender-crisp, 1 to 2 minutes.

COMPANY CABBAGE

This winter vegetable is especially good served with baked ham. Bake both at the same temperature, to help save energy.
BASIC RECIPE — MAKES 8 SERVINGS.

1 medium head cabbage
4 slices bacon
1 (10¾ oz.) can condensed cream of celery soup

⅓ c. milk
1 (3 oz.) can French-fried onion rings

Oven: 44 to 49 minutes cooking time

Cut cabbage in 8 wedges. Cook, covered, in 2″ boiling salted water in Dutch oven 10 minutes. Drain thoroughly. Meanwhile, cook bacon in skillet 6 minutes or until crisp. Drain on paper towels and crumble. Combine soup and milk. Stir in crumbled bacon. Place cabbage in 3-qt. casserole. Spoon soup mixture over cabbage. Cover. Bake in 350° oven 25 to 30 minutes or until sauce is bubbling. Top with onions. Bake, uncovered, 3 minutes longer.

 Microwave Oven (high setting): 22 to 27 minutes cooking time

Use ingredients listed in basic recipe, but add 2 tblsp. water and ½ tsp. salt. Cut cabbage as for cooking on Range Top. Place in 3-qt. glass casserole along with 2 tblsp. water and ½ tsp. salt. Cover and microwave (high setting) 12 to 15 minutes or until tender, re-distributing cabbage after 7 minutes. Drain. Place bacon on paper toweling in glass pie plate or dish. Cover with paper toweling. Microwave 3 minutes or until crisp. Crumble. Blend together soup and milk; stir in bacon. Spoon over cabbage. Cover and microwave 6 to 7 minutes. Sprinkle with onion. Microwave 1 to 2 minutes.

PENNSYLVANIA DUTCH CABBAGE

Cabbage is quickly cooked in this recipe because it is shredded first. It is seasoned much like a cabbage salad.

BASIC RECIPE — MAKES 6 SERVINGS.

6 slices bacon, cut up	½ tsp. salt
2 qts. shredded cabbage	¼ c. vinegar
1 tblsp. sugar	¼ c. water

 Range Top: 18 to 21 minutes cooking time

Cook bacon in skillet 6 minutes or until crisp. Remove and drain on paper towels. Pour off fat and reserve. Combine cabbage, bacon, sugar and salt in skillet. Add vinegar, water and 1 tblsp. bacon drippings. Cover and cook 12 to 15 minutes or until tender-crisp.

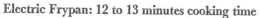 **Electric Frypan: 12 to 13 minutes cooking time**

Use ingredients listed in basic recipe. Put bacon in electric frypan; turn heat to 350°. Cook bacon in frypan 6 minutes or until crisp. Remove bacon and drain on paper towels. Pour off drippings and reserve. Combine cabbage, bacon, sugar and salt in skillet. Add vinegar, water and 1 tblsp. bacon drippings. Cover and simmer at 220°, with vent closed, 6 to 7 minutes or until cabbage is tender-crisp.

Pressure Cooker: 6 minutes cooking time

Use ingredients listed in basic recipe, but omit water. Cook bacon in 4-qt. pressure cooker 6 minutes or until crisp. Remove bacon and drain on paper towels. Pour off fat from pressure pan and reserve. Combine cabbage, bacon, sugar and salt in pressure cooker. Add vinegar and 1 tblsp. bacon drippings. Close cover securely. Place over high heat. Bring pressure up to 15 lbs., according to manufacturer's directions for pressure cooker. When pressure is reached (control will begin to jiggle), remove from heat. Reduce pressure instantly by placing cooker under cold running water.

SWEET-SOUR RED CABBAGE

Cabbage cooked to the tender-crisp stage has a much milder flavor than when it is steamed for a longer time.

BASIC RECIPE — MAKES 8 SERVINGS.

6 c. shredded red cabbage	3 tblsp. sugar
2 apples, pared and chopped	½ tsp. salt
½ c. vinegar	3 tblsp. butter or regular
½ c. water	margarine

Range Top: 13 to 15 minutes cooking time

Combine cabbage, apples, vinegar, water, sugar and salt in large saucepan. Cover and cook 12 to 14 minutes. Add butter; heat until melted, about 1 minute.

 Microwave Oven (high setting): 12 to 14 minutes cooking time

Use ingredients listed in basic recipe, but use ¼ c. instead of ½ c. water. Combine all ingredients in 3-qt. glass casserole. Cover and microwave (high setting) 12 to 14 minutes, stirring once.

CARROTS IN ORANGE-RAISIN SAUCE

The microwave oven cooks smaller quantities more efficiently than larger ones. That's why we reduce the size of basic recipe.

BASIC RECIPE — MAKES 8 SERVINGS.

4 c. sliced carrots	2 tblsp. brown sugar, firmly
¾ c. golden raisins	packed
1¼ c. orange juice	2 tsp. cornstarch
¾ c. water	¼ c. water
¼ tsp. salt	
2 tblsp. butter or regular	
margarine	

 Range Top: 25 to 30 minutes cooking time

Combine carrots, raisins, orange juice, ¾ c. water and salt in large saucepan. Cover and bring to a boil. Reduce heat to medium and cook 20 to 25 minutes or until carrots are tender. Stir in butter and brown sugar. Blend together cornstarch and remaining ¼ c. water. Add to carrot mixture. Cook and stir 5 minutes or until mixture thickens and boils.

Microwave Oven (high setting): 21 to 25 minutes cooking time

Use ingredients listed in basic recipe, but in different amounts. Combine 2 c. sliced carrots, ⅓ c. golden raisins, 1 c. orange juice and ⅛ tsp. salt in 2½-qt. glass casserole. Cover and microwave (high setting) 20 to 24 minutes or until carrots are tender, stirring 3 times. Stir in 1 tblsp. butter, 1 tblsp. brown sugar and a mixture of 2 tsp. cornstarch and 2 tblsp. water. Cover and microwave 1 minute. Stir. Makes 4 servings.

Pressure Cooker: 6 minutes cooking time

Use ingredients listed in basic recipe, but decrease orange juice from 1¼ c. to ½ c.; 2 tblsp. cornstarch instead of 2 tsp. and 2 tblsp. water instead of ¼ c. Melt butter in 4-qt. pressure cooker, about 1 minute. Stir in sliced carrots, raisins, brown sugar, salt and ½ c. orange juice. Close cover securely. Place over high heat. Bring to 15 lbs. pressure according to manufacturer's directions for your pressure cooker. When pressure is reached (control will begin to jiggle), reduce heat immediately and cook 3 minutes. Remove from heat. Reduce pressure instantly by placing cooker under cold running water. Blend together 2 tblsp. cornstarch and 2 tblsp. water. Add to carrot mixture. Cook 2 minutes, stirring constantly, until mixture bubbles and thickens.

GLAZED ORANGE CARROTS

An excellent choice for microwave cookery because it doesn't rely on browning to make dish attractive or tasty.

BASIC RECIPE — MAKES 4 SERVINGS.

3½ c. sliced carrots (1 lb.)
2 tblsp. butter or regular margarine
1 tsp. cornstarch

1 tsp. sugar
½ tsp. salt
1 tsp. grated orange rind
3 tblsp. orange juice

Range Top: 15 to 20 minutes cooking time

Cook carrots in boiling water in saucepan 10 to 15 minutes or until barely tender. Drain well. Add butter. Blend together cornstarch, sugar and salt; stir in orange rind and orange juice. Add to carrots. Cook, stirring constantly, until mixture comes to boiling and carrots are glazed, about 5 minutes.

 Microwave Oven (high setting): 16 to 17 minutes cooking time

Use ingredients listed in basic recipe. Place sliced carrots and butter in 1-qt. glass casserole. Cover and microwave (high setting) 15 to 16 minutes or until almost tender, stirring twice. Combine cornstarch, sugar, salt, grated orange rind and orange juice. Stir into carrots in casserole. Microwave 1 minute or until mixture boils. Stir before serving.

HONOLULU CARROTS

The pressure cooker method reduces the cooking time by two-thirds to only 5 minutes for this pineapple/carrot dish.

BASIC RECIPE — MAKES 6 SERVINGS.

4 c. sliced carrots	½ tsp. salt
1 (13½ oz.) can pineapple chunks	2 tblsp. butter or regular margarine

 Range Top: 17 minutes cooking time

Place carrots in saucepan. Drain pineapple, reserving juice. Add enough water to reserved juice to make 1 c. Add to carrots along with salt. Cover and cook 15 minutes or until carrots are tender. Add pineapple chunks and butter. Heat until pineapple is hot and butter is melted, about 2 minutes.

Microwave Oven (high setting): 16½ to 18½ minutes cooking time

Use ingredients listed in basic recipe. Drain pineapple, reserving ⅓ c. liquid. Combine carrots, salt and ⅓ c. pineapple juice in 1½-qt. glass casserole. Cover and microwave (high setting) 15 to 17 minutes or until carrots are tender, stirring once. Add butter and pineapple chunks. Microwave 1½ minutes or until pineapple is hot and butter is melted.

 Pressure Cooker: 5 minutes cooking time

Use ingredients listed in basic recipe. Place carrots in 4-qt. pressure cooker. Drain pineapple, reserving ½ c. juice. Add ½ c. pineapple juice and salt to carrots. Close cover securely. Place over high heat. Bring to 15 lbs. pressure, according to manufacturer's directions for your pressure cooker. When pressure is reached (control will begin to jiggle), reduce heat immediately and cook 3 minutes. Remove from heat. Reduce pressure instantly by placing cooker under cold running water. Add pineapple chunks and butter. Heat until pineapple is hot and butter is melted, about 2 minutes.

MARINATED CARROT SALAD

Your pressure cooker is such a timesaver! You can cook fresh carrots in only 3 minutes.

BASIC RECIPE — MAKES 8 SERVINGS.

2 lbs. carrots, sliced (4½ c.)

1 onion, sliced and separated into rings

1 green pepper, sliced

1 (10½ oz.) can condensed tomato soup

2 tblsp. ketchup

½ c. sugar

½ c. vinegar

½ c. salad oil

1 tsp. salt

⅛ tsp. pepper

 **Range Top: 7 minutes cooking time**

Place carrots in large saucepan; cover with boiling salted water. Bring to boiling and cook, covered, 7 minutes or until tender-crisp. Drain. Stir onion and green pepper into carrots. Blend together remaining ingredients. Stir into carrot mixture. Cover and refrigerate several hours or overnight.

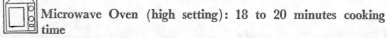 **Microwave Oven (high setting): 18 to 20 minutes cooking time**

Use ingredients listed in basic recipe. Place carrots and ½ c. water in 2-qt. glass casserole. Microwave (high setting), covered, 18 to 20 minutes or until tender-crisp, stirring once. Drain. Stir onion and green pepper into carrots. Blend together remaining ingredients. Stir into carrot mixture. Cover and refrigerate several hours or overnight.

Pressure Cooker: 3 minutes cooking time

Use ingredients in basic recipe. Place carrots and ½ c. water in 4-qt. pressure cooker. Close cover securely. Place over high heat. Bring to 15 lbs. pressure, according to manufacturer's directions for your pressure cooker. When pressure is reached (control will begin to jiggle), reduce heat immediately and cook 3 minutes. Remove from heat. Reduce pressure instantly by placing cooker under cold running water. Drain. Add onion and green pepper to carrots. Blend together remaining ingredients. Stir into carrot mixture. Cover and chill several hours or overnight.

PEPPY CAULIFLOWER

*The cauliflower is cooked whole and topped with an unusual cheese/
mayonnaise sauce spiked with a little mustard.*

BASIC RECIPE — MAKES 6 SERVINGS.

1 medium head cauliflower	1 tsp. prepared mustard
½ c. mayonnaise or salad dressing	½ tsp. salt
½ c. shredded Cheddar cheese	⅛ tsp. cayenne pepper

Oven: 23 to 30 minutes cooking time

Cook cauliflower in boiling salted water in saucepan 15 to 20 minutes or until tender. Meanwhile, combine remaining ingredients. Place cauliflower in 10×6×1½" glass baking dish (1½-qt.). Spread cheese mixture over it. Bake in 400° oven 8 to 10 minutes or until topping melts and bubbles.

Microwave Oven (high setting): 10½ to 13½ minutes cooking time

Use ingredients listed in basic recipe plus 3 tblsp. water. Place cauliflower and 3 tblsp. water in 1½-qt. glass casserole. Cover with waxed paper. Microwave (high setting) 9 to 11 minutes or until tender. Pour off water. Blend together remaining ingredients. Spread over cauliflower. Microwave 1½ to 2½ minutes or until topping melts and bubbles.

SESAME CAULIFLOWER

To save last-minute preparation, slice vegetables the night before and refrigerate. Stir-fry and serve in 8 minutes.

BASIC RECIPE — MAKES 6 SERVINGS.

1 medium head cauliflower (2 lbs.)	½ c. sliced green onions
3 tblsp. sesame seeds	⅓ c. water
¼ c. butter or regular margarine	¼ c. chopped fresh parsley
	1 tsp. salt
	⅛ tsp. pepper

 Range Top: 8 minutes cooking time

Prepare and assemble all ingredients before cooking. Break cauliflower into flowerets. Cut each floweret through stem into ¼" slices. Heat 12" skillet over medium-high heat. Add sesame seeds. Cook and stir until seeds are golden. Remove and reserve. Turn heat to medium. Add butter and melt. Stir in cauliflower and onions until vegetables are coated with butter. Add water. Cover and steam 8 minutes or until cauliflower is tender-crisp, stirring twice. Stir in parsley, sesame seeds, salt and pepper.

 Electric Frypan: 6 minutes cooking time

Use ingredients listed in basic recipe, but increase water from ⅓ to ½ c. Prepare and assemble all ingredients before cooking. Cut cauliflower as for Range Top. Heat electric frypan to 350°. Add sesame seeds. Cook, stirring constantly, until seeds are golden. Remove and reserve. Turn heat to 250°. Add butter and melt. Stir in cauliflower and onion until vegetables are coated with butter. Add ½ c. water. Cover and steam 6 minutes, with vent closed, or until cauliflower is tender-crisp, stirring once. Stir in parsley, sesame seeds, salt and pepper.

Electric Wok: 6 minutes cooking time

Use ingredients listed in basic recipe, but decrease water from ⅓ to ¼ c. Prepare and assemble all ingredients before cooking. Cut cauliflower as for Range Top. Turn wok to 350°. Add sesame seeds. Cook, stirring constantly, until seeds are golden. Remove and reserve. Turn heat to 250°. Add butter and melt. Stir in cauliflower and onion until vegetables are coated with butter. Add ¼ c. water, cover and steam 6 minutes or until cauliflower is tender-crisp, stirring once. Stir in parsley, sesame seeds, salt and pepper.

SCALLOPED CORN

Use your toaster-oven when it's just too hot to turn on your conventional oven. The perfect accompaniment for barbecued meats.

BASIC RECIPE — MAKES 4 TO 5 SERVINGS.

1 (17 oz.) can cream-style corn
1 (2 oz.) jar pimientos, drained and chopped
1 tsp. grated onion
1 egg, beaten

½ tsp. salt
⅛ tsp. pepper
¾ c. cracker crumbs
2 tblsp. butter or regular margarine
Paprika

 Oven: 22 minutes baking time

Combine corn, pimientos, onion, egg, salt, pepper and ½ c. of the cracker crumbs. Spread evenly in 8″ square baking pan. Melt butter in small saucepan, about 2 minutes. Toss with remaining ¼ c. cracker crumbs. Sprinkle crumbs over corn. Sprinkle with paprika. Bake in 350° oven 20 minutes.

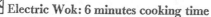 Microwave Oven (high setting): 9 to 11 minutes cooking time

Use ingredients listed in basic recipe. Combine corn mixture as for Oven. Spread evenly in 1-qt. glass casserole. Sprinkle with remaining

¼ c. cracker crumbs, dot with butter and sprinkle with paprika. Microwave (high setting) 9 to 11 minutes or until mixture is set in center. Let stand 4 to 5 minutes before serving.

 Toaster-Oven: 22 minutes cooking time
Use ingredients listed in basic recipe. Prepare as for Oven. Place in greased 8″ square baking pan. Bake at 350° for 20 minutes.

GREENS WITH HAM HOCKS

Use fresh turnip greens from your garden when they are in season. Just reduce cooking time according to your taste.
BASIC RECIPE — MAKES 6 SERVINGS.

3 lbs. smoked ham hocks or
   shanks
2 tblsp. cooking oil
1 onion, sliced
¼ tsp. ground savory

¼ tsp. pepper
4 c. water
3 (10 oz.) pkgs. frozen turnip
   greens

 Range Top: 3 hours cooking time
Brown ham hocks in hot oil in Dutch oven, about 10 minutes. Pour off drippings. Add onion, savory, pepper and water. Bring to boiling. Reduce heat and simmer, covered, 2 hours 30 minutes. Pour off cooking liquid. Skim off fat. Remove ham hocks and cut in bite-size pieces. Boil turnip greens in cooking liquid 20 minutes or until tender. Add ham hocks and reheat. Serve with vinegar.

 Pressure Cooker: 1 hour 15 minutes cooking time
Use ingredients listed in basic recipe, but decrease water from 4 c. to 1½ c. Brown ham hocks in hot oil in 4-qt. pressure cooker, about 10

minutes. Pour off drippings. Add onion, savory, pepper and 1½ c. water. Close cover securely. Place over high heat. Bring to 15 lbs. pressure, according to manufacturer's directions for your pressure cooker. When pressure is reached (control will begin to jiggle), reduce heat immediately and cook 25 minutes. Remove from heat. Let pressure drop of its own accord. Remove ham hocks and cut in bite-size pieces. Pour cooking liquid into 2-c. measuring cup. Skim off fat. If necessary, add water to make 2 c. Return liquid to pressure pan. Add turnip greens. Close cover securely. Place over high heat. Bring to 15 lbs. pressure, according to manufacturer's directions for your pressure cooker. When pressure is reached (control will begin to jiggle), reduce heat immediately and cook 10 minutes. Reduce pressure at once by placing cooker under cold running water. Add ham hocks to greens; reheat, about 10 minutes. Serve with vinegar.

WILTED LEAF LETTUCE

Your electric wok is so handy when preparing this salad. You heat dressing, toss and serve salad right in the wok.

BASIC RECIPE — MAKES 6 SERVINGS.

6 slices bacon	½ tsp. salt
¼ c. vinegar	2 qts. torn leaf lettuce
2 tblsp. water	¼ c. chopped green onions
2 tblsp. sugar	2 hard-cooked eggs, chopped

Range Top: 8 to 10 minutes cooking time

Cook bacon in skillet, 6 to 8 minutes or until crisp. Drain on paper towels, crumble and set aside. Pour off all but 3 tblsp. bacon drippings. Combine drippings with vinegar, water, sugar and salt. Heat to boiling, stirring to dissolve sugar, about 2 minutes. Combine lettuce, onions and bacon. Add hot vinegar mixture and toss to coat leaves. Garnish with hard-cooked eggs. Serve at once.

Microwave Oven (high setting): 7 to 9 minutes cooking time
Use ingredients listed in basic recipe, but chop bacon. Place bacon in a
2-qt. glass casserole. Cover with paper toweling. Microwave (high setting) 6 to 8 minutes or until crisp. Stir twice to prevent bacon pieces
from sticking together. Measure 3 tblsp. bacon drippings. Combine in
2-c. glass measuring cup with vinegar, water, sugar and salt. Microwave until boiling, about 1 minute. Stir to dissolve sugar. Combine lettuce, green onions and bacon. Pour hot vinegar mixture over lettuce
and toss to coat leaves. Top with hard-cooked eggs. Serve at once.

Electric Wok: 8 minutes cooking time
Use ingredients listed in basic recipe, but chop bacon. Heat electric
wok to 350°. Add bacon and cook 7 minutes, stirring frequently, or
until bacon is crisp. Remove bacon, drain on paper towels and set
aside. Pour off all but 3 tblsp. bacon drippings. Add vinegar, water,
sugar and salt. Heat to boiling, stirring to dissolve sugar, about 1 minute. Turn off heat. Add lettuce, onion and bacon and toss to coat
leaves. Serve at once in wok garnished with hard-cooked eggs.

FRENCH-FRIED ONIONS

*Now you can prepare crusty onion rings at home. To save time at the
last minute, fry ahead and reheat in 300° oven a few minutes.*
BASIC RECIPE — MAKES 6 SERVINGS.

2 large onions	Cooking oil
2 c. pancake mix	Salt
1⅓ c. water	

Range Top: 2 to 3 minutes cooking time
Cut onion in ¼" slices; separate into rings. Stir together pancake mix
and water to make a smooth batter. Pour 1" cooking oil into heavy

12″ skillet. Heat to 375° (use frying thermometer). Dip onion rings into batter with fork. Hold a few seconds over batter in bowl to catch drips. Cook, a few at a time, 2 to 3 minutes or until golden brown, turning once. Drain on paper toweling. Sprinkle with salt.

Electric Frypan: 2 to 3 minutes cooking time

Use ingredients listed in basic recipe. Prepare as for Range Top. Heat 1″ oil in electric frypan set at 400°. (This helps to maintain a temperature of 375° throughout the frying.) Cook, a few onion rings at a time, 2 to 3 minutes or until golden brown, turning once. Drain on paper toweling. Sprinkle with salt.

Electric Wok: 3 to 4 minutes cooking time

Use ingredients listed in basic recipe, but in decreased amounts. Cut 1 large onion in $1/4$″ slices; separate in rings. Stir together 1 c. pancake mix and $2/3$ c. water to make a smooth batter. Pour 1″ oil into electric wok. Set heat at 425°. Dip onion rings into batter with fork. Hold a few seconds over batter in bowl to catch drips. Cook, a few at a time, 3 to 4 minutes or until golden brown, turning once. Drain on paper toweling. Sprinkle with salt. Makes 3 servings.

TENDER-CRISP PEA PODS

If you've never tried stir-fried vegetables, try this recipe. Pea pods are especially suited to this cooking method.

BASIC RECIPE — MAKES 6 TO 8 SERVINGS.

3 tblsp. cooking oil
3 (6 oz.) pkgs. frozen pea pods
3 tblsp. chopped green onions
$3/4$ c. sliced water chestnuts

$1 1/2$ tsp. chicken bouillon
 granules
$1 1/2$ tblsp. soy sauce

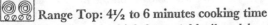 **Range Top: 4½ to 6 minutes cooking time**

Heat 12″ skillet over high heat. Add oil and heat. Add pea pods and onions. Stir and fry until pea pods are hot, but still crisp, about 4 to 5 minutes. Add water chestnuts, chicken bouillon granules and soy sauce. Cook and stir until water chestnuts are heated, 30 to 60 seconds.

Electric Frypan: 5 to 7 minutes cooking time

Use ingredients listed in basic recipe. Heat electric frypan to 400°. Add oil and heat. Add pea pods and onions. Stir and fry 4 to 5 minutes until pea pods are hot. Add water chestnuts, chicken bouillon granules and soy sauce; cook and stir until water chestnuts are heated, 1 to 2 minutes.

Microwave Oven (high setting): 5½ to 6½ minutes cooking time

Use ingredients listed in basic recipe, but in different amounts. Stir 2 tblsp. cooking oil, 2 (6 oz.) pkgs. frozen pea pods, ½ c. sliced water chestnuts and 2 tblsp. chopped green onions in 8″ square glass baking dish until vegetables are coated with oil. Cover with plastic wrap. Microwave (high setting) 5 to 6 minutes or until pea pods are tender-crisp, stirring once. Stir in 1 tsp. chicken bouillon granules and 1 tblsp. soy sauce. Microwave, covered, 30 seconds. Makes 5 servings.

Electric Wok: 3½ to 4 minutes cooking time

Use ingredients listed in basic recipe, but in different amounts. Heat wok to 375°. Add 2 tblsp. cooking oil and heat. Add 2 (6 oz.) pkgs. frozen pea pods and 2 tblsp. chopped green onions. Cook and stir 3 minutes or until pea pods are hot, but still crisp. Add ½ c. sliced water chestnuts, 1 tsp. chicken bouillon granules and 1 tblsp. soy sauce. Cook and stir until water chestnuts are heated, 30 to 60 seconds. Makes 5 servings.

CREAMED PEAS AND ONIONS

You can actually prepare this vegetable dish faster on top of the range than in the microwave oven.

BASIC RECIPE — MAKES 6 SERVINGS.

1 (10 oz.) pkg. frozen peas
1 (9 oz.) pkg. frozen onions in
  cream sauce
1 tblsp. chopped pimientos

⅓ c. dry bread crumbs
2 tblsp. butter or regular
  margarine, melted

Range Top: 4 minutes cooking time

Cook peas and onions as directed on packages in separate saucepans, about 4 minutes. Drain peas. Stir peas into onions; add pimientos. Toss together bread crumbs and melted butter. Pour vegetables into serving dish; sprinkle buttered crumbs on top.

Microwave Oven (high setting): 11½ to 14½ minutes cooking time

Use ingredients listed in basic recipe, but add ¼ tsp. salt. Combine peas and onions in 1½-qt. glass casserole. Add salt and pimientos. Cover and microwave (high setting) 10 to 12 minutes. Stir once during cooking. Microwave butter in small glass dish 30 seconds or until melted. Add bread crumbs to butter and toss. Sprinkle over vegetables. Microwave 1 to 2 minutes or until hot.

CARROT-POTATO KUGEL

In a hurry? You can cook this dish in one-quarter of the time if you microwave it. Sprinkle with red paprika before serving.
BASIC RECIPE — MAKES 6 SERVINGS.

2 c. grated raw potatoes	⅛ tsp. pepper
1 c. grated raw carrot	½ c. unsifted flour
⅓ c. grated onion	3 tblsp. cooking oil
1 tsp. salt	2 eggs, beaten

Oven: 40 to 45 minutes baking time

Thoroughly combine potato, carrot, onion, salt, pepper, flour and cooking oil in bowl. Stir in eggs; mix well. Spread in greased 8″ square baking pan. Bake in 350° oven 40 to 45 minutes or until wooden pick inserted in center comes out clean. Serve hot.

Microwave Oven (high setting): 10 to 11 minutes cooking time

Use ingredients listed in basic recipe. Prepare as for Oven. Spread in a lightly oiled 8″ square glass baking dish. Microwave, covered with waxed paper, 10 to 11 minutes or until wooden pick inserted in center comes out clean, giving dish quarter turns twice. Let stand 5 minutes before cutting. Serve hot.

Toaster-Oven: 40 minutes baking time

Use ingredients listed in basic recipe. Prepare as for Oven. Spread in greased 8″ square baking pan. Bake in toaster-oven at 350° for 40 minutes or until wooden pick inserted in center comes out clean. Serve hot.

GOLDEN CRUMBED POTATOES

Bake chicken alongside this delicious potato dish. You'll use your oven more efficiently this way.

BASIC RECIPE — MAKES 6 SERVINGS.

3 tblsp. butter or regular
   margarine
⅓ c. corn flake crumbs

1 tsp. seasoned salt
¼ tsp. pepper
6 medium potatoes, pared

Oven: 56 minutes cooking time

Melt butter in saucepan, about 1 minute. Combine corn flake crumbs, salt and pepper in small bowl. Roll potatoes in butter, then in crumb mixture. Place in shallow pan. Bake in 400° oven 55 minutes or until tender.

Microwave Oven (high setting): 17½ minutes cooking time

Use ingredients listed in basic recipe. Microwave (high setting) butter in small glass bowl 30 seconds or until melted. Roll potatoes in butter, then in mixture of corn flake crumbs, salt and pepper. Place in 8" square glass baking dish. Cover with paper towel. Microwave 17 minutes, giving dish a quarter turn once. Let stand 3 minutes.

HOT GERMAN POTATO SALAD

Use red or white-skinned salad potatoes for this recipe because they are waxy and hold their shape when sliced.

BASIC RECIPE — MAKES 6 SERVINGS.

5 medium potatoes	1½ tsp. salt
5 slices bacon	¼ tsp. pepper
½ c. chopped onion	½ c. water
2 tblsp. sugar	¼ c. vinegar
1 tblsp. flour	½ c. sliced red radishes

Range Top: 40 to 50 minutes cooking time

Cook unpared potatoes in boiling water 25 to 35 minutes or until tender. Meanwhile, fry bacon in skillet until crisp, about 6 minutes. Remove bacon, drain on paper towels and reserve. Cook onions in bacon drippings 5 minutes or until partially tender. Blend together sugar, flour, salt, pepper, water and vinegar. Add to onion mixture. Cook, stirring constantly, until mixture thickens and bubbles, about 2 minutes. Remove from heat. Peel and slice potatoes; crumble crisp bacon. Add potatoes to onion mixture; heat well, about 2 minutes. Add radishes and toss. Serve warm sprinkled with bacon.

Microwave Oven (high setting): 23 to 28 minutes cooking time

Use ingredients listed in basic recipe. Arrange potatoes in circle on paper towels in microwave oven. Microwave (high setting) 14 to 16 minutes, turning potatoes over once. Remove and set aside. Arrange bacon slices in 2-qt. glass casserole so they do not touch one another. Microwave 4 to 5 minutes or until crisp. Remove bacon. Add onion to drippings. Microwave, covered with paper towel, 2 to 3 minutes or until partially cooked. Blend together sugar, flour, salt, pepper, water and vinegar. Add to onion mixture. Microwave, uncovered, 2 to 3 minutes or until mixture boils. Meanwhile, peel and slice potatoes;

crumble bacon. Add potatoes to onion mixture; microwave 1 minute. Add radishes and toss. Serve hot topped with bacon.

Pressure Cooker: 28 minutes cooking time
Use ingredients listed in basic recipe, but add 1½ c. water for cooking potatoes. Fry bacon until crisp in 4-qt. pressure cooker, about 6 minutes. Remove bacon, drain, crumble and reserve. Cook onion in bacon drippings 5 minutes or until partially cooked. Remove onion mixture to bowl. Place unpeeled potatoes in pressure pan. Add 1½ c. water. Adjust cover securely. Place over high heat. Bring to 15 lbs. pressure, according to manufacturer's directions for your pressure cooker. When pressure is reached (control will begin to jiggle), reduce heat immediately and cook 15 minutes. Remove from heat. Reduce pressure instantly by placing cooker under cold running water. Drain. Peel and slice potatoes. Combine sugar, flour, salt, pepper, vinegar and remaining ½ c. water. Place in pressure cooker along with onion mixture. Cook and stir until mixture thickens and boils, about 2 minutes. Add potatoes and radishes. Toss gently. Serve warm sprinkled with bacon.

PARTY POTATOES

The potatoes are softer when cooked in the pressure cooker versus the other two appliances, but still are acceptable.

BASIC RECIPE — MAKES 6 SERVINGS.

4 c. pared, cubed potatoes (4 to 5 medium)	½ c. cottage cheese
¼ c. sliced green onions	1 tblsp. butter or regular margarine
¾ tsp. salt	¼ c. dry bread crumbs
½ c. dairy sour cream	

Range Top: 16 minutes cooking time
Place potatoes, green onions and salt in saucepan. Add enough water to cover. Bring to boiling. Cover and simmer 10 minutes or until vege-

tables are tender. Drain well. Stir in sour cream and cottage cheese. Heat 5 minutes, but do not boil. Meanwhile, melt butter in small saucepan, about 1 minute. Toss together butter and bread crumbs. Put vegetable mixture in serving dish; top with buttered crumbs.

Microwave Oven (high setting): 11 minutes cooking time

Use ingredients listed in basic recipe, but add ½ c. water. Place butter in 1-c. glass measuring cup. Microwave (high setting) 30 seconds or until melted. Add bread crumbs and toss. Place potatoes, green onions, salt and ½ c. water in 1½-qt. glass casserole. Cover and microwave 10 minutes, giving dish one quarter turn once. Drain well. Add sour cream and cottage cheese; mix well. Microwave 30 seconds, or until hot. Top with buttered crumbs.

Pressure Cooker: 9 minutes cooking time

Use ingredients listed in basic recipe, but add ½ c. water. Combine potatoes, green onions, salt and ½ c. water in 4-qt. pressure cooker. Close cover securely. Place over high heat. Bring to 15 lbs. pressure, according to manufacturer's directions for your pressure cooker. When pressure is reached (control will begin to jiggle), reduce heat immediately and cook 3 minutes. Remove from heat. Reduce pressure instantly by placing cooker under cold running water. Drain potatoes. Gently stir in sour cream and cottage cheese. Heat 5 minutes, but do not boil. Meanwhile, melt butter in small saucepan, about 1 minute. Add bread crumbs and toss. Put vegetable mixture in serving dish; top with buttered crumbs.

EASY SCALLOPED POTATOES

You can substitute any canned condensed cream soup for celery soup in this recipe.

BASIC RECIPE — MAKES 5 SERVINGS.

4 c. sliced, pared potatoes	1 (10¾ oz.) can condensed
¼ c. chopped onion	cream of celery soup
¾ tsp. salt	½ c. milk
⅛ tsp. pepper	

Oven: 1 hour 30 minutes baking time

Place half of potatoes in greased 1½-qt. casserole. Top with half of onion. Repeat layers. Sprinkle with salt and pepper. Blend together soup and milk. Pour over potatoes. Cover and bake in 350° oven 1 hour. Remove cover and continue baking 30 minutes.

Microwave Oven (high setting): 20 minutes cooking time

Use ingredients listed in basic recipe, but add a sprinkling of paprika. Combine ingredients in greased 2-qt. glass casserole as for Oven. Cover and microwave (high setting) 20 minutes, stirring every 5 minutes. Sprinkle with paprika. Let stand 5 minutes.

STUFFED BAKED POTATOES

These potatoes can be made ahead and refrigerated. Just heat quickly in any one of the following appliances.

BASIC RECIPE — MAKES 6 SERVINGS.

6 medium baking potatoes	1 tsp. salt
½ c. dairy sour cream	⅛ tsp. pepper
¼ c. butter or regular	1 tblsp. chopped green onions
margarine	¼ c. shredded Cheddar cheese
¼ c. milk	

Oven: 55 to 70 minutes baking time

Prick potatoes several times with kitchen fork. Bake in 425° oven 45 to 60 minutes or until tender. Cut slice from top of each potato. Scoop out insides, reserving shells. Combine potatoes, sour cream, butter, milk, salt and pepper in small mixing bowl. Beat until fluffy. Stir in onion and spoon into shells. Sprinkle with cheese. Heat in 375° oven 10 to 12 minutes or until hot and cheese is melted. (When potatoes are refrigerated, reheat 20 minutes, adding cheese the last 3 or 4 minutes.)

Microwave Oven (high setting): 18 to 20 minutes cooking time

Use ingredients listed in basic recipe, but increase shredded cheese from ¼ to ½ c. Prick potatoes several times with kitchen fork. Arrange in a circle on paper toweling in microwave oven. Leave at least 1″ space between potatoes. Microwave (high setting) 13 to 15 minutes or until tender, rearranging them once. Cut in half lengthwise. Scoop out insides, reserving shells. Combine as for Oven. Beat until fluffy. Add onion and spoon into shells. Arrange on serving plate. Microwave 4 minutes, giving plate a quarter turn once. Top with cheese. Microwave 1 minute or until cheese is melted. (When potatoes are refrigerated, microwave 6 minutes, giving plate a quarter turn once; top with cheese and microwave 1 minute longer.)

 Toaster-Oven: 55 to 70 minutes baking time

Use ingredients listed in basic recipe, but reduce amounts as follows. Prick 4 medium potatoes several times with kitchen fork and bake in toaster-oven at 425° for 45 to 60 minutes or until tender. Cut slice from top of each potato. Scoop out insides, reserving shells. Combine potatoes, ⅓ c. dairy sour cream, 3 tblsp. butter, 3 tblsp. milk, ¾ tsp. salt and a dash of pepper in small mixing bowl. Beat until fluffy. Stir in 2 tsp. chopped onion and spoon into shells. Sprinkle with 3 tblsp. shredded cheese. Heat in toaster-oven at 375° 10 minutes or until hot and cheese is melted. (When potatoes are refrigerated, reheat 20 minutes, adding cheese the last 3 or 4 minutes.) Makes 4 servings.

RATATOUILLE

Now you have a choice of three different appliances when you make this popular Mediterranean vegetable dish . . . serve hot or cold.

BASIC RECIPE — MAKES 8 SERVINGS.

1 c. chopped onion
1 clove garlic, minced
2 tblsp. cooking oil
1 lb. medium eggplant, pared and cubed (4¼ c.)
3 medium zucchini, sliced (3 c.)

1 green pepper, cut in strips
4 tomatoes, peeled and chopped
1 tsp. salt
½ tsp. basil leaves
½ tsp. thyme leaves
¼ tsp. pepper

Range Top: 35 to 50 minutes cooking time

Cook onion and garlic in hot oil in Dutch oven 5 minutes or until soft. Add remaining ingredients. Cover and cook over low heat 15 minutes. Uncover and continue cooking until vegetables are tender and juice is thickened, 15 to 30 minutes.

Microwave Oven (high setting): 27 to 32 minutes cooking time

Use ingredients listed in basic recipe, but use 1 tblsp. instead of 2 tblsp. cooking oil. Combine onion, garlic and 1 tblsp. oil in 2½-qt. glass casserole. Cover and microwave (high setting) 4 minutes or until onion is soft. Add eggplant, zucchini, and green pepper. Cover with paper towel. Microwave 8 minutes, stirring once. Stir in tomatoes, salt, basil, thyme and pepper. Microwave 15 to 20 minutes or until vegetables are tender. Let stand 5 minutes.

 Slow Cooker: 4 hours 5 minutes cooking time

Use ingredients listed in basic recipe. Cook onion and garlic in hot oil in small skillet 5 minutes or until soft. Place sauteed onion mixture and remaining ingredients in slow cooker. Stir well. Cover and cook on high 4 hours.

BUFFET SPINACH

Frozen rarebit makes a tasty cheese sauce for this dish. French-fried onion rings make a delicious and attractive garnish.

BASIC RECIPE — MAKES 6 SERVINGS.

6 slices bacon
2 (10 oz.) pkgs. frozen chopped
  spinach
½ c. sliced water chestnuts

1 (10 oz.) pkg. frozen Welsh
  rarebit, thawed
1 (3 oz.) can French-fried
  onions

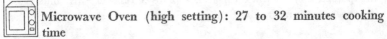 **Oven: 46 minutes cooking time**

Cook bacon in skillet 6 minutes or until crisp. Drain on paper towels and crumble. Meanwhile, cook spinach in 1 c. boiling salted water in saucepan 10 minutes or until tender. Drain spinach by pressing in sieve. Combine spinach, water chestnuts, rarebit and half of onions.

Turn into greased 1½-qt. casserole. Bake in 350° oven 20 minutes. Top with bacon and remaining onions. Continue baking 10 more minutes.

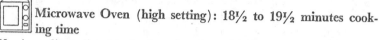 **Microwave Oven (high setting): 18½ to 19½ minutes cooking time**

Use ingredients listed in basic recipe, but add ¼ tsp. salt. Layer bacon and paper towels in 10×6×1½" glass baking dish (1½-qt.). Microwave (high setting) 5 to 6 minutes or until crisp, giving dish one quarter turn. Remove bacon. Pour off fat. Place spinach in same baking dish. Cover and microwave 8 minutes, stirring once to break up. Drain spinach by pressing in sieve. Combine drained spinach, water chestnuts, half of onions, rarebit and salt. Crumble bacon on top. Microwave 5 minutes, giving dish one quarter turn. Top with remaining onions; microwave 30 seconds.

Toaster-Oven: 46 minutes cooking time

Use ingredients listed in basic recipe. Cook bacon and spinach as for Oven. Place in greased 8" square baking pan. Bake at 350° for 20 minutes. Top with bacon and remaining onions. Continue baking 10 minutes.

HOT SPINACH SALAD

The electric wok makes an attractive serving dish for a buffet supper. Just toss salad with dressing and serve immediately.

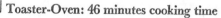

BASIC RECIPE — MAKES 6 SERVINGS.

2 qts. torn spinach, stems removed (10 oz.)
½ c. chopped onion
1 c. halved cherry tomatoes
2 tblsp. sugar
½ tsp. salt

¼ tsp. dry mustard
2 tblsp. lemon juice
1 tblsp. ketchup
½ tsp. Worcestershire sauce
6 slices bacon, chopped

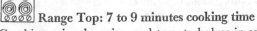 Range Top: 7 to 9 minutes cooking time

Combine spinach, onion and tomato halves in salad bowl. Stir together sugar, salt and mustard. Add lemon juice, ketchup and Worcestershire sauce to sugar mixture. Cook bacon in skillet 6 to 8 minutes or until crisp. Drain bacon on paper towels; set aside. Pour off all but 3 tblsp. bacon drippings. Add lemon juice mixture to skillet. Bring to a boil, about 1 minute. Add bacon to spinach mixture. Pour hot dressing over all; toss well. Serve at once.

Microwave Oven (high setting): 7 to 9 minutes cooking time

Use ingredients listed in basic recipe. Combine spinach, onion and tomato halves in salad bowl. Stir together sugar, salt and mustard in 2 c. glass measure. Add lemon juice, ketchup and Worcestershire sauce to sugar mixture. Place bacon in 2-qt. casserole. Microwave (high setting) 6 to 8 minutes or until crisp. Stir twice to prevent bacon pieces from sticking together. Remove bacon pieces; drain on paper towels; set aside. Pour off all but 3 tblsp. bacon drippings. Add lemon juice mixture to casserole. Microwave until boiling, about 1 minute. Stir to dissolve sugar. Add bacon to spinach mixture. Pour hot dressing over all; toss well. Serve at once.

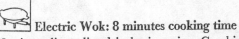 Electric Wok: 8 minutes cooking time

Use ingredients listed in basic recipe. Combine spinach, onion and tomato halves in bowl. Stir together sugar, salt and mustard. Add lemon juice, ketchup and Worcestershire sauce to sugar mixture. Heat wok to 350°. Add bacon and cook, stirring frequently, 7 minutes or until crisp. Remove bacon and drain on paper towels; set aside. Pour off all but 3 tblsp. bacon drippings. Add lemon juice mixture to wok. Bring to a boil, about 1 minute. Turn off heat. Add spinach mixture and bacon. Toss quickly. Serve at once using wok as serving dish.

SPINACH-CHEESE CASSEROLE

We've reduced the size of the basic recipe for the microwave version so it would cook more evenly and efficiently.

BASIC RECIPE — MAKES 8 TO 10 SERVINGS.

3 eggs
¼ c. flour
1 tsp. salt
3 (10 oz.) pkgs. frozen spinach,
   thawed

2 c. cream-style cottage cheese
1 c. cubed sharp, process
   American cheese

 Oven: 1 hour baking time

Beat eggs in large mixing bowl; beat in flour and salt. Drain spinach thoroughly by pressing in sieve. Stir spinach, cottage cheese and American cheese into egg mixture. Place in greased 2-qt. casserole. Cover and bake in 325° oven 1 hour.

 Microwave Oven (high setting): 10 to 12 minutes cooking time

Use ingredients in basic recipe, but in different amounts. Beat 2 eggs in mixing bowl; beat in 2 tblsp. flour and ½ tsp. salt. Drain 2 (10 oz.) pkgs. frozen spinach, thawed, by pressing in sieve. Stir spinach, 1⅓ c. cream-style cottage cheese and ⅔ c. cubed sharp, process American cheese into egg mixture. Place in an 8″ round glass baking dish. Cover with waxed paper. Microwave (high setting) 10 to 12 minutes, giving dish one quarter turn. Makes 6 servings.

SUMMER SQUASH BAKE

You can make the casserole ahead and refrigerate it. Simply add 10 more minutes to baking time in oven method.

BASIC RECIPE — MAKES 6 SERVINGS.

2 qts. sliced yellow summer
    squash or zucchini
¼ c. chopped onion
1 (10½ oz.) can condensed
    cream of celery soup

1 c. dairy sour cream
½ tsp. salt
2 tblsp. butter or regular
    margarine
1 c. herb stuffing mix

Oven: 27 to 37 minutes cooking time

Place squash and onion in large saucepan. Add water to cover. Cook, covered, 5 to 10 minutes or until tender. Drain thoroughly. Blend together celery soup, sour cream and salt in bowl. Fold into squash. Spread into greased 13×9×2″ baking pan. Melt butter in small saucepan, about 2 minutes. Add stuffing mix and toss. Sprinkle on top of squash mixture. Bake in 350° oven 20 to 25 minutes.

Microwave Oven (high setting): 27 minutes cooking time

Use ingredients listed in basic recipe, but use ¼ c. water. Microwave (high setting) butter in small glass bowl 1 minute or until melted. Add stuffing mix and toss. Combine squash, onion, ¼ c. water and salt in large glass mixing bowl. Cover and microwave 20 minutes or until squash is tender-crisp. Stir every 5 minutes. Drain. Blend together soup and sour cream. Stir into squash. Spoon mixture into 12×8×2″ glass baking dish (2-qt.). Microwave 6 minutes, stirring once. Sprinkle with stuffing mixture.

NEW ENGLAND-STYLE SWEET POTATOES

This sweet potato recipe adapts well to all four appliances. Choose the one that fits your time schedule best.

BASIC RECIPE — MAKES 6 SERVINGS.

6 sweet potatoes or yams, peeled
 and cut lengthwise in quarters
 (about 2½ lbs.)
1 c. maple-flavored syrup

3 tblsp. butter or regular
 margarine, melted
1½ tsp. salt

Range Top: 25 minutes cooking time
Place sweet potatoes in 10″ skillet. Combine remaining ingredients; pour over potatoes. Bring to boiling; reduce heat. Cover and simmer 25 minutes or until potatoes are tender. Turn potatoes once or twice during cooking to glaze evenly.

Electric Frypan: 35 to 45 minutes cooking time
Use ingredients listed in basic recipe. Place sweet potatoes in electric frypan. Combine remaining ingredients; pour over potatoes. Cover and cook at 225°, with vent closed, 35 to 45 minutes or until potatoes are tender. Turn potatoes once or twice during cooking to glaze evenly.

Microwave Oven (high setting): 15 to 17 minutes cooking time
Use ingredients listed in basic recipe, but omit water. Place potatoes in 12×8×2″ glass baking dish (2-qt.). Combine maple-flavored syrup, butter and salt. Pour over potatoes. Cover with plastic wrap. Microwave (high setting) 15 to 17 minutes or until potatoes are tender. Stir once or twice during cooking.

Pressure Cooker: 12 minutes cooking time

Use ingredients listed in basic recipe. Place sweet potatoes in 4-qt. pressure cooker. Combine remaining ingredients; pour over potatoes. Close cover securely. Place over high heat. Bring to 15 lbs. pressure, according to manufacturer's directions for your pressure cooker. When pressure is reached (control will begin to jiggle), reduce heat immediately and cook 7 minutes. Remove from heat. Reduce pressure instantly by placing cooker under cold running water. Remove sweet potatoes to serving dish; keep warm. Cook liquid in pressure cooker on high heat about 5 minutes to reduce by about one-half. Pour over potatoes and serve.

SWEET POTATO-APPLE CASSEROLE

You can make better use of your oven space if you bake this dish alongside either roast pork or baked ham. An energy saver!

BASIC RECIPE — MAKES 8 SERVINGS.

6 medium sweet potatoes	½ tsp. salt
6 tblsp. butter or regular margarine	⅓ c. brown sugar, firmly packed
2 apples, pared and sliced	

Oven: 1 hour 42 minutes cooking time

Prick sweet potatoes with fork. Bake in 400° oven 40 minutes or until tender. Melt butter in small skillet, about 2 minutes. When potatoes are cool enough to handle, peel and slice sweet potatoes. Place half of potatoes in greased 2-qt. casserole. Top with half of apples, salt, brown sugar and butter. Repeat layers. Cover and bake in 350° oven 1 hour or until apples are tender.

Microwave Oven (high setting): 33½ minutes cooking time
Use ingredients listed in basic recipe. Prick sweet potatoes with fork.
Arrange on paper toweling in a circle in microwave oven, leaving at
least 1″ between potatoes. Microwave (high setting) 18 minutes or
until tender, re-arranging potatoes once. When cool enough to handle,
peel and slice. Microwave butter in small glass bowl 30 seconds or
until melted. Place half of potatoes in greased 2-qt. casserole. Top with
half of apples, salt, brown sugar and butter. Repeat layers. Cover and
microwave 15 minutes or until apples are tender, giving casserole one
quarter turn.

SWEET POTATO BOATS

*Such an attractive way to serve sweet potatoes. Stuff the potato shells a
day ahead and just reheat at dinner time.*

BASIC RECIPE   —   MAKES 6 SERVINGS.

6 medium sweet potatoes
1 (8½ oz.) can crushed
   pineapple
3 tblsp. butter or regular
   margarine

1 tblsp. brown sugar, firmly
   packed
½ tsp. salt
Chopped pecans

 Oven: 1 hour 12 minutes cooking time
Prick sweet potatoes with fork. Bake in 400° oven 40 minutes or until
tender. Drain pineapple, reserving liquid. Cut slice from top of each
potato. Scoop out insides and place in bowl. Add butter, brown sugar
and salt. Beat until smooth, adding enough reserved pineapple liquid
to moisten. Stir in pineapple. Stuff into sweet potato shells. Top with
chopped pecans. Bake in 400° oven 12 minutes or until hot. Or cool
stuffed sweet potatoes, cover and refrigerate. To serve, bake in 400°
oven 20 minutes or until hot.

Microwave Oven (high setting): 24 to 28 minutes cooking time

Use ingredients listed in basic recipe. Prick sweet potatoes with fork. Arrange on paper toweling in microwave oven in a circle at least 1″ apart. Microwave (high setting) 16 to 18 minutes or until potatoes are tender. Re-arrange sweet potatoes once during cooking. Drain pineapple, reserving liquid. Cut slice from top of each potato. Scoop out insides and place in bowl. Add butter, brown sugar and salt. Beat until smooth, adding enough pineapple liquid to moisten. Stir in pineapple. Stuff into sweet potato shells. Top with chopped pecans. Microwave 3 to 4 minutes or until hot. Or cool, cover and refrigerate. To serve, microwave 8 to 10 minutes or until hot.

BAKED TOMATOES

Heat these tomato halves in your oven while you are baking a beef roast or ham—takes only 20 minutes.

BASIC RECIPE — MAKES 4 SERVINGS.

4 tomatoes	2 tblsp. grated Parmesan cheese
½ c. chopped fresh parsley	1 tsp. seasoned salt

Oven: 20 minutes baking time

Core tomatoes; cut in half crosswise. Place cut side up in greased 13×9×2″ baking pan. Combine remaining ingredients. Sprinkle over tomatoes. Bake in 375° oven 20 minutes.

Microwave Oven (high setting): 6 minutes cooking time

Use ingredients listed in basic recipe. Prepare as for Oven. Place tomatoes cut side up in 12×8×2″ glass baking dish (2-qt.). Combine remaining ingredients; sprinkle over tomatoes. Microwave (high setting) 6 minutes, giving dish one quarter turn.

MEDITERRANEAN ZUCCHINI

This vegetable combo can be cooked quickly whether you choose top of the range or the microwave oven option.

BASIC RECIPE — MAKES 4 SERVINGS.

3 medium zucchini, sliced
(about 1 qt.)
1 (4 oz.) can mushroom stems
and pieces, drained
2 tblsp. chopped onion
1 clove garlic, minced

1 (8 oz.) can tomatoes, cut up
½ tsp. salt
¼ tsp. pepper
2 tblsp. butter or regular
margarine
¼ c. grated Parmesan cheese

Range Top: 8 to 10 minutes cooking time
Combine zucchini, mushrooms, onion, garlic, tomatoes, salt and pepper in saucepan. Cook 6 to 8 minutes or until zucchini is tender. Add butter; stir until melted, about 2 minutes. Serve in individual sauce dishes and sprinkle with Parmesan cheese.

Microwave Oven (high setting): 10 minutes cooking time
Use ingredients listed in basic recipe. Combine zucchini, mushrooms, onion, garlic, tomatoes, salt, pepper and butter in 1½-qt. glass casserole. Cover and microwave (high setting) 10 minutes or until zucchini is tender, giving casserole one quarter turn. Serve sprinkled with Parmesan cheese.

ZUCCHINI PROVENCAL

Try this "end of summer" vegetable dish to use up abundant supplies of fresh zucchini, tomatoes and green peppers from your garden.
BASIC RECIPE — MAKES 4 SERVINGS.

1 onion, thinly sliced and separated into rings
1 green pepper, cut in thin strips
1 clove garlic, minced
2 tblsp. cooking oil
3 medium zucchini, thinly sliced

3 medium tomatoes, peeled and chopped
4 tblsp. tomato paste
¼ c. sliced ripe olives
1 bay leaf
1 tsp. oregano leaves
¾ tsp. salt
¼ tsp. pepper

Range Top: 25 minutes cooking time
Cook onion, green pepper and garlic in hot oil in 12″ skillet 5 minutes, stirring frequently. Add remaining ingredients. Cover and cook over medium heat 10 minutes, stirring frequently. Remove cover. Continue cooking, stirring frequently, until vegetables are tender, about 10 minutes.

Microwave Oven (high setting): 20 minutes cooking time
Use ingredients listed in basic recipe. Stir together onions, green pepper, garlic and oil in 2½-qt. glass casserole. Microwave (high setting), covered, 5 minutes. Stir in zucchini. Microwave, covered, 5 minutes, stirring once. Add remaining ingredients; microwave 10 minutes or until vegetables are tender, stirring 3 times. Cover and let stand 5 minutes.

MIXED VEGETABLE CASSEROLE

Here's a great vegetable dish for the winter months when fresh vegetables are not readily available.

BASIC RECIPE — MAKES 6 TO 8 SERVINGS.

1 (24 oz.) pkg. frozen mixed
   broccoli, cauliflower and
   carrots
1 (10¾ oz.) can condensed
   cream of celery soup
⅓ c. milk
1 tsp. Worcestershire sauce

1 c. shredded sharp process
   American cheese
½ c. sliced water chestnuts
¼ tsp. salt
½ c. coarse rich round cracker
   crumbs

Oven: 25 to 30 minutes baking time

Cook vegetables as directed on package; drain. Blend together soup, milk and Worcestershire sauce in large bowl. Stir in cheese, water chestnuts and salt. Stir in drained vegetables. Spread in greased 13×9×2″ baking pan. Top with cracker crumbs. Bake in 350° oven 25 to 30 minutes.

Microwave Oven (high setting): 15 to 19 minutes cooking time

Use ingredients listed in basic recipe, but instead of milk use ¼ c. water. Place frozen vegetables in 12×8×2″ glass baking dish (2-qt.). Add ¼ c. water. Cover with waxed paper. Microwave (high setting) 8 to 9 minutes or until vegetables are tender, stirring once. Do not drain. Stir in soup, cheese, water chestnuts, Worcestershire sauce and salt. Sprinkle evenly with cracker crumbs. Microwave 7 to 10 minutes or until hot.

CHAPTER SIX

Hospitality Foods

If you are interested in quick, tasty food to share with friends, this chapter is for you. Its recipes are for versatile, informal refreshments that fit into a busy person's schedule.

Take Peppy Ham-Cheese Rollups for an example. You can get them ready, except for heating, before company arrives. It takes from 1 to 5 minutes, depending on the appliance you use, to turn them into piping hot tidbits. Serve them with a beverage or as an accompaniment to a fruit or vegetable salad at a light lunch. For something simpler, consider Zippy Cheese Crackers. Almost everyone likes them. Both the crackers and rollups complement bowls of steaming soup on cold days.

Or if your family likes food served on sticks, turn to the recipe pages that follow. You will find choices of several tempters, such as Deviled Chicken Livers, Peppy Hot Dogs and Teriyaki Beef Bites. And do not overlook Stuffed Mushroom Appetizers. They are a perfect send-off for many beverages and also for hamburgers you want to glorify when serving guests. Lay them on the plates alongside the burgers.

Dips also appear in this recipe chapter. Chili-Cheese Dip with corn chips and Hot Crab Dip are among the several here that will win smiles from family or friends.

Styles in refreshments are changing. Few hosts or hostesses have time to fuss over fancy desserts and elaborate baked foods for most of their entertaining. Concern for good nutrition and a desire to hold down the calorie intake also are incentives to switch to simpler more healthful types of food. But you'll find specialties here that help meet all these needs.

STUFFED MUSHROOM APPETIZERS

To store fresh mushrooms before using, spread on tray, cover with moistened paper towels and refrigerate up to three days.

BASIC RECIPE — MAKES 16.

¼ c. finely chopped onion
¼ c. finely chopped green
   pepper
¼ c. finely chopped celery
3 tblsp. butter or regular
   margarine
1 (3 oz.) pkg. cream cheese,
   softened

⅓ c. dry bread crumbs
½ tsp. salt
⅛ tsp. pepper
1 tblsp. lemon juice
1 tsp. Worcestershire sauce
16 mushroom caps
Paprika

 Oven: 26 to 27 minutes cooking time

Cook onion, green pepper and celery in butter in skillet 6 to 7 minutes or until tender. Combine with cream cheese, bread crumbs, salt, pepper, lemon juice and Worcestershire sauce. Fill mushroom caps with mixture, heaping it. Place in greased 8″ square baking pan. Sprinkle with paprika. Bake in 350° oven 20 minutes. Serve with cocktail picks.

Microwave Oven (high setting): 8¼ minutes cooking time

Use ingredients listed in basic recipe. Place cream cheese in small glass bowl. Microwave (high setting) 15 seconds to soften. Place onion, green pepper, celery and butter in 1-qt. glass casserole. Cover and microwave 4 minutes, stirring once. Stir cream cheese into onion mixture. Add bread crumbs, salt, pepper, lemon juice and Worcestershire sauce. Fill mushroom caps with mixture, heaping it. Place in 8″ square glass baking dish. Sprinkle generously with paprika. Microwave 4 minutes, turning dish once. Serve with cocktail picks.

Toaster-Oven: 26 to 27 minutes cooking time

Use ingredients listed in basic recipe. Prepare them as for Oven. Place filled mushrooms in greased 8″ square baking pan. Sprinkle with paprika. Bake in toaster-oven at 350° for 20 minutes. Serve with cocktail picks.

COCKTAIL SHRIMP ON CREAM CHEESE

This unusual cheese mold is made ahead and topped with hot shrimp sauce just before serving. So easy and delicious.

BASIC RECIPE — MAKES 1 APPETIZER MOLD.

1 (8 oz.) pkg. cream cheese,
   softened
2 tblsp. chopped green onions
   with tops

½ c. cocktail sauce
1 c. small frozen, cooked
   cocktail shrimp
Assorted crackers

Range Top: 5 minutes cooking time

Combine cream cheese and green onions. Mold in foil-lined small bowl or 10-oz. custard cup. Chill. To serve, unmold on serving plate; remove foil. Combine cocktail sauce and shrimp in small saucepan. Stir over low heat 5 minutes or until shrimp are thawed and sauce is hot. Pour over cream cheese. Serve with knife for slicing cheese and with assorted crackers.

Microwave Oven (high setting): 4 to 5 minutes cooking time

Use ingredients listed in basic recipe, but soften cream cheese by microwaving 60 seconds. Stir in green onions. Mold and chill as for Range Top. To serve, unmold on serving plate; remove foil. Measure cocktail sauce in 2-c. glass measuring cup. Add shrimp and microwave (high setting) 3 to 4 minutes or until shrimp are thawed and sauce is hot. Stir once after 2 minutes. Pour over cream cheese. Serve with knife for slicing cheese and with assorted crackers.

DEVILED CHICKEN LIVERS

Coat livers with crumbs early in the day and refrigerate. Then cook livers and prepare sauce at the last minute.

BASIC RECIPE — MAKES 20 APPETIZERS.

8 oz. chicken livers (about 10)	2 tblsp. prepared mustard
3 tblsp. butter or regular margarine, melted	1 tblsp. ketchup
½ c. dry bread crumbs	1 tblsp. water
1 tblsp. butter or regular margarine	2 tsp. Worcestershire sauce
	½ tsp. seasoned salt
	¼ tsp. onion salt

 Oven: 19 minutes cooking time

Cut chicken livers in half. Roll in 3 tblsp. melted butter, then in bread crumbs. Place in greased 13×9×2″ baking pan. Bake in 350° oven 18 minutes. (To check doneness, cut one liver in half. They may be done on the inside, but look pink on the outside.) Melt 1 tblsp. butter in small saucepan, about 1 minute. Add mustard, ketchup, water, Worcestershire sauce, seasoned salt and onion salt. Bring mixture to a boil; pour into bowl. Serve livers on wooden picks with sauce for dipping.

Microwave Oven (high setting): 6½ minutes cooking time

Use ingredients listed in basic recipe. Cut chicken livers in half. Place 3 tblsp. butter in small glass bowl. Microwave (high setting) 30 seconds or until melted. Dip livers in melted butter and then roll in bread crumbs. Place in 10×6×1½″ glass baking dish (1½-qt.). Microwave, uncovered, 5 minutes or until livers are done. Turn and rearrange once during cooking. (Cut into liver to check doneness. It may be done on the inside, but look pink on the outside.) Combine 1 tblsp. butter, mustard, ketchup, water, Worcestershire sauce, seasoned salt and onion salt in small glass bowl. Microwave 60 seconds or until hot; stir to blend. Serve livers on wooden picks with sauce for dipping.

CHICKEN LIVER PATE

You'll need a blender to whirl liver mixture after cooking. Then mixture is refrigerated one day to blend flavors.
BASIC RECIPE — MAKES 2 CUPS.

½ c. butter or regular
    margarine
1 lb. chicken livers
¼ c. chopped onion
1 garlic clove, minced
½ tsp. salt

¼ tsp. pepper
¼ tsp. dried thyme leaves
1 tsp. Worcestershire sauce
⅛ tsp. hot pepper sauce
⅓ c. water

 Range Top: 12 minutes cooking time

Melt butter in skillet, about 2 minutes. Add chicken livers, onion and garlic; cook 5 minutes, stirring occasionally. Add salt, pepper, thyme, Worcestershire sauce, hot pepper sauce and water. Bring to a boil. Reduce heat and simmer, covered, 5 minutes. Place mixture in blender container. Cover and whirl until smooth. Cover and chill in refrigerator at least one day to blend flavors. Serve with melba toast or assorted crackers.

 Microwave Oven (high setting): 9 to 12 minutes cooking time

Use ingredients listed in basic recipe. Place butter in 12×8×2″ glass baking dish (2-qt.). Microwave (high setting) 2 to 3 minutes or until melted. Add livers, onion, garlic, salt, pepper, thyme, Worcestershire sauce and hot pepper sauce. Cover with waxed paper and microwave 7 to 9 minutes or until livers lose pink color inside. Place liver mixture and water in blender container. Cover and whirl until smooth. Cover and chill in refrigerator at least one day before serving. Serve with melba toast or assorted crackers.

BARBECUED CHICKEN WINGS

You can refrigerate this cooked appetizer ahead so you need only to arrange it on a plate when it's time to serve. Pass napkins.

BASIC RECIPE — MAKES 16.

1½ lbs. chicken wings
¾ c. bottled barbecue sauce

Oven: 30 minutes baking time

Remove and discard wing tips. Cut wings in two pieces at joint. Dip in barbecue sauce. Place in greased 13×9×2″ baking pan. Bake, uncovered, in 350° oven 30 minutes. Remove and chill. Serve chicken with extra barbecue sauce for dipping.

Microwave Oven (high setting): 10 to 12 minutes cooking time

Use ingredients in basic recipe. Prepare chicken wings as for Oven. Place 12×8×2″ glass baking dish (2-qt.). Cover with waxed paper. Microwave (high setting) 5 minutes. Rearrange wing pieces. Continue microwaving 5 to 7 minutes or until done. Remove and chill. Serve with extra barbecue sauce for dipping.

PEPPY HAM-CHEESE ROLLUPS

Prepare ham rolls ahead of time and refrigerate. Heating requires only minutes, no matter which appliance you choose.

BASIC RECIPE — MAKES 10.

4 oz. boiled ham, thinly sliced
Dijon-style mustard
3 oz. Muenster cheese (about)

Oven: 3 to 5 minutes baking time

Cut ham slices in half to make 4×2″ strips. Spread with mustard. Cut cheese in thin 3×1″ strips. Place a strip of cheese on ham. Roll as for jelly roll, starting at 2″ side. Fasten with cocktail pick. Repeat until ham is used. Place in 8″ square baking pan. Bake in 400° oven 3 to 5 minutes or just until cheese begins to melt.

 Microwave Oven (high setting): 1 to 1½ minutes cooking time

Use ingredients listed in basic recipe. Prepare them as for cooking in oven. Place rollups in 8″ square glass baking dish. Microwave (high setting) 1 to 1½ minutes or just until cheese begins to melt.

 Toaster-Oven: 3 to 5 minutes cooking time

Use ingredients listed in basic recipe. Place rollups in 8″ square baking pan. Bake in toaster-oven at 400° for 3 to 5 minutes or just until cheese begins to melt.

TERIYAKI BEEF BITES

You can marinate this appetizer several hours, if it suits your schedule. Then cook and serve on heated plate.

BASIC RECIPE — MAKES ABOUT 3 DOZEN.

1 lb. beef tenderloin, 1″ thick	¼ c. soy sauce
¼ c. sherry	2 tsp. lemon juice
¼ c. honey	

 Oven: 6 to 8 minutes baking time

Cut tenderloin in 1″ cubes. Combine sherry, honey, soy sauce and lemon juice in deep bowl. Add meat and stir to coat well. Marinate at least 1 hour. Arrange meat pieces in 13×9×2″ baking pan. Bake in 475° oven 6 to 8 minutes. Serve with wooden picks.

 Microwave Oven (high setting): 8 to 10 minutes cooking time
Use ingredients listed in basic recipe. Prepare ingredients as for Oven. Arrange marinated meat pieces in 12×8×2″ glass baking dish (2-qt.). Microwave (high setting) 8 to 10 minutes, giving dish a half turn once. Serve with wooden picks.

 Toaster-Oven: 7 to 9 minutes cooking time
Use ingredients listed in basic recipe. Prepare ingredients as for Oven. Arrange marinated meat pieces in 8″ square baking pan. Bake at 475° for 7 to 9 minutes. Serve with wooden picks.

ST. PATRICK'S DAY DIP

Keep dip hot in fondue pot and serve with lots of crisp raw vegetables and corn chips or potato chips.
BASIC RECIPE — MAKES 3 CUPS.

½ c. chopped onion
½ c. chopped celery
¼ c. butter or regular
  margarine
3 tblsp. flour
1 (10¾ oz.) can condensed
  cream of celery soup

1 (6 oz.) roll process garlic
  cheese food, cut up
1 (10 oz.) pkg. frozen chopped
  broccoli, thawed
¼ tsp. salt
6 to 8 drops hot pepper sauce

 Range Top: 17 minutes cooking time
Cook onion and celery in melted butter in medium saucepan 5 minutes or until soft, but do not brown. Stir in flour. Add soup, cheese,

broccoli, salt and hot pepper sauce; mix well. Cook over medium heat, stirring constantly, 12 minutes or until cheese is melted and mixture thickens and comes to a boil. Serve hot.

Microwave Oven (high setting): 11 to 14 minutes cooking time

Use ingredients listed in basic recipe. Place onion, celery and butter in medium glass bowl. Microwave (high setting), uncovered, 5 to 6 minutes or until onion is soft. Stir twice during cooking. Stir in flour. Add soup, cheese, broccoli, salt and hot pepper sauce; mix well. Microwave, uncovered, 6 to 8 minutes or until cheese is melted and dip is thickened and hot. Stir every 2 minutes. Serve hot.

Slow Cooker: 2 hours 35 minutes cooking time

Cook onion and celery in melted butter in small skillet 5 minutes or until soft, do not brown. Stir in flour. Place in lightly greased slow cooker. Stir in soup, cheese, broccoli, salt and hot pepper sauce. Cover and cook on high setting 30 minutes or until cheese is melted, stirring twice. Turn to low setting and cook, covered, 2 hours. Serve hot.

TUNA TANTALIZERS

Although the microwave takes almost as long to heat all the appetizers, it will not heat up your kitchen as the oven does.

BASIC RECIPE — MAKES 27 APPETIZERS.

1 (7 oz.) can tuna, drained and flaked
½ c. finely chopped celery
2 tblsp. finely chopped sweet pickle

⅓ c. mayonnaise
2 tsp. lemon juice
1 tsp. prepared mustard
3 slices process American cheese
27 rich round crackers

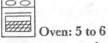 Oven: 5 to 6 minutes baking time

Combine tuna, celery, pickle, mayonnaise, lemon juice and mustard in bowl; blend well. Cut each cheese slice crosswise in thirds, then lengthwise to make 9 small squares. Spread tuna mixture on crackers. Top with cheese. Place on baking sheet. Bake in 350° oven 5 to 6 minutes or until cheese melts.

 Microwave Oven (high setting): 2 minutes cooking time

Use ingredients listed in basic recipe. Prepare tuna-topped crackers as for Oven. Place half of crackers in 12×8×2″ glass baking dish (2-qt.). Microwave (high setting) 60 seconds or until cheese melts. Repeat with remaining crackers.

 Toaster-Oven: 9 to 12 minutes cooking time

Use ingredients listed in basic recipe. Prepare tuna-topped crackers as for Oven. Place 9 crackers in 8″ square baking pan. Bake at 350° for 3 to 4 minutes or until cheese melts. Repeat twice to heat remaining crackers.

PEPPY HOT DOGS

Serve this delicious sweet-sour appetizer in a chafing dish or fondue pot to keep warm for up to two hours.

BASIC RECIPE — MAKES 3½ CUPS.

½ c. plum jelly
½ c. prepared mustard
1 lb. smoked cocktail
   frankfurters or frankfurters
   cut in 1″ lengths*

1 (13½ oz.) can pineapple
tidbits, drained

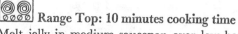 Range Top: 10 minutes cooking time

Melt jelly in medium saucepan over low heat, stirring often, about 2 minutes. Blend in mustard. Stir in frankfurters and pineapple. Cook over low heat 8 minutes or until thoroughly heated, stirring occasionally. Serve with wooden picks.

Microwave Oven (high setting): 8½ minutes cooking time

Use ingredients listed in basic recipe. Place jelly in 2-qt. glass casserole. Microwave (high setting) 1½ minutes or until jelly is melted. Blend in mustard. Stir in frankfurters and pineapple. Microwave 7 minutes or until hot, stirring once. Serve with wooden picks.

* Note: You can use plain cocktail or frankfurters instead of smoked frankfurters in this recipe.

HOT CRAB DIP

This recipe can also be chilled and served as a spread for crackers or small rye rounds.

BASIC RECIPE — MAKES 5 CUPS.

2 (8 oz.) pkgs. cream cheese, cut up
2 (6½ oz.) cans crabmeat, drained, flaked and cartilage removed
2 (5 oz.) jars sharp process American cheese spread
½ c. chopped green onions
¼ c. milk
2 tsp. Worcestershire sauce

Range Top: 8 to 10 minutes cooking time

Combine all ingredients in 3-qt. saucepan. Cook over medium-low heat, stirring constantly, 8 to 10 minutes or until dip is hot and cheeses are melted. Serve hot with chips or melba toast.

Microwave Oven (high setting): 8 to 10 minutes cooking time

Use ingredients listed in basic recipe. Combine all ingredients in 2-qt. glass bowl or casserole. Microwave (high setting) 8 to 10 minutes or until hot and cheeses are melted. Stir after first 3 minutes of cooking and then every 2 minutes. Makes 4½ cups.

 Slow Cooker: 3½ hours cooking time

Use ingredients listed in basic recipe. Combine all ingredients in lightly greased slow cooker. Cover and cook on high setting 30 minutes or until cheeses begin to melt, stirring occasionally. Continue cooking on high, covered, until mixture is smooth and cheese is melted. Turn to low setting and cook, covered, 3 hours or until hot. Makes 4¼ cups.

CEREAL-NUT SCRAMBLE

A favorite American snack that's been adapted to two modern appliances, the microwave and the slow cooker.

BASIC RECIPE — MAKES ABOUT 7 CUPS.

2 c. bite-size shredded wheat squares
2 c. bite-size shredded corn squares
2 c. thin pretzel sticks
1 c. dry roasted peanuts

½ c. butter or regular margarine, melted
1 tblsp. Worcestershire sauce
½ tsp. seasoned salt
¼ tsp. garlic salt

 Oven: 20 minutes baking time

Combine wheat squares, corn squares, pretzel sticks and peanuts in mixing bowl. Combine butter, Worcestershire sauce, seasoned salt and garlic salt. Pour over cereal mixture and toss gently. Spread evenly in 13×9×2″ baking pan. Bake in 350° oven 20 minutes, stirring several times.

Microwave Oven (high setting): 7½ to 9½ minutes cooking time

Use ingredients listed in basic recipe, except do not melt butter. Combine wheat squares, corn squares, pretzel sticks and peanuts in mixing bowl. Place butter, Worcestershire sauce, seasoned salt and garlic salt in 2-cup glass measuring cup. Microwave (high setting) 1½ minutes or until butter is melted. Pour over cereal mixture and toss gently. Spread evenly in 12×8×2″ glass baking dish (2-qt.). Microwave (high setting) 6 to 8 minutes, stirring every 2 minutes.

 Slow Cooker: 3 to 4 hours cooking time

Use ingredients listed in basic recipe. Combine wheat squares, corn squares, pretzel sticks and peanuts in slow cooker. Combine butter, Worcestershire sauce, seasoned salt and garlic salt. Pour over cereal mixture and toss gently. Cover and cook on low setting 3 to 4 hours. Uncover the last 30 to 40 minutes.

HOT CLAM/CHEESE DIP

No need to shred cheese for this quick dip . . . just use process cheese spread and heat until melted. Serve with chips.

BASIC RECIPE — MAKES 1 CUP.

1 (6½ oz.) can minced clams, drained	1 tblsp. finely chopped green pepper
1 (5 oz.) jar sharp process cheese spread	1 tblsp. finely chopped green onions

 Range Top: 5 minutes cooking time

Combine all ingredients in double boiler top. Place over boiling water and cover. Cook, stirring frequently, 5 minutes or until cheese is melted and mixture is smooth. Serve hot with corn or potato chips.

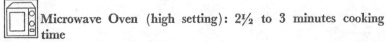

Microwave Oven (high setting): 2½ to 3 minutes cooking time

Use ingredients listed in basic recipe. Combine ingredients in 1-qt. glass casserole. Microwave (high setting) 2½ to 3 minutes or until cheese is melted and mixture is smooth, stirring every minute.

CHILI-CHEESE DIP

You can begin to heat this dip in the slow cooker before your guests arrive. No need to worry that it will burn.

BASIC RECIPE — MAKES ABOUT 3½ CUPS.

- 1 (1 lb.) pkg. pasteurized process cheese spread
- 1 (10½ oz.) can chili without beans
- ½ c. chopped green onions
- 1 (4 oz.) can green chili peppers, drained, seeded and chopped (about ½ c.)

Range Top: 10 to 12 minutes cooking time

Combine all ingredients in 2-qt. saucepan. Cook over low heat, stirring frequently, 10 to 12 minutes or until cheese is melted. Serve hot with tortilla or corn chips.

Microwave Oven (high setting): 6 to 7 minutes cooking time

Use ingredients listed in basic recipe. Combine ingredients in 2-qt. glass bowl. Microwave (high setting) 6 to 7 minutes or until cheese is melted. Stir every 2 minutes to blend ingredients.

Slow Cooker: 2½ to 3 hours cooking time

Use ingredients listed in basic recipe. Combine ingredients in slow cooker. Cover and cook on low setting 2½ to 3 hours or until cheese is melted. Stir two or three times to blend ingredients.

ZIPPY CHEESE CRACKERS

You will note that the microwave oven and toaster-oven time doubles because you will need to heat the crackers in two batches.
BASIC RECIPE — MAKES 24.

1 (3 oz.) pkg. cream cheese
¼ c. crumbled blue cheese
¼ c. chopped almonds
½ tsp. Worcestershire sauce

Few drops bottled hot pepper
  sauce
24 shredded wheat crackers

 Oven: 5 minutes baking time

Stir together cream cheese, blue cheese, almonds, Worcestershire sauce and hot pepper sauce. Spread mixture on crackers. Place in 13✕9✕2″ baking pan. Bake in 400° oven 5 minutes. Serve hot.

Microwave Oven (high setting): 2 minutes cooking time

Use ingredients listed in basic recipe. Combine cheese mixture as in Oven method. Spread on crackers. Place 12 crackers in 8″ square glass baking dish. Microwave (high setting) 45 to 60 seconds. Repeat with remaining crackers. Serve hot.

Toaster-Oven: 10 minutes baking time

Use ingredients listed in basic recipe. Combine cheese mixture as for Oven. Spread on crackers. Put 12 crackers in 8″ square baking pan. Bake at 400° for 5 minutes. Repeat with remaining 12 crackers.

HOT LIVERWURST CANAPES

Since the capacity of the toaster-oven is smaller than the regular oven, you need to bake these canapes in three batches.

BASIC RECIPE — MAKES ABOUT 30.

3 oz. liverwurst
1 (3 oz.) pkg. cream cheese, softened
1 tblsp. milk
1 tblsp. chopped chives
½ tsp. Worcestershire sauce

½ tsp. prepared mustard
Few drops hot pepper sauce
Rye cocktail crackers (about 30)
Sliced pimiento-stuffed olives

Oven: 3 to 5 minutes baking time

Blend together liverwurst, cream cheese and milk in bowl using a fork. Stir in chives, Worcestershire sauce, mustard and hot pepper sauce. Spread on crackers. Top each with a stuffed olive slice. Place on baking sheet. Bake in 400° oven 3 to 5 minutes or until hot.

Microwave Oven (high setting): 2½ minutes cooking time

Use ingredients listed in basic recipe. Place liverwurst and cream cheese in glass bowl. Microwave (high setting) 30 seconds or until softened. Add milk; blend into liverwurst mixture with fork. Stir in chives, Worcestershire sauce, prepared mustard and hot pepper sauce. Spread on crackers. Top each with a stuffed olive slice. Place 15 in 12×8×2″ glass baking dish (2-qt.). Microwave 60 seconds or until bubbly. Repeat with remaining canapes.

Toaster-Oven: 9 to 12 minutes cooking time

Use ingredients listed in basic recipe. Prepare canapes as for Oven. Place 9 canapes in an 8″ square baking pan. Bake in 400° toaster-oven 3 to 4 minutes or until hot. Repeat until all canapes are baked.

NACHOS

The yield of the basic recipe has been adjusted to use each appliance as efficiently as possible.

BASIC RECIPE — MAKES 24 NACHOS.

24 tortilla chips   Sliced Monterey Jack cheese,
½ c. Jalapeno bean dip   cut in 24 (1") squares

Oven: 5 minutes baking time

Place tortilla chips in 13×9×2" baking pan. Top each with 1 tsp. bean dip, then a square of cheese. Bake in 400° oven 5 minutes or until cheese is melted.

Microwave Oven (high setting): 1½ minutes cooking time

Use ingredients list in basic recipe, but use 15 tortilla chips, 5 tblsp. bean dip and 15 (1") squares cheese. Place tortilla chips in 12×8×2" glass baking dish (2-qt.). Top each tortilla chip with 1 tsp. bean dip, then a square of cheese. Microwave (high setting) 60 to 90 seconds or until cheese is melted, giving dish one half turn during cooking. Makes 15 nachos.

Toaster-Oven: 5 minutes cooking time

Use ingredients listed in basic recipe, but use 10 tortilla chips, ¼ c. bean dip and 10 (1") squares cheese. Place 10 tortilla chips in 8" square baking pan. Top each with 1 tsp. bean dip and then a square of cheese. Bake in toaster-oven at 400° for 5 minutes or until cheese is melted. Makes 10 nachos.

Winning Breads and Desserts

This book would not be complete without a section on quick breads and desserts. What is miraculous about the following recipes is that you can cook them your way, adapting your selections to your time and appliances.

Take Pumpkin Bread, a delightful spicy loaf, as an example. The recipe for it accommodates busy women by offering them a choice of five ways to cook it—baking in the conventional range's oven or toaster-oven, steaming in a kettle on range top, microwaving and cooking in the slow cooker. Not all the breads from the same recipe, but cooked with different appliances, are identical, but all of them taste wonderful when sliced thin and spread with butter or cream cheese.

Honey-Nut Rolls are fun to eat and easy to make. You start with a tube of refrigerator biscuits. If you bake them in the conventional oven as a coffee ring, it takes 20 minutes, around 2½ hours in the slow cooker. You can put the rolls in the cooker and forget them until they are done. If timed correctly, you can bring out the yummy, pull-apart, hot loaf at serving time—to the delight of everyone. Be sure to have plenty of paper napkins handy.

Brownie Pudding Cake, shiny with self-made fudge sauce, and plump Raisin-Stuffed Apples tie for blue ribbons in this chapter's dessert collection. Delicious as they are, these two desserts do not surpass all others in taste and good looks, but the recipes for them are the most adaptable. Both dishes may be cooked with four different appliances. This provides considerable leeway in the choice of a meal ending to prepare in the time available.

Raisin-Stuffed Apples, for instance, need to bake 45 minutes in the

conventional oven and 9 to 10 minutes in the microwave oven, although the number of apples is reduced from 6 to 4 apples for microwaving. Even if you microwave a second quartet of apples, the total
minutes required are amazingly brief. In the slow cooker, they cook
about 8 hours, a convenience if you are away from your kitchen.

At the end of the chapter, we've included a few favorite confections
and also a recipe for Chocolate Fudge. Our home economist remarked
that she will never make fudge the old-fashioned way again after testing this recipe in the microwave oven. She liked not having to stir the
fudge constantly during cooking.

BANANA BREAD

*Now we bring old-fashioned banana bread up to date. You can choose
to steam or bake it depending on your schedule.*

BASIC RECIPE — MAKES 1 LOAF.

⅓ c. shortening	½ tsp. baking soda
½ c. sugar	½ tsp. ground cinnamon
2 eggs	1 c. mashed ripe bananas (2
1¾ c. unsifted flour	medium or 3 small)
1 tsp. baking powder	½ c. chopped walnuts

Oven: 45 to 50 minutes baking time

Cream together shortening and sugar in large mixing bowl; add eggs
and beat well. Stir together flour, baking powder, baking soda and cinnamon. Add to creamed mixture alternately with banana. Mix in walnuts. Turn into well-greased 9×5×3″ loaf pan. Bake in 350° oven 45
to 50 minutes or until done. Remove from pan; cool on rack. Slice
thinly and serve warm or cold with butter or cream cheese.

Range Top: 2 hours cooking time

Use ingredients listed in basic recipe. Prepare as for Oven. Turn into
well-greased 2-qt. bowl. Cover tightly with foil. Place on rack in big

kettle or Dutch oven. Pour in boiling water to depth of 1″, adding more water if necessary. Cover and steam over low heat for 2 hours or until done. Remove from bowl; cool on rack. To slice, cut loaf lengthwise in half and then slice thin. Serve warm or cold with butter or cream cheese.

Slow Cooker: 2 hours to 2 hours 30 minutes cooking time
Use ingredients listed in basic recipe. Prepare as for Oven. Turn into well-greased 2-lb. coffee can or 6-c. mold. Place in slow cooker. Cover and cook on high 2 to 2 hours 30 minutes. Remove from can; cool on rack. Serve warm or cold. Cut cylindrical loaf lengthwise to slice. Serve with butter or cream cheese.

PUMPKIN BREAD

This versatile bread can be steamed in slow cooker or on range top. It can also be baked in oven and toaster-oven or microwaved.

BASIC RECIPE — MAKES 1 LOAF.

1 c. unsifted flour
1 tsp. pumpkin pie spice
¾ tsp. baking soda
½ tsp. salt
⅔ c. canned pumpkin
⅔ c. sugar

⅓ c. buttermilk
1 egg
1 tblsp. butter or regular
   margarine, melted
½ c. chopped walnuts

Oven: 45 to 50 minutes baking time
Stir together flour, pumpkin pie spice, baking soda and salt. Combine pumpkin, sugar, buttermilk, egg and butter in mixing bowl; beat until thoroughly combined. Add dry ingredients; beat just until smooth. Stir in walnuts. Turn batter into well-greased 8½×4½×2½″ loaf pan. Bake in 350° oven 45 to 50 minutes or until toothpick inserted in center of loaf comes out clean. Remove from pan; cool on rack. Serve warm or cold.

Range Top: 3 hours 30 minutes cooking time

Use ingredients listed in basic recipe. Combine as for Oven. Turn batter into well-greased 2-lb. coffee can or a 4 to 5-cup pudding mold. Cover with foil. Place on rack in deep kettle. (Three metal screw bands may be used to make a rack.) Add 1" boiling water to kettle. Cover and steam on low heat 3 hours 30 minutes or until done, adding more water if needed. Remove from can or mold to cooling rack. Serve warm or cold.

Microwave Oven (high setting): 6 to 7 minutes cooking time

Use ingredients listed in basic recipe. Combine as for Oven. Turn batter into well-greased 8" square glass baking dish. Microwave (high setting) 6 to 7 minutes or until toothpick comes out clean, turning dish 3 quarter turns during cooking. Cool 10 minutes. Remove from baking dish; cool on rack. Serve warm or cold.

Slow Cooker: 3 hours 30 minutes cooking time

Use ingredients listed in basic recipe. Combine as for Oven. Turn batter into greased and floured 2-lb. coffee can or 4 to 5-c. mold. Cover with foil. Place on rack in slow cooker. Cover and cook on high 3 hours 30 minutes. Remove from can or mold; cool on rack. Serve warm or cold.

Toaster-Oven: 45 minutes baking time

Use ingredients listed in basic recipe. Prepare as for Oven. Turn into well-greased 8½×4½×2½" loaf pan. Bake in toaster-oven at 350° for 30 minutes. Cover top with foil to prevent excessive browning. (Do not let foil touch heating elements.) Continue baking 15 minutes. Remove from baking pan; cool on rack. Serve warm or cold.

DATE-NUT BREAD

If it's too hot to turn on your oven to bake this bread, just microwave it. You and your kitchen will stay cooler.

BASIC RECIPE — MAKES 1 LOAF.

1 c. chopped dates	¾ c. boiling water
¾ c. chopped walnuts	2 eggs, beaten
1½ tsp. baking soda	1 tsp. vanilla
½ tsp. salt	1½ c. sifted flour
3 tblsp. shortening	1 c. sugar

Oven: 50 to 55 minutes baking time

Combine dates, walnuts, baking soda and salt in bowl. Add shortening and water; mix until shortening is melted. Cool 20 minutes. Stir in eggs and vanilla. Combine flour and sugar; beat into date mixture. Spread in greased 8½×4½×2½" loaf pan. Bake in 350° oven 50 to 55 minutes or until toothpick inserted off-center comes out clean. Remove from pan and cool on rack. Wrap and store in refrigerator overnight before slicing.

Microwave Oven (high setting): 8 to 9 minutes cooking time

Use ingredients listed in basic recipe. Prepare as for Oven. Spread in greased 8½×4½×2½" glass loaf dish. Microwave (high setting) 8 to 9 minutes, giving dish a quarter turn every 2 minutes. Let stand in pan 10 minutes. Remove from dish; cool on rack. When cool, wrap and store in refrigerator overnight before slicing.

RAISIN-OATMEAL MUFFINS

You get two more muffins in the microwave version because the batter rises higher than in the conventional oven.

BASIC RECIPE — MAKES 12 MUFFINS.

1½ c. quick-cooking oats
1⅓ c. milk
1¼ c. unsifted flour
2 tsp. baking powder
½ tsp. salt
¼ tsp. ground cinnamon
⅛ tsp. ground nutmeg
2 eggs, beaten

½ c. shortening, melted
⅓ c. brown sugar, firmly packed
½ c. raisins
1 tblsp. butter or regular
   margarine, melted
1 tblsp. sugar
½ tsp. ground cinnamon

Oven: 25 to 30 minutes baking time

Stir together oats and milk in bowl. Let stand 20 to 30 minutes. Stir together flour, baking powder, salt, ¼ tsp. cinnamon and nutmeg in mixing bowl. Mix eggs, shortening, brown sugar and raisins into oatmeal mixture. Make well in dry ingredients. Add oatmeal mixture all at once and stir until mixture is moistened. Fill 12 greased muffin-pan cups ⅔ full. Bake in 400° oven 25 to 30 minutes. Brush muffin tops with melted butter. Sprinkle with mixture of sugar and remaining ½ tsp. cinnamon.

Microwave Oven (high setting): 7 to 9 minutes cooking time

Use ingredients listed in basic recipe. Combine as for Oven. Line 14 (5-oz.) custard cups with paper baking cups. Fill ½ full of batter. Arrange 7 cups in circle in microwave oven. Microwave (high setting) 3½ to 4½ minutes or until tops of muffins are dry. Repeat with remaining batter. Brush muffin tops with melted butter. Sprinkle with mixture of sugar and ½ tsp. cinnamon. Makes 14 muffins.

REFRIGERATOR BRAN MUFFINS

Serve homemade muffins without last-minute preparation. This batter can be stored for 3 days in refrigerator before baking.

BASIC RECIPE — MAKES 18 MUFFINS.

½ c. boiling water
1½ c. whole bran cereal
1 c. buttermilk
¾ c. sugar
⅓ c. shortening

2 eggs
2 c. sifted flour
1¼ tsp. baking soda
½ tsp. salt

 Oven: 20 minutes baking time

Pour boiling water over bran cereal in bowl. Mix well; let cool. Stir in buttermilk. Cream together sugar and shortening in mixing bowl until fluffy. Add eggs and beat well. Sift together flour, baking soda and salt. Stir cooled bran mixture into creamed mixture. Add dry ingredients all at once; stir just until moistened. (Batter will not be smooth.) Store in tightly covered container in refrigerator overnight or until needed. Batter can be stored up to 3 days. To bake, fill greased muffin cups two-thirds full; bake in 425° oven about 20 minutes or until toothpick inserted in center of muffin comes out clean.

 Microwave Oven (high setting): 30 to 45 seconds cooking time per muffin

Use ingredients listed in basic recipe. Prepare as for Oven. Line 6-oz. custard cups with paper baking cups. Place 3 tblsp. batter in each custard cup. Microwave one muffin 45 seconds; two muffins, 1 minute 20 seconds and four muffins, 2 minutes, or until muffins are no longer doughy on top.

 Toaster-Oven: 20 minutes baking time

Use ingredients listed in basic recipe. Prepare as for Oven. Grease 6-cup muffin pan; fill cups two-thirds full. Bake in toaster-oven at 425° about 20 minutes or until toothpick inserted in center of muffin comes out clean.

HONEY-NUT ROLLS

Transform ordinary refrigerated biscuits into a coffee ring that can be baked in the oven or steamed in the slow cooker.

BASIC RECIPE — MAKES 1 COFFEE RING.

2 tblsp. butter or regular
  margarine, melted
¼ c. honey
¼ tsp. ground cinnamon

1 (8 oz.) pkg. refrigerated
  biscuits (10)
1 c. chopped walnuts

Oven: 20 minutes baking time

Combine butter, honey and cinnamon; mix well. Dip biscuits in honey mixture, then in walnuts. Place in well-greased 6 or 6½-cup ring mold. Bake in 350° oven 20 minutes or until done. Turn out immediately, scraping any extra honey-nut mixture from pan onto rolls. Serve warm.

Slow Cooker: 2 hours 30 minutes cooking time

Use ingredients listed in basic recipe. Prepare as for Oven. Place in well-greased 1-lb. coffee can. Place in slow cooker. Cover and cook on high 2 to 2½ hours or until done. Turn out immediately. Serve warm, bottom side up.

SPEEDY STREUSEL COFFEE CAKE

Special microwave cookware isn't needed for this coffee cake. Just use a round glass baking dish with a custard cup in center.

BASIC RECIPE — MAKES 8 SERVINGS.

1½ c. sifted flour	⅓ c. melted butter or regular
2½ tsp. baking powder	margarine
½ tsp. salt	½ c. milk
1 egg, beaten	1 tsp. vanilla
¾ c. sugar	Streusel Topping (recipe
	follows)

 Oven: 25 to 30 minutes baking time

Sift together flour, baking powder and salt into mixing bowl. Combine egg, sugar, butter, milk and vanilla in small bowl; beat with rotary beater until blended. Add milk mixture to flour mixture all at once, stirring just until blended. Spread batter in greased 8-inch square baking pan. Sprinkle with Streusel Topping. Bake in 375° oven 25 to 30 minutes or until toothpick inserted in center comes out clean. Serve warm.

Microwave Oven (high setting): 5 to 7 minutes cooking time

Use ingredients listed in basic recipe. Prepare as for Oven. Place a 6-oz. custard cup bottom-side down in greased 8-inch round glass baking dish. Spread batter in baking dish. Sprinkle with Streusel Topping. Microwave (high setting) 5 to 7 minutes or until toothpick inserted in center comes out clean. Cool 2 minutes in dish. Cut in wedges. Serve warm.

Streusel Topping: Combine ½ c. firmly packed brown sugar, 2 tblsp. flour and ¾ tsp. ground cinnamon in bowl. Cut in 2 tblsp. soft butter or regular margarine until crumbly. Stir in ½ c. chopped walnuts.

HOMEMADE DOUGHNUT BALLS

This easy-to-make doughnut recipe eliminates the rolling and cutting steps. Just drop dough by spoonfuls into hot oil.

BASIC RECIPE — MAKES ABOUT 3 DOZEN.

2 eggs	⅛ tsp. ground nutmeg
½ c. sugar	2 tblsp. butter or regular
½ c. half-and-half	margarine, melted
2 c. sifted flour	Cooking oil
1½ tsp. baking powder	⅓ c. sugar
½ tsp. salt	¼ tsp. ground cinnamon

 Range Top: 2 to 4 minutes frying time for 8 balls

Beat eggs in bowl; beat in ½ c. sugar and half-and-half. Sift together flour, baking powder, salt and nutmeg. Stir into egg mixture, one-third at a time. Fold in melted butter. Pour 1″ oil into heavy 12″ skillet. Heat to 375°. Drop small teaspoonfuls of dough into hot oil, 8 at a time. Fry until brown, 2 to 4 minutes, turning once. Drain on paper toweling. Shake doughnuts, a few at a time, in plastic bag containing mixture of ⅓ c. sugar and cinnamon.

Electric Frypan: 2 to 4 minutes frying time for 8 balls

Use ingredients listed in basic recipe. Prepare as for Range Top. Heat 1″ oil in 12″ electric frypan. Set heat at 400°. (This helps to maintain a temperature of 375°.) Drop small teaspoonfuls of dough into hot oil, 8 at a time. Fry, drain and sugar balls as directed for Range Top.

Electric Wok: 2 to 4 minutes frying time for 6 balls

Use ingredients listed in basic recipe, but in smaller amounts. Beat 1 egg; beat in ¼ c. sugar and ¼ c. half-and-half. Sift together 1 c. sifted flour, ¾ tsp. baking powder, ¼ tsp. salt and a dash of nutmeg. Stir into egg mixture, one-third at a time. Fold in 1 tblsp. melted butter. Pour 1″ oil into electric wok. Set heat at 400°. (This helps to maintain a temperature of 375°.) Drop small teaspoonfuls of dough into hot oil, 6 at a time. Fry until brown, 2 to 4 minutes, turning once. Drain on paper toweling. Shake balls, a few at a time, in plastic bag containing mixture of 3 tblsp. sugar and ⅛ tsp. cinnamon. Makes 1½ dozen.

HIGHLAND SCONES

Imagine serving homemade scones on a hot summer day without turning on the oven. Bake them in your electric frypan.

BASIC RECIPE — MAKES 12 SCONES.

1 c. unsifted flour	⅓ c. shortening
3 tblsp. sugar	½ c. quick-cooking oats
2 tsp. baking powder	½ c. currants
½ tsp. salt	2 eggs, beaten

Oven: 8 to 10 minutes baking time

Stir together flour, sugar, baking powder and salt in bowl. Cut in shortening with pastry blender until mixture is crumbly. Stir in oats and currants. Stir in eggs until mixture is moistened. Turn out on well-floured board; knead lightly 10 to 12 times. Roll or pat dough to an 8×7″ rectangle, about ½″ thick. Cut in 12 (2×2½″) rectangles. Place on ungreased baking sheet. Bake in 450° oven 8 to 10 minutes or until golden brown. Serve warm.

Electric Frypan: 20 to 22 minutes baking time

Use ingredients listed in basic recipe. Prepare scones as for Oven. Brush skillet lightly with shortening. Set heat at 275°. Add scones and bake, covered, vent closed, 10 to 12 minutes or until golden brown on the bottom. Turn and brown on the other side in covered skillet, vent closed, about 10 more minutes. Serve warm.

ITALIAN CROUTONS

These homemade croutons have more flavor than purchased ones. Prepare them on a less busy day and store until needed.

BASIC RECIPE — MAKES 3 CUPS.

1 qt. bread cubes
2 tblsp. Parmesan cheese
1 tsp. mixed Italian herb
seasoning

¼ tsp. garlic salt
⅓ c. butter or regular
margarine, melted

 Oven: 25 to 30 minutes baking time

Spread bread cubes in 13×9×2″ baking pan. Bake in 300° oven 10 to 15 minutes or until cubes begin to dry. Combine cheese, herb seasoning and garlic salt. Sprinkle over bread cubes. Drizzle with butter, tossing to coat cubes. Spread out and continue baking 15 minutes or until crisp and dry, stirring twice.

 Microwave Oven (high setting): 7 to 10 minutes cooking time

Use ingredients listed in basic recipe, but melt butter in microwave oven. Place butter in small glass bowl and microwave (high setting) 60 seconds or until melted. Place bread cubes in 12×8×2″ glass baking dish (2-qt.). Microwave 2 to 4 minutes or until cubes begin to dry. Sprinkle with cheese, herb seasoning and garlic salt. Drizzle with butter, tossing to coat cubes. Microwave 5 to 6 minutes or until crisp and dry, stirring once.

CHERRY COBBLER

We changed the basic recipe to compensate for the lack of browning in the electric frypan and microwave so it would look appealing.

BASIC RECIPE — MAKES 6 TO 8 SERVINGS.

2 c. biscuit mix

1 (21 oz.) can cherry pie filling

½ tsp. ground cinnamon

⅓ c. water

Oven: 25 to 30 minutes baking time

Prepare biscuit mix as directed on package. Roll ½″ thick. Cut in 6 to 8 (2½″) circles. Combine cherry pie filling, cinnamon and water in 9″ square baking pan. Top with biscuits. Bake in 400° oven 25 to 30 minutes or until biscuits are golden brown. Delicious served warm with cream or ice cream.

Electric Frypan: 30 minutes baking time

Use ingredients listed in basic recipe, but add ¼ c. butter or regular margarine. Prepare biscuit mix as directed on package, roll and cut as for Oven. Melt butter in electric frypan at 250°, about 2 minutes. Add biscuits, turning to coat with butter on both sides. Cover. Bake, with vent closed, 15 minutes or until browned. Turn and continue baking, covered, 8 more minutes. Combine cherry pie filling, cinnamon and water. Spoon around biscuits. Cover and heat through, 5 minutes.

Microwave Oven (high setting): 6½ to 7½ minutes cooking time

Use ingredients listed in basic recipe, but add 2 tblsp. butter or regular margarine and ¾ c. honey graham cereal, crushed. Prepare, roll and cut biscuits as for Oven. Microwave (high setting) butter in glass dish 30 seconds or until melted. Dip biscuits in butter to coat both sides, then in honey graham cereal. Combine cherry pie filling, cinnamon and water in 8" square glass baking dish. Top with biscuits. Microwave uncovered 6 to 7 minutes, or until biscuits are done, giving dish 3 quarter turns while cooking.

SPICY APRICOT CRISP

If you cannot find the small size cake mix in your supermarket, you can use one-half of the 18½ oz. package yellow cake mix.

BASIC RECIPE — MAKES 6 SERVINGS.

1 (21 oz.) can apricot pie filling	2 tblsp. brown sugar, packed
1 (9 oz.) pkg. yellow cake mix	1 tsp. ground cinnamon
¼ c. butter or regular margarine, melted	¼ c. finely chopped walnuts

Oven: 35 to 40 minutes baking time

Spread pie filling evenly in 8" square baking pan. Sprinkle with cake mix. Drizzle butter evenly over cake mix. Combine brown sugar, cinnamon and walnuts; sprinkle over mixture. Bake in 350° oven 35 to 40 minutes or until top is golden brown. Delicious served warm or cold with whipped cream, whipped topping or vanilla ice cream.

Microwave Oven (high setting): 11½ minutes cooking time

Use ingredients listed in basic recipe. Spread pie filling evenly in 8" square glass baking dish. Sprinkle with cake mix. Place butter in cup. Microwave (high setting) 30 seconds or until melted. Drizzle butter evenly over cake mix. Combine brown sugar, cinnamon and walnuts; sprinkle over mixture. Microwave 11 minutes, giving dish a half turn once. Delicious served with whipped cream, whipped topping or vanilla ice cream.

Toaster-Oven: 35 to 40 minutes baking time

Use ingredients listed in basic recipe. Place ingredients in 8″ square baking pan as for Oven. Bake at 350° for 35 to 40 minutes or until golden brown. Cover with foil if necessary to avoid excessive browning.

GRANDMA'S APPLE BETTY

The toaster-oven is so handy when you want to bake one item—no need to heat the large one—saves on energy, too!

BASIC RECIPE — MAKES 4 TO 6 SERVINGS.

½ c. butter or regular
   margarine
4 c. bread cubes (½″ cubes)
¾ c. brown sugar, packed
¾ tsp. ground cinnamon

⅛ tsp. ground nutmeg
⅛ tsp. salt
4 c. chopped, pared cooking
   apples (6 medium)

Oven: 40 to 45 minutes baking time

Melt butter in saucepan, about 2 minutes. Toss bread cubes with butter, brown sugar, cinnamon, nutmeg and salt in a large mixing bowl. Place one half of apples in bottom of greased 8″ square glass baking dish. Top with one half of bread mixture. Repeat layers. Bake in 375° oven 40 to 45 minutes or until apples are tender. Serve warm.

Toaster-Oven: 45 minutes baking time

Use ingredients listed in basic recipe. Prepare as for Oven, but use 8″ square baking pan. To prevent excessive browning, cover with foil, crimping foil to rim of pan to hold it in place. Be sure foil will not touch heating elements when you place pan in toaster-oven. Bake at 375° for 30 minutes. Remove pan from oven; remove foil; return pan to oven and bake 15 minutes more or until apples are tender and top is crispy. Serve warm.

Microwave Oven (high setting): 10 to 12 minutes baking
time
Use ingredients listed in basic recipe. Prepare as for Oven. Cover with
waxed paper. Microwave (high setting) 5 minutes. Give dish one half
turn and microwave 5 to 7 minutes longer or until apples are tender.
Serve warm.

 Slow Cooker: 2 to 2¼ hours cooking time.
Use ingredients listed in basic recipe. Prepare as for Oven, except
place layers of apples and bread cubes in slow cooker. Cover and cook
on high 2 to 2¼ hours or until apples are tender. Serve warm.

PEACHY COBBLER

*A lovely cobbler that can be cooked on top of the range. Slightly
spiced peach filling topped with fluffy steamed dumplings.*
BASIC RECIPE — MAKES 6 TO 8 SERVINGS.

3 tblsp. brown sugar, packed
3 tblsp. cornstarch
½ tsp. ground cinnamon
Dash of salt
1 (29 oz.) can sliced peaches
1 tblsp. lemon juice
2 tblsp. butter or regular
  margarine

1 c. biscuit mix
⅓ c. milk
2 tblsp. brown sugar, packed
2 tblsp. finely chopped walnuts
Whipped cream or prepared
  whipped topping

 Range Top: 23 minutes cooking time
Combine 3 tblsp. brown sugar, cornstarch, cinnamon and salt in 10″
skillet. Stir in undrained peaches, lemon juice and butter. Cook and
stir over low heat until thickened and bubbly, about 3 minutes. Keep
hot. Mix biscuit mix with milk in bowl. Drop mixture by tablespoonfuls over hot peaches. Combine remaining 2 tblsp. brown sugar

and walnuts; sprinkle over dumplings. Cook, uncovered, over low heat
10 minutes. Cover and cook 10 more minutes or until dumplings are
fluffy and done. Serve with whipped cream or topping.

 Microwave Oven (high setting): 17 minutes cooking time
Use ingredients listed in basic recipe. Combine 3 tblsp. brown sugar,
cornstarch, cinnamon and salt in 8″ square glass baking dish. Stir in
undrained peaches, lemon juice and butter. Microwave (high setting)
11 minutes, or until thickened and bubbly, stirring after first 6 minutes, then every 2 minutes. Mix biscuit mix with milk in bowl. Drop
by tablespoonfuls over hot peaches. Combine the remaining 2 tblsp.
brown sugar and walnuts; sprinkle over dumplings. Microwave 6 minutes or until dumplings are fluffy and done, giving dish a half turn after 3 minutes. Serve with whipped cream or topping.

STRAWBERRY-PINEAPPLE CRISP .

*Your family can enjoy this crisp in the middle of winter. It's so easy to
prepare and is delicious topped with a pour of cream.*
BASIC RECIPE — MAKES 6 SERVINGS.

1 (10 oz.) pkg. frozen sliced strawberries, thawed	½ c. quick-cooking oats
	¼ c. brown sugar, packed
1 (20 oz.) can pineapple chunks	2 tblsp. flour
	2 tblsp. butter or regular margarine
2 tblsp. brown sugar, packed	
2 tblsp. cornstarch	⅛ tsp. ground cinnamon

Oven: 30 minutes cooking time
Drain strawberries, reserving syrup. Drain pineapple, reserving syrup.
Add enough pineapple syrup to strawberry syrup to make 1 c. Combine 2 tblsp. brown sugar and cornstarch in small saucepan. Blend in
fruit syrup. Cook over medium heat, stirring constantly, until mixture

bubbles and thickens, about 5 minutes. Combine strawberries, pineapple and syrup mixture in greased 10×6×2″ glass baking dish (1½-qt.). Combine oats, ¼ c. brown sugar and flour in bowl. Cut in butter until crumbly. Sprinkle over fruit mixture. Sprinkle with cinnamon. Bake in 350° oven 25 minutes.

Microwave Oven (high setting): 6 to 7 minutes cooking time
Use ingredients listed in basic recipe. Drain strawberries and pineapple and combine syrups as for Oven. Blend together 2 tblsp. brown sugar and cornstarch in 10×6×2″ glass baking dish (1½-qt.). Blend in syrup mixture. Microwave (high setting) 1 minute; stir. Continue microwaving until mixture is bubbly and thickened, 2 to 3 minutes, stirring every 30 seconds. Stir in strawberries and pineapple. Combine oats, ¼ c. brown sugar and flour in bowl. Cut in butter until crumbly. Sprinkle over fruit mixture. Sprinkle with cinnamon. Microwave, uncovered, 3 minutes or until bubbly. Give dish a quarter turn once.

APPLE CRISP

If you like apple crisp with a crusty, golden brown topping, you'll prefer the oven or toaster-oven cooking methods.
BASIC RECIPE — MAKES 6 SERVINGS.

6 sliced, pared apples
¾ c. brown sugar, packed
½ c. unsifted flour
½ c. quick-cooking oats

½ tsp. ground cinnamon
⅓ c. butter or regular
    margarine

Oven: 35 minutes baking time
Place apples in 8″ square baking pan. Combine brown sugar, flour, oats and cinnamon in bowl. Cut in butter until crumbly. Sprinkle over apples. Bake in 375° oven 35 minutes or until apples are tender.

Microwave Oven (high setting): 14 minutes cooking time

Use ingredients listed in basic recipe. Place apples in 8″ square glass baking dish. Combine brown sugar, flour, oats and cinnamon in bowl. Cut in butter until crumbly. Sprinkle over apples. Microwave (high setting), uncovered, 14 minutes or until apples are tender.

Toaster-Oven: 35 minutes baking time

Use ingredients listed in basic recipe. Prepare as for Oven. Bake at 375° for 35 minutes. Cover with foil, if necessary, to avoid excessive browning.

HONEYED DATE CUPS

This unusual dessert requires little preparation time and combines two country favorites: honey and dates.

BASIC RECIPE — MAKES 6 SERVINGS.

¼ c. butter or regular
  margarine
1 c. honey
3 eggs
1¼ c. quick-cooking oats

¾ c. chopped dates
⅛ tsp. salt
1 tsp. vanilla
¼ tsp. ground cinnamon

Oven: 40 minutes baking time

Beat together butter and honey in bowl until creamy. Add eggs; beat well. Stir in oats, dates, salt and vanilla. Turn into 6 buttered (6-oz.) custard cups. Sprinkle with cinnamon. Place in 13×9×2″ baking pan. Pour about 1″ hot water around custard cups. Bake in 325° oven 40 minutes or until knife inserted off center comes out clean.

Electric Frypan: 40 minutes cooking time
Use ingredients listed in basic recipe. Combine as for Oven. Set filled custard cups in electric frypan. Pour cold water around them to a depth of 1″. Cover. Set heat at 220°. Cook, with vent closed, 40 minutes or until knife inserted off center comes out clean.

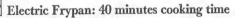 **Microwave Oven (high setting): 7 to 8 minutes cooking time**
Use ingredients in basic recipe, but in smaller amounts. Beat together 3 tblsp. butter or regular margarine and ⅔ c. honey in mixing bowl until creamy. Add 2 eggs; beat well. Stir in ¾ c. quick-cooking oats, ½ c. chopped dates, a dash of salt and ¾ tsp. vanilla. Turn into 4 buttered (6-oz.) custard cups. Sprinkle with ⅛ tsp. cinnamon. Place in 8″ square glass baking dish. Pour about 1″ hot water around them. Microwave (high setting) 7 to 8 minutes or until knife inserted off center comes out clean, giving dish 3 quarter turns. Makes 4 servings.

VERSATILE CREAM PUDDING

You can make four different flavored cream puddings as well as choose from two cooking methods in this recipe.
BASIC RECIPE — MAKES 4 SERVINGS.

½ c. sugar	1 egg, well beaten
2 tblsp. cornstarch	2 tblsp. butter or regular
¼ tsp. salt	margarine
1⅔ c. milk	2 tsp. vanilla

Range Top: 9 minutes cooking time
Combine sugar, cornstarch and salt in medium saucepan. Gradually stir in milk. Cook and stir over medium heat until thickened and bubbly, about 5 minutes. Cook and stir 2 more minutes. Remove from heat. Stir a small amount of hot mixture into egg; gradually return to

hot mixture in saucepan. Cook and stir 2 more minutes. Remove from heat; add butter and vanilla. Stir until butter melts. Pour into dessert dishes; cool slightly. Chill until serving time. Serve with sweetened whipped cream if desired.

Microwave Oven (high setting): 6½ minutes cooking time
Use ingredients listed in basic recipe. Combine sugar, cornstarch and salt in a 1½-qt. glass bowl or casserole. Gradually stir in milk; mix well. Microwave (high setting), uncovered, 3 minutes. Stir and microwave 3 minutes longer, stirring at the end of each minute. Remove from oven. Gradually stir a small amount of hot mixture into egg; return to hot mixture and mix well. Microwave 30 seconds, stirring after each 15 seconds. Remove from oven. Add butter and vanilla. Stir until butter melts. Pour into dessert dishes; cool slightly. Chill until serving time.

Variations
Coconut Cream Pudding: Follow directions for Versatile Cream Pudding, but stir in ½ c. flaked coconut with butter and vanilla.
Butterscotch Cream Pudding: Follow directions for Versatile Cream Pudding, but substitute brown sugar for white sugar and increase butter to 3 tblsp.
Chocolate Cream Pudding: Follow directions for Versatile Cream Pudding, but increase sugar to ⅔ c. and add 1½ (1 oz.) squares unsweetened chocolate with the milk.

PUMPKIN CUSTARD PUDDING

The puddings baked conventionally have a browner top than the ones cooked in the electric frypan and the microwave oven.
BASIC RECIPE — MAKES 6 SERVINGS.

1½ c. canned pumpkin	3 tblsp. sugar
1½ c. milk	2 tsp. pumpkin pie spice
3 eggs	½ tsp. salt
½ c. brown sugar, packed	

 Oven: 50 to 60 minutes baking time

Combine all ingredients in bowl and beat with rotary beater until smooth. Pour into 6 (6 oz.) custard cups. Place in 13×9×2″ baking pan. Add very hot water to the depth of 1″. Bake in 325° oven 50 to 60 minutes or until knife inserted off center comes out clean. Serve warm or chilled.

Electric Frypan: 35 to 40 minutes cooking time

Use ingredients listed in basic recipe. Combine all ingredients in bowl and beat with rotary beater until smooth. Pour into 6 (6 oz.) custard cups. Place in electric frypan. Pour in 1″ cold water around custards. Cover. Set at 220°. Cook, with vent closed, 35 to 40 minutes or until knife inserted off center comes out clean.

Microwave Oven (high setting): 10 to 12 minutes cooking time

Use ingredients listed in basic recipe, but reduce them as follows. Combine 1 c. canned pumpkin, 1 c. milk, 2 eggs, 1/3 c. brown sugar, packed, 2 tblsp. sugar, 1½ tsp. pumpkin pie spice and ¼ tsp. salt in bowl. Beat with rotary beater until smooth. Pour into 4 (6 oz.) custard cups. Place in 8″ square glass baking dish. Add very hot water to the depth of 1″. Microwave (high setting) 10 to 12 minutes or until knife inserted off center comes out clean. Give baking dish a quarter turn every 3 minutes. Makes 4 servings.

CUP CUSTARD

Soft and creamy cup custard no matter how you cook it. This versatile multiple-method recipe suits any day's schedule.

BASIC RECIPE — MAKES 6 SERVINGS.

2 c. milk	1/8 tsp. salt
3 eggs, beaten	3/4 tsp. vanilla
1/4 c. sugar	Ground nutmeg

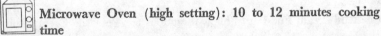

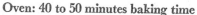 **Oven: 40 to 50 minutes baking time**

Scald milk. Combine eggs, sugar, salt and vanilla in bowl. Gradually stir hot milk into egg mixture. Pour through fine wire sieve into 6 (6 oz.) custard cups. Sprinkle with nutmeg. Place on oven rack in baking pan. Pour very hot water around custards to depth of 1″. Bake in 325° oven 40 to 50 minutes or until knife inserted just off center comes out clean. Serve warm or chilled.

 **Electric Frypan: 30 to 40 minutes cooking time**

Use ingredients listed in basic recipe. Prepare custards as for Oven. Place filled custard cups in electric frypan. Pour cold water around custards to a depth of 1″. Cover. Simmer at 220°, with vent closed, 30 to 40 minutes or until knife inserted just off center comes out clean. Serve warm or chilled.

Microwave Oven (high setting): 4 minutes cooking time

Use ingredients listed in basic recipe, but reduce the amounts as follows. Measure 1⅓ c. milk into a 4-c. glass measuring cup and microwave (high setting) 2 to 2½ minutes or until very hot. Combine 2 beaten eggs, 3 tblsp. sugar, dash of salt and ½ tsp. vanilla in bowl. Gradually stir hot milk into egg mixture. Pour through fine wire sieve into 4 (6 oz.) custard cups. Sprinkle with nutmeg. Place in 8″ square glass baking dish. Pour very hot water around custards to a depth of 1″. Microwave 4 minutes or until custards test done. Serve warm or chilled. Makes 4 servings.

DATE TAPIOCA PUDDING

Chopped dates make this version of a favorite American pudding different. Now you have two ways to cook it, too.
BASIC RECIPE — MAKES 6 SERVINGS.

2 c. milk	2 eggs, separated
¼ c. sugar	2 tblsp. sugar
¼ c. quick-cooking tapioca	1 tsp. vanilla
¼ tsp. salt	½ c. chopped dates

 Range Top: 6 to 8 minutes cooking time

Combine milk, ¼ c. sugar, tapioca, salt and beaten egg yolks in saucepan. Beat egg whites in another bowl until foamy; gradually beat in 2 tblsp. sugar and beat until soft peaks form. Cook milk mixture over medium heat, stirring constantly until it comes to a full rolling boil, 6 to 8 minutes. Remove from heat. Fold hot tapioca mixture into egg whites. Fold in vanilla and dates. Cover and let stand 20 minutes. Stir. Serve warm or chilled.

Microwave Oven (high setting): 5½ to 6½ minutes cooking time

Use ingredients listed in basic recipe. Measure milk into 4-c. glass measuring cup. Add ¼ c. sugar, tapioca, salt and beaten egg yolks. Stir well. Microwave (high setting) 3 minutes; stir. Continue microwaving 2½ to 3½ minutes, stirring every minute. Beat egg whites until foamy; gradually beat in 2 tblsp. sugar and beat until soft peaks form. Fold hot tapioca mixture into egg whites. Fold in vanilla and dates. Cover and let stand 20 minutes. Stir. Serve warm or chilled.

BROWNIES

Since brownies are already brown in color, the lack of browning in the microwave oven is unnoticed. A cake-like brownie.

BASIC RECIPE — MAKES 4 TO 5 DOZEN.

1¼ c. unsifted flour
¾ tsp. baking soda
¼ tsp. salt
¾ c. soft butter or regular margarine
1½ c. brown sugar, packed
3 eggs

2 tsp. vanilla
3 (1 oz.) squares unsweetened chocolate, melted and cooled
¾ c. milk
¾ c. chopped walnuts
Chocolate Frosting (recipe follows)

 Oven: 25 minutes baking time

Stir together flour, baking soda and salt; set aside. Place butter, brown sugar, eggs, vanilla and chocolate in large mixing bowl. Beat with electric mixer at medium speed until thoroughly combined (1½ minutes). Blend in milk. Stir in dry ingredients and walnuts. Spread batter evenly in greased 15½×10½×1" jelly roll pan. Bake in 350° oven 25 minutes or until done. Cool in pan on rack. Spread with Chocolate Frosting.

Chocolate Frosting: Combine 6 tblsp. butter or margarine and 2 (1 oz.) squares unsweetened chocolate, melted and cooled. Blend in 2 c. sifted confectioners sugar. Stir in 1½ tsp. vanilla and 2 to 3 tblsp. milk. Beat until mixture is smooth and of spreading consistency.

 Electric Frypan: 40 to 45 minutes cooking time

Use ingredients listed in basic recipe, but use 2¼ c. flour. Preheat frypan, with vent closed, to 275°. Stir together 2¼ c. flour, baking soda and salt; set aside. Place butter, sugar, eggs, melted chocolate and vanilla in large mixer bowl. Beat with electric mixer at medium speed until thoroughly combined (1½ minutes). Blend in milk; stir in dry ingredients and nuts. Brush skillet with shortening. Spread batter evenly in skillet. Cover and cook, with vent closed, until top no longer is sticky, about 40 to 45 minutes. Open vent the last 5 minutes. Invert on rack. When cool, spread with Chocolate Frosting as for Oven.

 Microwave Oven (high setting): 9 to 11½ minutes cooking time

Use ingredients listed in basic recipe, but in different amounts. Place 2 (1 oz.) squares unsweetened chocolate in 6 oz. custard cup. Microwave (high setting) 3 to 3½ minutes or until melted. Set aside to cool. Stir together ¾ c. unsifted flour, ½ tsp. baking soda and ⅛ tsp. salt. Place ½ c. soft butter or regular margarine, 1 c. brown sugar, packed, 2 eggs, cooled chocolate and 1½ tsp. vanilla in large mixer bowl. Beat with electric mixer at medium speed until thoroughly combined (1½ minutes). Blend in ½ c. milk. Stir in dry ingredients and ½ c. chopped walnuts. Spread batter evenly in greased 12×8×2″ glass baking dish (2-qt.). Microwave 6 to 8 minutes, giving dish a half turn after 3 minutes of cooking. Cool in pan on rack. Frost with Chocolate Frosting as follows. Makes 3 dozen brownies.

Chocolate Frosting: Place 1½ (1 oz.) squares unsweetened chocolate in 6 oz. custard cup. Microwave (high setting) for 3 minutes. Cool. Thoroughly combine 4 tblsp. soft butter or regular margarine and cooled chocolate. Blend in 1½ c. sifted confectioners sugar. Stir in 1 tsp. vanilla and 1 to 2 tblsp. milk. Beat until mixture is smooth and of spreading consistency.

DATE NUT PUDDING CAKE

Although the top of this dessert does not brown in the microwave, it looks appealing when topped with ice cream or whipped cream.
BASIC RECIPE — MAKES 6 SERVINGS.

¾ c. boiling water	2 tsp. baking powder
½ c. chopped dates	½ tsp. salt
2 tblsp. soft butter or regular margarine	¼ tsp. ground cinnamon
½ c. sugar	½ c. chopped walnuts
¼ c. brown sugar, packed	1¾ c. boiling water
1 egg	¾ c. brown sugar, packed
1 c. unsifted flour	1 tblsp. butter or regular margarine

Oven: 40 minutes baking time

Combine ¾ c. boiling water and dates in bowl. Cool to room temperature. Cream together 2 tblsp. butter, sugar, ¼ c. brown sugar and egg in mixing bowl until well combined. Blend in the cooled date mixture. Stir together flour, baking powder, salt and cinnamon. Add to creamed mixture and beat just until well combined. Stir in walnuts. Spread batter evenly in greased 8″ square baking pan. Combine 1¾ c. boiling water, ¾ c. brown sugar and 1 tblsp. butter in bowl; blend well. Pour gently over cake batter. Bake in 350° oven 40 minutes. Delicious served warm with ice cream, whipped cream or whipped dessert topping.

Microwave Oven (high setting): 14 minutes cooking time

Use ingredients listed in basic recipe, but use cold water instead of boiling water. Place ¾ c. water in 2-c. glass measuring cup. Microwave (high setting) 2 minutes or until water boils. Add dates and cool. Microwave 2 tblsp. butter in large glass bowl 30 seconds or until melted. Blend in sugar, ¼ c. brown sugar and egg. Add the cooled date mixture. Stir together flour, baking powder, salt and cinnamon. Blend into date mixture until smooth. Stir in walnuts. Spread batter evenly in ungreased 8″ square glass baking dish. Microwave 1¾ c. water in a 1-qt. measuring cup until boiling, about 3½ minutes. Add ¾ c. brown sugar and 1 tblsp. butter, stirring until combined. Pour gently over cake batter. Microwave, uncovered, 8 minutes, giving dish three quarter turns. Serve warm with ice cream, whipped cream or whipped dessert topping.

ORANGE-CARROT CAKE

This carrot cake is a little unusual because it uses mashed cooked carrots instead of shredded raw carrots.

BASIC RECIPE — MAKES 12 SERVINGS.

2 c. sifted flour
1 tsp. baking soda
1 tsp. baking powder
1 tsp. ground cinnamon
½ tsp. salt
¼ c. butter or regular
   margarine
1 c. sugar
2 eggs, beaten

1 c. mashed cooked carrots,
   cooled (4 medium)
¼ c. orange juice
1 tsp. grated orange rind
½ c. raisins
½ c. chopped walnuts
Cream Cheese Frosting (recipe
   follows)

Oven: 25 to 30 minutes baking time

Sift together flour, baking soda, baking powder, cinnamon and salt; set aside. Cream together butter and sugar in bowl until light and fluffy. Thoroughly beat in eggs. Beat in carrots, orange juice and orange rind (batter looks curdled at this stage). Stir in flour mixture with spoon. Stir in raisins and walnuts. Spread in 2 greased and floured 8″ round layer cake pans. Bake in 350° oven 25 to 30 minutes or until cake tests done. Cool in pans on racks 10 minutes. Remove from pans; cool on racks. When cooled, spread Cream Cheese Frosting between layers, on sides and top of cake. Store in refrigerator.

Microwave Oven (high setting): 10 minutes cooking time
Use ingredients listed in basic recipe, but reduce baking powder from
1 to ½ tsp. Prepare cake batter as for Oven. Spread in 2 waxed paper-
lined 8″ round glass baking dishes. (Do not grease sides of dishes.)
Cook 1 layer at a time. Microwave (high setting) 5 minutes, giving
dish a quarter turn after 2½ minutes. Repeat with remaining layer.
Cool layers in dishes on racks 5 minutes. Turn out on cake racks.
When cooled, frost with Cream Cheese Frosting between layers, on
sides and top of cake. Store in refrigerator.

Cream Cheese Frosting: Combine ½ c. soft butter or regular margarine, 1 (8 oz.) pkg. cream cheese and 1 tsp. vanilla in mixing bowl.
Beat until smooth and creamy. Gradually beat in 1 (1 lb.) pkg. confectioners sugar, sifted. If mixture is too thick to spread, add a little
milk.

BROWNIE PUDDING CAKE

*The pudding is covered with aluminum foil halfway through the bak-
ing time in the toaster-oven to prevent excessive browning.*
BASIC RECIPE — MAKES 6 SERVINGS.

1 c. unsifted flour	2 tblsp. cooking oil
¾ c. sugar	1 tsp. vanilla
2 tblsp. baking cocoa	⅓ c. chopped walnuts
2 tsp. baking powder	¾ c. brown sugar, packed
½ tsp. salt	¼ c. baking cocoa
½ c. milk	1¼ c. hot water

Oven: 40 minutes baking time
Stir together flour, sugar, 2 tblsp. cocoa, baking powder and salt in
bowl. Add milk, oil and vanilla; stir until smooth. Mix in walnuts.
Spread evenly in greased 8″ square baking pan. Combine brown sugar,

¼ c. cocoa and hot water in another bowl; mix well. Gently pour over batter. Bake in 350° oven 40 minutes or until top springs back when touched lightly with fingertip. Serve warm or cold, plain or with ice cream.

 Electric Frypan: 15 minutes baking time

Use ingredients listed in basic recipe but in different amounts. Stir together 1½ c. unsifted flour, 1¼ c. sugar, 3 tblsp. cocoa, 1 tblsp. baking powder and ¾ tsp. salt in bowl. Add ¾ c. milk, 3 tblsp. cooking oil and 2 tsp. vanilla; stir until smooth. Mix in ½ c. chopped walnuts. Spread in greased frypan preheated to 275°. Combine 1 c. brown sugar, packed, ⅓ c. baking cocoa and 2½ c. hot water in another bowl. Mix well. Gently pour over batter. Cover. Bake, with vent closed, 15 minutes or until cake tests done. Serve warm or cold, plain or with ice cream. Makes 10 to 12 servings.

 Microwave Oven (high setting): 11 to 13 minutes cooking time

Use ingredients listed in basic recipe. Prepare batter as for Oven. Spread evenly in greased 8″ square glass baking dish. Combine brown sugar, ¼ c. baking cocoa and hot water in another bowl. Mix well. Gently pour over batter. Microwave (high setting) 11 to 13 minutes or until cake tests done. Give dish 3 quarter turns during baking. Serve warm or cold, plain or with ice cream.

 Toaster-Oven: 40 minutes baking time

Use ingredients listed in basic recipe. Prepare them for Oven. Bake in toaster-oven at 350° for 20 minutes. Cover with foil to prevent excess browning and continue baking 20 minutes or until cake tests done. Serve warm or cold, plain or with ice cream.

CARAMEL-COCONUT OATMEAL CAKE

No one could guess which cake was baked conventionally or which was microwaved when these were placed side by side in our Kitchens.

BASIC RECIPE — MAKES 8 TO 12 SERVINGS.

1½ c. water
1 c. quick-cooking oats
½ c. butter or regular
   margarine
1 c. brown sugar, packed
½ c. sugar
2 eggs
1½ tsp. vanilla

1⅓ c. sifted flour
1 tsp. baking soda
1 tsp. ground cinnamon
½ tsp. salt
¼ tsp. ground nutmeg
Caramel-Coconut Topping
  (recipe follows)

Oven: 32 minutes cooking time

Combine water and oats in medium saucepan. Bring to a boil; cook 1 minute or until thickened, stirring occasionally. Remove from heat. Cream together butter and sugars in bowl until light and fluffy, using electric mixer at medium speed. Add eggs, one at a time, beating well after each addition. Blend in vanilla. Stir in oatmeal mixture; mix well with spoon. Sift together flour, baking soda, cinnamon, salt and nutmeg. Stir into creamed mixture. Turn into greased 12×8×2″ glass baking dish (2-qt.). Bake in 350° oven 30 minutes or until cake tests done. Remove from oven; place on rack. Prepare topping.

Caramel-Coconut Topping: Combine 1 c. flaked coconut, ½ c. finely chopped walnuts, ½ c. packed brown sugar, ⅓ c. milk, ¼ c. butter or regular margarine and dash of salt in medium saucepan. Bring to boiling. Reduce heat and simmer, stirring constantly, 1 minute or until mixture thickens slightly. Spread over warm cake. Cake is delicious served slightly warm or cold.

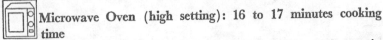 **Microwave Oven (high setting): 16 to 17 minutes cooking time**

Use ingredients listed in basic recipe. Combine water and oats in 2½-qt. glass bowl. Microwave (high setting) 3 minutes or until mixture thickens, stirring once. Remove from oven; stir and set aside. Cream together butter and sugars in bowl until light and fluffy, using electric mixer at medium speed. Add eggs, one at a time, beating well after each addition. Blend in vanilla. Stir in oatmeal mixture; mix well with spoon. Sift together flour, baking soda, cinnamon, salt and nutmeg. Stir into creamed mixture. Grease 12×8×2″ glass baking dish (2-qt.) on bottom only. Turn mixture into dish. Microwave (high setting) 10 to 11 minutes, giving dish 3 quarter turns during cooking. Cake is done when a toothpick placed in center comes out almost clean. The top of the cake is moist and slightly shiny in appearance. Remove from oven and place on rack. Prepare topping.

Caramel-Coconut Topping: Use ingredients listed in basic recipe. Combine all ingredients in 1-qt. glass bowl. Microwave (high setting), uncovered, 2½ to 3 minutes or until slightly thickened, stirring once after 1½ minutes. Remove and stir again. Spread on warm cake. Cake is delicious served slightly warm or cold.

APPLE GINGERBREAD TORTE

A quick-fix dessert that takes only about 9 minutes to cook in the microwave. Topping is especially delicious.

BASIC RECIPE — MAKES 9 SERVINGS.

1 (14 oz.) pkg. gingerbread
  mix
1½ c. applesauce

2 c. thawed frozen whipped
  topping
½ c. chopped walnuts

Oven: 40 minutes baking time

Prepare gingerbread by package directions, but reduce water by ½ c. and add 1 c. of the applesauce. Spread batter in greased 8″ square baking pan. Bake in 350° oven 40 minutes or until wooden toothpick inserted in center comes out clean. Cool in pan on rack. Fold remaining ½ c. applesauce into topping. Spread on top of gingerbread. Sprinkle with walnuts. Refrigerate until serving time.

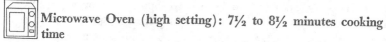

Microwave Oven (high setting): 7½ to 8½ minutes cooking time

Use ingredients listed in basic recipe. Prepare gingerbread by package directions but omit ½ c. water and add 1 c. of the applesauce. Grease bottom only of an 8″ square glass baking dish. Spread batter in dish. Microwave (high setting) 7½ to 8½ minutes or until gingerbread tests done, giving dish quarter turns three times. Cool in pan on rack. Fold remaining ½ c. applesauce into topping. Spread on top of gingerbread; sprinkle with walnuts. Refrigerate until serving time.

Toaster-Oven: 35 to 40 minutes baking time

Use ingredients listed in basic recipe. Prepare batter as for Oven. Spread in greased 8″ square baking pan. Bake at 350° in toaster-oven 25 minutes. Cover lightly with foil to prevent excessive browning. Continue baking until gingerbread tests done, 10 to 15 minutes. Cool in pan on rack. Fold remaining ½ c. applesauce into topping. Spread on top of gingerbread. Sprinkle with walnuts. Refrigerate until serving time.

CRANBERRY CAKE

Make better use of your oven heat by baking this dessert alongside a roast and baked potatoes.

BASIC RECIPE — MAKES 6 TO 8 SERVINGS.

2 tblsp. butter or regular margarine

1 (16 oz.) can whole cranberry sauce

1 large apple, pared, cored and chopped (1 c.)

1 (9 oz.) pkg. yellow cake mix

Sweetened whipped cream or whipped topping

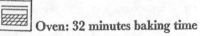 Oven: 32 minutes baking time

Melt butter in 8″ square baking pan in oven, about 2 minutes. Combine cranberry sauce and apple in bowl. Spoon over butter in baking dish. Prepare cake mix as directed on package. Spoon evenly over cranberry mixture. Bake in 350° oven 30 minutes or until cake tests done. Let stand 2 to 3 minutes. Invert on serving plate. Serve with sweetened whipped cream.

Microwave Oven (high setting): 11½ to 14½ minutes cooking time

Use ingredients listed in basic recipe. Microwave (high setting) butter in 8″ square glass baking dish 30 seconds or until melted. Combine cranberry sauce and apple; spoon evenly over butter in baking dish. Prepare cake mix as directed on package. Spoon evenly over cranberry mixture. Microwave 11 to 14 minutes. Give dish three quarter turns during cooking. Let stand 2 to 3 minutes. Invert on serving plate. Serve topped with sweetened whipped cream.

Toaster-Oven: 30 minutes baking time

Use ingredients listed in basic recipe. Prepare ingredients as for Oven. Bake at 350° for 30 minutes or until cake tests done. Let stand 2 to 3 minutes. Cover with foil, if necessary, to avoid excessive browning. Invert on serving plate. Serve topped with sweetened whipped cream.

CHOCOLATE CHEESE SWIRL PIE

These pies are identical no matter which way they are cooked. An attractive cheese pie swirled with melted chocolate.

BASIC RECIPE — MAKES 8 SERVINGS.

4 (3 oz.) pkgs. cream cheese, softened
½ c. sugar
2 eggs

1½ tsp. vanilla
1 (9″) Crumb Pie Shell (recipe follows)
½ c. semisweet chocolate pieces

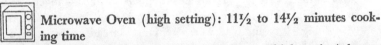

Oven: 22 to 27 minutes baking time

Beat cream cheese, sugar, eggs and vanilla in small mixer bowl until smooth. Pour into Crumb Pie Shell. Melt chocolate pieces over low heat, about 2 minutes. Drop melted chocolate evenly by teaspoonfuls over pie. Swirl chocolate through filling with fork. Bake in 325° oven 20 to 25 minutes or until center appears set. Cool and chill.

Crumb Pie Shell: Combine 6 tblsp. melted butter or regular margarine, 1¼ c. graham cracker crumbs and ¼ c. sugar in bowl; mix well. Press firmly into 9″ pie plate.

Microwave Oven (high setting): 6½ minutes cooking time

Use ingredients listed in basic recipe. Prepare pie filling as for Oven. Pour into Crumb Pie Shell. Place chocolate pieces in small glass bowl. Microwave (high setting) 1½ minutes to melt. Drop by teaspoonfuls evenly on pie. Swirl chocolate through filling with fork. Microwave 5 minutes or until center appears set, giving dish a quarter turn every minute. Cool and chill.

Crumb Pie Shell: Use ingredients listed in basic recipe, but microwave (high setting) butter in small glass bowl until melted, about 1 minute. Combine with graham cracker crumbs and sugar; mix well. Press firmly into 9″ glass pie plate.

COFFEE CHOCOLATE LAYER PIE

Both methods take exactly the same amount of cooking time. The range top does require constant stirring during cooking.

BASIC RECIPE — MAKES 6 TO 8 SERVINGS.

½ c. butter or regular margarine

2 c. vanilla wafer crumbs

1 (3⅝ oz.) pkg. chocolate pudding and pie filling

2 c. milk

1 (1½ oz.) env. whipped topping mix

¼ c. sifted confectioners sugar

1½ tsp. instant coffee granules or powder

½ c. cold milk

½ tsp. vanilla

¼ c. toasted slivered almonds

Range Top: 8 minutes cooking time

Melt butter in small skillet, about 3 minutes. Combine butter and vanilla wafer crumbs. Press firmly into 9″ pie plate. Set aside. Prepare chocolate pudding with 2 c. milk according to package directions for pie filling, about 5 minutes. Pour into crumb crust and chill. Combine whipped topping mix, confectioners sugar and coffee granules in small mixing bowl. Add remaining ½ c. milk and vanilla. Beat until light and fluffy, using electric mixer at high speed. Spread over chilled chocolate layer in crust. Top with almonds and chill 3 to 4 hours.

Microwave Oven (high setting): 7 to 8 minutes cooking time

Use ingredients listed in basic recipe. Microwave (high setting) butter in glass bowl 1 minute or until melted. Combine butter with crumbs. Press firmly into 9″ pie plate. Set aside. Combine chocolate pudding mix with 2 c. milk in 4-cup glass measuring cup or bowl. Microwave, uncovered, until mixture thickens and bubbles, 6 to 7 minutes. Stir after 3 minutes, then every minute. Pour pudding into crumb crust and chill. Combine whipped topping mix, confectioners sugar and coffee granules in small mixer bowl. Add remaining ½ c. milk and vanilla. Beat until light and fluffy, using electric mixer at high speed. Spread over chilled chocolate layer in crust. Top with almonds and chill 3 to 4 hours.

RHUBARB-STRAWBERRY DESSERT SAUCE

Welcome spring with this delightful dessert sauce. Pour over ice cream, yellow cake squares or vanilla pudding.

BASIC RECIPE — MAKES 3 CUPS.

3 c. cut-up fresh rhubarb, 1″ pieces

1 c. sugar

⅓ c. water

1 c. halved fresh strawberries

1 tblsp. cornstarch

2 tblsp. water

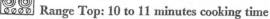 Range Top: 10 to 11 minutes cooking time

Combine rhubarb, sugar and ⅓ c. water in saucepan. Bring to a boil; reduce heat. Cover and simmer 5 minutes. Add strawberries. Continue cooking until strawberries are tender, 2 to 3 minutes. Blend together cornstarch and 2 tblsp. water. Add to rhubarb mixture. Cook, stirring constantly, until mixture thickens and boils, about 3 minutes. Remove from heat. Chill in refrigerator until serving time.

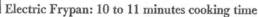 Electric Frypan: 10 to 11 minutes cooking time

Use ingredients listed in basic recipe, but double all of them except the water for cooking. Increase water to 1 c. Combine 6 c. rhubarb, 2 c. sugar and 1 c. water in electric frypan. Turn heat setting to 400°. Bring to a boil. Reduce heat to 250°. Cover and cook, with vent open, 5 minutes. Add 2 c. strawberries. Continue cooking until strawberries are tender, 2 to 3 minutes. Blend together 2 tblsp. cornstarch and ¼ c. water. Add to rhubarb mixture. Cook, stirring constantly, until mixture thickens and boils, about 3 minutes. Remove from heat. Chill in refrigerator until serving time. Makes 6 cups.

Microwave Oven (high setting): 10 minutes cooking time

Use ingredients listed in basic recipe, but use ½ c. water. Combine rhubarb, sugar and cornstarch in 1½-qt. glass casserole. Stir in ½ c. water. Cover. Microwave (high setting) 8 minutes, stirring once. Add strawberries. Cover and continue cooking 2 minutes or until mixture is thickened and bubbly. Remove from oven. Chill in refrigerator until serving time.

HOT BANANA SUNDAE

Use any of these three cooking methods for a special dessert that is ready in only minutes.

BASIC RECIPE — MAKES 6 SERVINGS.

3 tblsp. butter or regular
   margarine
¼ c. red currant jelly
⅓ c. brown sugar, packed
⅓ c. sherry

3 medium green-tinged bananas
3 tblsp. lime or lemon juice
1 qt. vanilla ice cream
½ c. flaked coconut

 Oven: 5 to 7 minutes cooking time

Melt butter and jelly in saucepan over low heat, stirring to blend, about 2 minutes. Stir in brown sugar and sherry. Remove from heat; set aside. Cut peeled bananas in half crosswise, then lengthwise. Brush banana quarters with lime juice. Add remaining lime juice to the sauce. Place bananas in 12×8×2″ glass baking dish (2-qt.). Spoon sauce over bananas. Bake in 350° oven 3 to 5 minutes. Serve two warm banana quarters topped with ice cream, then with the sauce and coconut.

 Electric Frypan: 3 to 4 minutes cooking time

Use ingredients listed in basic recipe, but increase butter from 3 to 4 tblsp. Preheat frypan to 220°. Add butter and jelly, stirring until melted and blended, about 2 minutes. Stir in brown sugar and sherry. Cut peeled bananas in half crosswise, then lengthwise. Brush with lime juice. Add remaining lime juice to sauce. Place bananas in sauce, spooning sauce over. Cover and simmer, with vent closed, 3 to 4 minutes or until bananas are tender. Serve two warm banana quarters topped with ice cream, sauce and coconut.

Microwave Oven (high setting): 5½ minutes cooking time
Use ingredients listed in basic recipe. Microwave (high setting) butter
in a small glass bowl 30 seconds or until melted. Add jelly and melt,
about 1 minute. Add brown sugar and sherry; stir until well blended.
Cut peeled bananas in half crosswise, then lengthwise. Brush them
with lime juice. Add remaining lime juice to sauce. Place bananas in
12×8×2″ glass baking dish (2-qt.). Spoon sauce over bananas. Microwave (high setting), uncovered, 2 minutes; give dish one half turn.
Continue cooking 2 minutes. Serve two warm banana quarters topped
with ice cream, sauce and coconut.

RAISIN-STUFFED APPLES

*Now you have a choice of five cooking methods for "baked" apples.
The cooking times vary from 9 minutes to 8 hours.*
BASIC RECIPE — MAKES 6 SERVINGS.

6 baking apples	¾ c. raisins
2 tblsp. butter or regular	3 tblsp. chopped walnuts
margarine	½ c. water
¼ c. brown sugar, packed	

Oven: 45 to 55 minutes baking time
Core apples. Peel a strip around apples one-third way below stem end
to help prevent splitting. Blend together butter and brown sugar; stir
in raisins and walnuts. Stuff into apple cavities. Place apples in 9″
round baking pan. Add water to pan. Bake in 350° oven 45 to 55 minutes or until tender, basting occasionally with syrup.

Electric Frypan: 25 to 30 minutes cooking time
Use ingredients listed in basic recipe. Prepare stuffed apples as for
Oven. Place stuffed apples in electric frypan. Add water. Set at 325°.

Bring to a boil and cover. Cook, with vent open, at 220°. Cook 25 to 30 minutes or until apples are tender, basting occasionally with syrup.

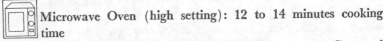

Microwave Oven (high setting): 12 to 14 minutes cooking time

Use ingredients listed in basic recipe, but use 6 tblsp. water. Core and stuff apples as for Oven. Place each stuffed apple in a 10-oz. glass casserole. Spoon 1 tblsp. water over each apple. Cover with waxed paper. Arrange casseroles in a circle in microwave oven. Microwave (high setting) 12 to 14 minutes or until tender, re-arranging casseroles once.

Slow Cooker: 8 hours cooking time

Use ingredients listed in basic recipe. Prepare stuffed apples as for Oven. Place stuffed apples in cooker. Add water. Cover and cook on low 8 hours.

Toaster-Oven: 45 to 55 minutes cooking time

Use ingredients listed in basic recipe, but reduce the size of recipe as indicated. Core 2 medium baking apples. Peel a strip around apples one-third way below stem end to prevent splitting. Blend together 2 tsp. butter and 1 tblsp. brown sugar; stir in ¼ c. raisins and 1 tblsp. chopped walnuts. Stuff into apple cavities. Place each apple in a 10-oz. casserole. Spoon 1 tblsp. water over each apple. Cover with aluminum foil. Bake in toaster-oven at 350° for 45 to 55 minutes or until tender. Makes 2 servings.

SPICY PRUNES

Try garnishing your next roast pork or ham with these prunes. Place them on orange slices and add a few sprigs of parsley.

BASIC RECIPE — MAKES 5 SERVINGS.

1 medium orange	5 whole allspice
2 c. dried prunes	3 whole cloves
3 tblsp. brown sugar, packed	1½ c. water
1 (3″) stick cinnamon	

Range Top: 6 minutes cooking time

Cut 2 (3×¼″) strips of peel from orange. Remove white membrane from peel. Combine with remaining ingredients in saucepan. Cook over medium heat until mixture boils, about 5 minutes. Boil 1 minute. Cool and chill. Remove spices.

Microwave Oven (high setting): 5 to 6 minutes cooking time

Use ingredients listed in basic recipe, but heat water to boiling before combining with other ingredients. Combine brown sugar, cinnamon, allspice, cloves and hot water in 1½-qt. glass casserole. Stir until sugar is dissolved. Cut orange strips as for Range Top. Add with prunes to spicy mixture. Cover and microwave (high setting) 4 to 5 minutes or until water starts to boil. Microwave 1 minute longer. Cool and chill. Remove spices.

CHOCOLATE FUDGE

Now you can make homemade marshmallow fudge in your microwave oven and it takes only 9 minutes to cook.

BASIC RECIPE — MAKES 78 PIECES.

3 c. sugar
¾ c. butter or regular
  margarine
⅔ c. evaporated milk
¼ tsp. salt
1 (12 oz.) pkg. semisweet
  chocolate pieces

1 (7 oz.) jar marshmallow
  creme (2 c.)
2 tsp. vanilla
1 c. chopped walnuts

Range Top: 15 minutes cooking time

Combine sugar, butter, evaporated milk and salt in 3-qt. heavy saucepan or Dutch oven. Bring to a full rolling boil, stirring constantly, about 10 minutes. Cook 5 more minutes over medium heat, stirring constantly. Remove from heat and stir in chocolate pieces; continue to stir until chocolate is melted. Add marshmallow creme and vanilla; mix until thoroughly combined. Stir in walnuts. Pour into buttered 13×9×2″ baking pan. Cool and cut in 1½×1″ pieces.

Microwave Oven (high setting): 8 to 9 minutes cooking time

Use ingredients listed in basic recipe. Combine sugar, butter, evaporated milk and salt in large glass mixing bowl. Microwave (high setting) 8 to 9 minutes, stirring well three or four times during cooking. Remove and stir in chocolate pieces; continue to stir until chocolate is melted. Add marshmallow creme and vanilla; mix until thoroughly combined. Stir in walnuts and pour into buttered 13×9×2″ baking pan. Cool and cut in 1½×1″ pieces.

CARAMEL CEREAL CONFECTION

If your children like sweets, this confection is a good choice. It contains protein-rich cereal flakes and peanuts.
BASIC RECIPE — MAKES 32.

1 (14 oz.) pkg. caramel candies	8 c. high-protein cereal flakes
¼ c. butter or regular margarine	1 (6½ oz.) can salted peanuts
¼ c. water	1 (6 oz.) pkg. semisweet chocolate pieces

 Range Top: 15 minutes cooking time

Place candies, butter and water in large, heavy saucepan. Cook, covered, 15 minutes over low heat until candies are melted, stirring occasionally. After candies are melted, stir vigorously until smooth. Pour over cereal, peanut and chocolate pieces in large mixing bowl. Stir to coat well. Press firmly into buttered 13×9×2″ baking pan. Chill in refrigerator until firm, about 1 hour. Cut in 2×1½″ bars.

Microwave Oven (high setting): 6 minutes cooking time

Use ingredients listed in basic recipe. Place candies in single layer in 3-qt. glass casserole. Cut butter in 4 pieces and place on top candies. Add water. Cover and microwave (high setting) 6 minutes or until mixture can be stirred until smooth. Stir in cereal flakes, about a quarter of them at a time. Stir to coat well. Stir in peanuts, then chocolate. Press firmly into buttered 13×9×2″ baking pan. Chill in refrigerator until firm, about 1 hour. Cut in 2×1½″ bars.

CHOCOLATE-NUT BARS

These bars are a cross between a cookie and a candy. A great deal of time is saved when cooked in the microwave.

BASIC RECIPE — MAKES 20.

1½ c. graham cracker crumbs
1 (14 oz.) can sweetened
   condensed milk
1 (6 oz.) pkg. semisweet
   chocolate pieces

¾ c. chopped pecans
½ tsp. vanilla

Oven: 30 to 35 minutes baking time

Stir together all ingredients until crumbs are moistened. Spread in greased 8″ square baking pan. Bake in 350° oven 30 to 35 minutes. Cool in pan on rack. Cut in 2×1½″ bars.

Microwave Oven (high setting): 8 minutes cooking time

Use ingredients listed in basic recipe. Stir together all ingredients until crumbs are moistened. Spread in greased 8″ square glass baking dish. Microwave (high setting) 8 minutes or until top of mixture is dry, giving dish a quarter turn 3 times. Cool in pan on rack. Cut in 2×1½″ bars.

COCONUT-NUT BARS

If you microwave these bars, remove them while the top is still moist—
they continue to cook and the top dries.

BASIC RECIPE — MAKES 20.

⅓ c. butter or regular
    margarine
⅓ c. brown sugar, packed
¾ c. sifted flour
½ tsp. baking soda
½ tsp. salt
¾ c. quick-cooking oats

2 eggs
¾ c. brown sugar, packed
1 tblsp. flour
1 tblsp. lemon juice
¾ c. flaked coconut
½ c. chopped walnuts

Oven: 25 to 30 minutes baking time
Cream together butter and ⅓ c. brown sugar in mixing bowl until light and fluffy. Stir together ¾ c. flour, baking soda and salt. Add to creamed mixture along with oats. Press into bottom of greased 8" square baking pan. Beat eggs in another bowl. Stir in remaining ingredients. Spread over oat mixture. Bake in 350° oven 25 to 30 minutes or until brown on top. Cool in pan on racks. Cut in 1½ ✕ 1" bars.

Microwave Oven (high setting): 5 to 7 minutes cooking time
Use ingredients listed in basic recipe. Cream together butter and ⅓ c. brown sugar in mixing bowl until light and fluffy. Sift together ¾ c. flour, baking soda and salt. Add to creamed mixture along with oats. Press into bottom of waxed paper-lined 8" square glass baking dish. Beat eggs in another bowl. Stir in remaining ingredients. Spread over oat mixture. Microwave (high setting) 5 to 7 minutes, giving dish a quarter turn twice. Cool in pan on rack. Cut in 1½ ✕ 1" bars.

Toaster-Oven: 25 minutes baking time
Use ingredients listed in basic recipe. Prepare as for Oven. Bake in greased 8″ square baking pan. Bake at 350° for 20 minutes or until browned. Cover with aluminum foil and continue baking 5 minutes. Cool in pan on rack. Cut in 1½×1″ bars.

CRISPY PEANUT BARS

Quick-to-fix confections that can be prepared at the last minute for snacking or for packing in lunch boxes.
BASIC RECIPE — MAKES 36 BARS.

½ c. sugar
½ c. light corn syrup
⅛ tsp. salt
1 c. chunky peanut butter

2 c. crisp rice cereal
Brown Sugar Frosting (recipe
  follows)

Range Top: 6 minutes cooking time
Combine sugar, corn syrup and salt in medium saucepan. Bring mixture to boiling, about 3 minutes. Boil gently 1 minute to dissolve sugar. Remove from heat. Blend in peanut butter and then gently stir in rice cereal. Pat evenly in aluminum foil-lined 8″ square baking pan. Spread Brown Sugar Frosting on top. Cool. Peel off foil and cut in bars.

Brown Sugar Frosting: Combine ¼ c. butter or regular margarine and ¼ c. brown sugar, packed, in small saucepan. Cook and stir over low heat until butter is melted and sugar is dissolved, about 2 minutes. Remove from heat and stir in 1 tblsp. milk and ½ tsp. vanilla. Add ¼ c. sifted confectioners sugar and beat until smooth and of spreading consistency. Spread evenly over bars and sprinkle with ¼ c. chopped dry roasted peanuts.

Microwave Oven (high setting): 5½ to 7 minutes cooking time

Use ingredients listed in basic recipe. Combine sugar, corn syrup and salt in 2-qt. glass casserole. Microwave (high setting) about 3½ to 4½ minutes or until sugar is dissolved. Blend in peanut butter and then gently stir in rice cereal. Pat evenly in aluminum foil-lined 8″ square baking pan. Spread Brown Sugar Frosting on top. Cool. Remove foil and cut in bars.

Brown Sugar Frosting: Use ingredients listed in basic recipe. Combine butter and brown sugar in small glass bowl. Microwave (high setting) 2 to 2½ minutes or until butter is melted and sugar is dissolved. Stir once during cooking. Stir in milk and vanilla; add confectioners sugar and beat until smooth and of spreading consistency. Spread evenly over bars and sprinkle with chopped dry roasted peanuts.

CHOCOLATE PEANUT DROPS

Once you've melted chocolate in the microwave oven, you'll want to use it every time. No need to watch it while it melts.

BASIC RECIPE — MAKES 2½ DOZEN.

1 (6 oz.) pkg. semisweet chocolate pieces	2 tblsp. confectioners sugar
¼ c. light corn syrup	⅛ tsp. salt
2 tsp. vanilla	1½ c. dry roasted peanuts

 Range Top: 3 minutes cooking time

Combine chocolate pieces and corn syrup in medium saucepan. Cook over low heat, stirring constantly, until chocolate is melted, about 3 minutes. Remove from heat and stir in remaining ingredients; mix well. Drop by teaspoonfuls onto waxed paper. Let stand 2 or 3 hours or until set.

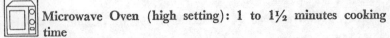 Microwave Oven (high setting): 1 to 1½ minutes cooking time

Combine chocolate pieces and corn syrup in glass mixing bowl. Microwave (high setting) 1 to 1½ minutes or until chocolate is melted. Add remaining ingredients; mix well. Drop by teaspoonfuls onto waxed paper. Let stand 2 or 3 hours or until set.

APPLIANCE INDEX

INDEX